Scriptures
of the East

Scriptures of the East

SECOND EDITION

edited by

James Fieser
University of Tennessee at Martin

John Powers
Australian National University

Boston   Burr Ridge, IL   Dubuque, IA   Madison, WI   New York
San Francisco   St. Louis   Bangkok   Bogotá   Caracas   Kuala Lumpur
Lisbon   London   Madrid   Mexico City   Milan   Montreal   New Delhi
Santiago   Seoul   Singapore   Sydney   Taipei   Toronto

Higher Education

SCRIPTURES OF THE EAST, SECOND EDITION

Published by McGraw-Hill, a business unit of The McGraw-Hill Companies, Inc., 1221 Avenue of the Americas, New York, NY 10020. Copyright © 2004 by The McGraw-Hill Companies, Inc. All rights reserved. Previous edition(s) 1998. All rights reserved. No part of this publication may be reproduced or distributed in any form or by any means, or stored in a database or retrieval system, without the prior written consent of The McGraw-Hill Companies, Inc., including, but not limited to, in any network or other electronic storage or transmission, or broadcast for distance learning.

Some ancillaries, including electronic and print components, may not be available to customers outside the United States.

This book is printed on acid-free paper containing 10% postconsumer waste.

4 5 6 7 8 9 0 DOC/DOC 0 9 8 7

ISBN-13: 978-0-07-286522-6 World
ISBN-10: 0-07-286522-9 World

ISBN-13: 978-0-07-286523-3 East
ISBN-10: 0-07-286523-7 East

Vice president and editor-in-chief: *Thalia Dorwick*
Publisher: *Chris Freitag*
Sponsoring editor: *Jon-David Hague*
Marketing manager: *Lisa G. Berry*
Project manager: *Richard H. Hecker*
Production supervisor: *Enboge Chong*
Design coordinator: *Mary Kazak*
Cover image: *© Getty Images, © Corbis*
Compositor: *Shepherd, Inc.*
Typeface: *10/12 Palatino*
Printer: *R. R. Donnelley/Crawfordsville, IN*

Library of Congress Cataloging-in-Publication Data

Scriptures of the east/edited by James Fieser, John Powers—2nd ed
    p. cm
  Includes bibliography references.
  ISBN 0-07286523-7 (softcover : alk. paper)
  1. Sacred books. 2. Asia—Religion. I. Fieser, James. II. Powers, John, 1957–
BL1010.S36 2004
291.8'2—dc21

2003048701

www.mhhe.com

About the Authors

JAMES FIESER is an assistant Professor of Philosophy at the University of Tennessee at Martin. He received his BA from Berea College (1980), and his MA and PhD from Purdue University's Department of Philosophy (1983, 1986). He is author, co-author, and editor of seven books, including *A Historical Introduction to Philosophy* (Oxford University Press, 2003) and *Socrates to Sartre and Beyond* (McGraw-Hill, 2003). He as edited and annotated the ten-volume *Early Responses to Hume* (Thoemmes Press, 1999–2003) and the five-volume *Scottish Common Sense Philosophy* (Thoemmes Press, 2000). He has published articles on the topics of David Hume, moral skepticism, rights theory, environmental ethics, business ethics, virtue theory, and natural law. He is founder and general editor of the *Internet Encyclopedia of Philosophy* web site.

JOHN POWERS is Reader in the Faculty of Asian Studies, Australian National University. He received his PhD from the University of Virginia in Buddhist Studies. His research interests include Indo-Tibetan Mahayana Buddhism, Indian philosophy, and contemporary human rights issues. He is the author of 7 books and 35 articles, including *Introduction to Tibetan Buddhism* (Ithaca: Snow Lion, 1995) and *Hermeneutics and Tradition in the Samdhinirmocana-sutra* (Leiden: E J Brill, 1993). He teaches courses on Asian Religions, Methodology, and Contemporary India.

Contents

Shinto

Preface

Several avenues are open for understanding the world's religions. One could dialog with believers of the various religions, visit their sacred sites and temples, or attend classes for converts. A more practical approach would be to read surveys of the various religions, some written by believers defending their faith, others by critics, and even more by academic historians, anthropologists, psychologists, and philosophers. Yet another avenue is to examine the collected sacred texts revered by these religions. Each of these approaches offers only a single perspective on one of the most complex phenomena of world civilization, and none alone can claim primacy.

This book introduces the world's religions through selections from their scriptures. There are special benefits to this avenue of exploration. In most cases the sacred texts are the oldest written documents in the tradition, and we gain a sense of immediate connection by studying the same documents that followers have been reading for millennia. The texts are also foundational to a religion's most important doctrines, rituals, social and ethical positions. Thus, they explain the authoritative basis of traditions that might otherwise seem incomprehensible, or even groundless. Finally, the texts have become the most sacred symbols of these traditions, implying that we are on holy ground each time a sentence is read.

We have prepared our selection of scriptures in three formats. The volume titled *Scriptures of the East* contains the sacred writings of Hinduism, Jainism, Buddhism, Sikhism, Confucianism, Daoism, Shinto, and Australian Aboriginal religions of the East. *Scriptures of the West* contains those of Zoroastrianism, Judaism, Christianity, Islam, the Baha'i Faith, and indigenous religions of the West. The volume titled *Scriptures of the World's Religions* contains all the material in the East and West volumes.

Since very few scriptures were originally written in the English language, these are selections of *translated* scriptures. Efforts have been made to find the most recent and readable translations available. A few scriptures are still available only in older translation, such as the Shinto Nihongi, and therefore are the default choice. We modernized some of these translations in view of recent scholarship. We have also been sensitive in our selection among competing translations. For example, in the Judaism chapter we opted for the

Jewish Publication Society's translation of the *Tanakh* rather than translations of the Old Testament that are more associated with Christianity. Similarly, in the Christianity chapter we used the Scholars Version of the New Testament gospels, a new translation that was prepared free of ecclesiastical and religious control. Unique to this anthology are several scriptures in Asian languages newly translated by John Powers.

An exhaustive collection of world scriptures would be over a thousand volumes in length. Selectivity, therefore, is inevitable. The first difficult choice was to confine the texts to those of religions that are practiced today. This excludes dead traditions that are mainly of academic interest, such as ancient Greek, Mesopotamian, and Egyptian religions. Second, preference is given to texts that discuss the lives and teachings of religious founders and present central doctrines. These are not only of greater intrinsic interest, but assure that the essential differences between religions emerge. Third, the scriptures selected are those accessible to lay practitioners, and not those intended mainly for theologians. Finally, emphasis is placed on religions that have a wide sphere of influence, specifically Hinduism, Buddhism, Judaism, Christianity, and Islam. Less influential religions, specifically Jainism, Shinto, Sikhism, Zoroastrianism, and the Baha'i Faith, are covered more briefly.

In spite of the above boundaries of inclusion, the notion of *scripture* used here is sufficiently broad to include three strata of religious texts. The first stratum involves texts that the religions themselves deem most sacred. The term *protocanonical* is typically used in reference to this level, which includes the Buddhist *Pali Canon,* the Muslim *Qur'an,* and the Jewish *Tanakh.* The second stratum involves more peripheral sacred texts, often termed *deuterocanonical,* that are usually derived from oral tradition. This includes collections of oral law, such as the Jewish *Talmud* and the Muslim *Hadith,* as well as texts on the lives of religious founders, such as the Sikh *Janam-sakhi.* The third stratum involves sectarian texts that at some time in the history of that religion were considered scripture by members of that sect. This final category allows for a broader range of texts than is found in most scripture anthologies, and includes sacred writings from sectarian movements and mystical traditions. Examples are the Christian *Book of Mormon* and the Jewish *Zohar.*

A high priority was placed on including material that supports the interests of women, presents women in positions of leadership, or is written by women. Some of these are Judaism's *Song of Deborah* in the *Tanakh,* the Christian *Gnostic Gospel of Mary,* the mystical sayings of Rabi'a in Islam, Buddhism's *Liberation Songs of the Nuns,* and the Jain debates on enlightenment of women.

The readings within each religion are categorized according to the inherent structure of the scriptural canons themselves, following a sequence of historical narrative or their dates of composition. This is preferred over topical arrangement, influenced by anthropological studies of religion, which eliminates narrative and historical context. We believe that our arrangement is more harmonious with the way each religion understands its own canon and that it is more consistent with how religious studies scholars understand a given religion's scriptures. In addition, it allows readers to gain a sense of the historical development of ideas and practices. This is important since all religious traditions are dynamic systems that create new paradigms in response to changing social conditions and religious ideals, while striving to maintain a perceived connection with their origins. The dynamic relation between tradition and innovation is critical to understanding and interpreting living religious systems. It is hoped that through our arrangement of texts in a roughly chronological sequence, readers will gain a sense of the relations between the origins of religions as reported in early canonical works and subsequent developments.

The most visible change to this second edition is the inclusion of two new sections: Australian Aboriginal Religions of the East, and Indigenous Religions of the West. Transliteration of Chinese terms now follows the Pinyin system, rather than the older Wade-Giles one. In the section on Judaism, new selections are added from the Talmud and on statements of faith. In the Christianity section, new selections are added on early Church fathers, Protestant statements of faith, and recent sectarian movements. In the Islam section, new selections are added from the Hadith and statements of faith.

We thank friends and colleagues who have generously offered advice on this book. Alphabetically, they are Stephen Benin, Ronald C. Bluming, Christopher Buck, Stevan L. Davies, Richard Detweiler, Richard Elliot Friedman, Charles Johnson, Habib Riazati, Norman Lillegard, William Magee, Rochelle Millen, Moojan Momen, Randall Nadeau, Joseph H. Peterson, Richard Pilgrim, Kenneth Rose, Betty Rosian, Aziz Sachedina, Chaim E. Schertz, Robert Stockman, Mark Towfiq, and Mark Tyson.

Scriptures of the East

Hinduism

INTRODUCTION

Contemporary Hindus commonly refer to their tradition as the "universal truth" (*sanatana-dharma*), implying that it is a meta-tradition which is able to embrace the truths of all other systems of thought while transcending them through its expansive ability to embrace truth in multiple manifestations. Hinduism is the dominant religious tradition of the Indian subcontinent, and currently over 700 million people consider themselves to be Hindus.

Hinduism is, however, a difficult tradition to define. Its dominant feature is diversity, and its adherents are not required to accept any doctrine or set of doctrines, to perform any particular practices, or to accept any text or system as uniquely authoritative. Many Hindus, for example, are monotheists and believe that there is only one God, despite the proliferation of gods in Hinduism. They assert that God has many manifestations, and that God may appear differently to different people and different cultures.

Other Hindus are polytheists who believe that the various gods they worship are distinct entities, while pantheistic Hindus perceive the divine in the world around them, as a principle that manifests in natural phenomena, particular places, flora and fauna, or other humans. Some Hindus consider themselves to be agnostic, contending that God is in principle unknown and unknowable. Other Hindus are atheists who do not believe in the existence of any gods, but this position does not lead to their excommunication by their fellow Hindus. Even more confusing, in daily practice it is common to see one person or community sequentially manifesting combinations of these attitudes in different circumstances.

Hinduism has a plethora of doctrines and systems, but there is no collection of tenets that could constitute a universally binding Hindu creed, nor is there any core belief that is so fundamental that it would be accepted by all Hindus. Hinduism has produced a vast collection of sacred texts, but no one has the authority of the Christian Bible, the Jewish Torah, or the Muslim Qur'an. Perhaps the most widely revered sacred texts are the Vedas ("Wisdom Texts"), most of which were written over 2,000 years ago, but despite their generally accepted authoritativeness, few Hindus today are even able to read them, and the *brahmins* (priests) whose sacred task is to memorize and recite them generally are unable to explain what they mean.

In searching for a way to define the boundaries of Hinduism, the term "Hindu" may provide some help. It was originally coined by Persians who used it to refer to the people they encountered in northern India. Thus, the term "Hindu" originally referred to the inhabitants of a geographical area, and in later centuries it was adopted by people of India who identified themselves with the dominant religious tradition of the subcontinent.

Contemporary Hinduism is still delimited more by geography than by belief or practice: a Hindu is someone who lives on the Indian subcontinent or is descended from people of the region, who considers himself or herself to be a Hindu, and who is accepted as such by other Hindus. There are no distinctive doctrines whose acceptance would serve as a litmus test of orthodoxy, no ecclesiastical authority that is able to declare some to be Hindus in good standing or label others as heretics, and no ceremony whose performance would serve as a definitive rite of passage into the tradition. There is no founder of the tradition; it has no dominant system of theology or single moral code. Contemporary Hinduism embraces groups whose respective faiths and practices have virtually nothing in common with each other.

This is not to say, however, that Hinduism lacks distinctive doctrines, practices, or scriptures; in fact, the exact opposite is the case. Hinduism has developed a plethora of philosophical schools, rituals, and sacred texts, and its adherents commonly assert a belief in a shared heritage, historical continuity, and family relationships between the multiple manifestations of their tradition. The selections given below represent only a small sampling of the vast corpus of Hindu religious literature. In addition, it should be noted that this literature represents only a tiny part of the Hindu tradition, and primarily reflects the views and practices of a small intellectual elite. The vast majority of Hindus have been—and continue to be—primarily illiterate agricultural workers with little if any knowledge of the sacred scriptures. Their practices are generally derived from local cults and beliefs that often have little in common with the religion and philosophy of the authors of the scriptures. Furthermore, these texts do not form a coherent system, but are as diverse as Hinduism itself. They were written over the course of millennia and reflect shifting paradigms and political, religious, and social agendas, geographical differences, and varying ideas about how people should worship, think, live, and interact.

History of Hinduism and Hindu Scriptures

Hinduism may be compared to a complex symphony in which new themes are introduced as the piece develops, while old ones continue to be woven into its texture. Nothing is ever truly lost, and elements of the distant past often return to prominence at unexpected times, although often in forms that are altered in accordance with the intellectual and religious currents of a particular time and place. The scriptures of Hinduism reflect its diversity and its complex history. They include ancient hymns to anthropomorphic gods and liturgical texts detailing how priests should prepare sacrifices, mystical texts that speculate on the nature of ultimate reality, devotional literature to a variety of deities, philosophical texts of great subtlety and insight, and combinations of these and related themes.

The earliest stratum of Indian sacred literature that is accessible today is found in the Vedas, which evolved into their present form between 1400 and 400 B.C.E. The earliest of these were brought to India around 1300 B.C.E. by seminomadic tribes who referred to themselves as Aryans, meaning "noble" or "wise." Upon their arrival, the newcomers encountered indigenous inhabitants, who were dubbed "slaves" (*dasa* or *dasyu*).The Vedas are referred to by Hindus as "revelation" (*shruti*, literally "what is heard"), in contrast to other scriptures referred to as "tradition" (*smriti*, literally "what is remembered"). Both classes are regarded as canonical, but the latter is not considered to have the same level of authoritativeness as the Vedas. The Vedas, being completely transcendent, are not subject to human imperfections, but are products of direct revelation.

There are four Vedas: (1) the *Rig Veda*, so named because it is composed of stanzas (*rik*); (2) the *Sama Veda* (composed mostly of hymns taken from the *Rig Veda* and set to various melodies, or *saman*); (3) the *Yajur Veda* (composed of *yajus*, selected ritual prayers, mostly taken from the *Rig Veda*); and (4) the *Atharva Veda* (a collection of ritual texts named after the sage Atharvan). The Vedas contain several primary types of literature: (1) chants or hymns (*samhita*), generally directed toward the gods (*deva*) of the Vedic pantheon; (2) ritual texts (*brahmana*), which detail the sacrifices performed by brahmins; (3) mystical texts concerned with the quest for ultimate truth (*aranyakas* and *upanishads*). According to tradition, the Vedas are not the product of human composition (*apaurusheya*), but are a part of the very fabric of reality. They were directly perceived by "seers" (*rishi*), whose mystical contemplations— aided by ingestion of an intoxicating beverage called *soma*—enabled them to intuit primordial sounds reverberating throughout the universe, and rendered into human language as the books of the Vedas.

Aryan Religion and Society

Contemporary scholars commonly refer to the indigenous people of the subcontinent as Dravidians, and recent archeological evidence suggests that they attained a high degree of social development prior to the arrival of the Aryans, although their society was probably in decline by the time the Aryans began to enter India. The Aryans were of European stock, and described themselves as tall, fair-skinned, blond-haired, and civilized, while they characterized the indigenous people as short, snub-nosed, curly-haired, barbaric, and immoral. They viewed their coming as a positive development that introduced righteousness and civilization to the region, and during the next several centuries they gradually subjugated the Dravidians, who were generally relegated to the lowest levels of Aryan society.

From an early period, the Aryans and their descendants propounded the idea that human society should ideally be stratified, with each social class having clearly defined functions and duties. At the top of the hierarchy were the brahmins, the priestly class, whose sacred duty was to perform sacrifices to the gods described in the Vedas. Many of these gods were personifications of natural phenomena, such as the sun and moon, wind, and so forth. Many gods were believed to have dominion over a particular natural force or phenomenon, and the rituals of the Vedas were commonly directed to either one god or a small group of gods who were considered to have the ability to affect a particular sphere of divine provenance.

The role of the priests was central in this system: They were expected to remain ritually pure and to preserve the sacred texts, along with the sacred lore of priestcraft. Their social function prevented them from engaging in manual labor, trade, agriculture, or other nonpriestly occupations, since these were considered polluting. In exceptional circumstances occasioned by special need they were allowed to earn a living by other means, but ideally their lives should be devoted to study of the sacred Vedas and performance of Vedic rituals. This was crucial to the maintenance of the system of "upholding the world" (*loka-samgraha*), which was a core concern of Vedic religion. In this system, the brahmins performed a pivotal function in offering sacrifices to the gods. The sacrifices were generally transmuted into smoke through the agency of Agni, god of fire (who is manifested in the ritual fire, as well as other forms of combustion). Smoke converted the material of the sacrifice into a subtle essence suitable for the gods' consumption, and the process required that the brahmins remain ritually pure, since any pollution they acquired was passed on to their sacrifices. The gods would naturally be insulted if offered unclean food and would respond by denying the requests the brahmins made on behalf of the sponsors of the sacrifices.

The Vedic system was based on a symbiosis of gods and humans: The gods required the sacrificial offerings, and humans needed the gods to use their supernatural powers to maintain cosmic order (*rita*). The system assumed that humans only prosper in a stable and ordered cosmos, an idea that is reflected in the story of the slaying of the demon Vritra ("Obstructer") by Indra, the king of the gods in the Vedas. Demons thrive in chaos, and at the beginning of time Vritra rules over a chaotic cosmos until Indra, after a mighty battle, slays him and thus makes it possible for the gods to establish order. This primordial battle reflects the crucial role played by the gods in establishing and maintaining cosmic law.

The concerns of Vedic literature are primarily practical and this-worldly. They focus on particular pragmatic goals, such as bountiful crops, fertility, peace, stability, wealth, and so forth. The results of the sacrifices are believed to accrue in the present life, and although a world of the dead is mentioned, it does not play a major role in the early Vedic tradition.

The Upanishads and Yoga

The focus shifts in the later Vedic period, in which texts of speculative philosophy and mysticism begin to appear. Referred to as Aranyakas and Upanishads, they were written by sages who often expressed dissatisfaction with the ritualism and this-worldly focus of the early Vedic texts. Their authors sought the ultimate power behind the sacrifices, the force that gives rise to gods, humans, and all the other phenomena of the universe. They found this through a process of inward-looking meditation that sought an unchanging essence beyond the transient phenomena of existence. The present life was no longer viewed as the beginning and end of one's existence; rather, living beings were said to be reborn in successive lives in accordance with their actions (*karma*). The actions of the present result in opposite and equal reactions in the future, and one's present life was said to be a result of the karma accrued in the past. The cycle of existence (*samsara*) was said by the sages of the Upanishads to be beginningless, but it may be ended. It is perpetuated by a basic misunderstanding of the true nature of reality (*avidya*, "ignorance"), but one may escape it by attaining correct understanding of truth, which is found only by people who shift their attention from external things to find the truly real.

By following the path of wisdom that correctly discriminates the real from the unreal, the truly important from the merely pleasant, and the changeless from the transitory, the sage eventually discovers that within everyone is an eternal, unchanging essence, an immortal soul referred to as the "self" (*atman*). The Upanishads declare that this essence alone survives death, that it has been reborn countless times in an infinite variety of different bodies, while itself remaining unchanged by the multiple identities we all develop in successive lifetimes. It is characterized by three qualities: being, consciousness, and bliss (*sat cit ananda*), meaning that it is pure, unchanging being, and its nature is never altered, despite the changing external circumstances of our lives; it is pure consciousness that takes no notice of the vicissitudes of our lives; and it remains unaffected by our joys, sorrows, hopes, disappointments, pleasures, or pains, and so it is in a continuous state of equanimity. Moreover, the Upanishadic sages identified the self with the cosmic ultimate, something supremely mysterious, hidden from ordinary perception but all-pervasive, supremely subtle, the essence of all that is. This ultimate was said to be beyond words or conceptual thought, and was referred to as "Brahman," because it is the purest and most sublime principle of existence, just as in human society brahmins are the purest and holiest class.

According to this system, the perceptions of ordinary beings are profoundly distorted by ignorance, and the only way to attain correct knowledge is through a process of discipline (*yoga*) in which one's thoughts and body are gradually brought under control, and one's attention is turned away from sense objects and directed within. These premises are shared with the system outlined in the *Yoga Aphorisms* (*Yoga-sutra*) of Patanjali, who is credited with gathering together the principal practices and premises of the yoga system. Patanjali's system, however, differs in significant ways from that of the Upanishads, although both use the term "yoga" to describe their respective training programs. The Upanishads outline a monistic system in which the sole reality is said to be Brahman, while everything else is based on mistaken perceptions. Patanjali, by contrast, contends that both matter (*prakriti*) and spirit (*purusha*) are real entities, and the goal of his system is separation (*kaivalya*) of spirit from matter, while the Upanishads aim at a final apotheosis in which all dualities are transcended and one realizes the fundamental identity of the self and Brahman. The final goal of the Upanishads is expressed in the greatest of the "great statements" (*mahavakya*) that sum up the central insights of the Upanishadic sages: "That is you" (*tat tvam asi*), which expresses the identity of the individual soul and Brahman. Patanjali's goal, by contrast, is separation that liberates one's spiritual essence from matter.

The goal of both systems is liberation (*moksha*) from the cycle of existence, but each conceives release differently. Both consider yoga to be the primary practice for attaining the final goal, and for both yoga is a program of introspective meditation that begins with physical discipline, control of random, ignorant thoughts, and development of insight into unchanging truth, but the ontological presuppositions and ultimate goals of the two systems differ in significant details.

Social Structure

The Upanishads and Patanjali's yoga system represent a shift from the primacy of sacrifices to the gods in the early Vedic period to a general acceptance of the idea that the final goal of the religious path is *moksha*. As final liberation from cyclic existence came to be viewed as the supreme goal, sacrifices aimed at maintaining the order of the world and the acquisition of mundane benefits were consequently devalued as inferior to the pursuit of knowledge of truth. As an apparent reaction to this trend, orthodox elements began to stress the importance of performing one's social duties (*dharma*). Texts like the *Laws of Manu* and the *Bhagavad-gita* emphasized the importance of selfless, devout adherence to the duties of one's social class (*varna*): the brahmins, the warriors and rulers (*kshatriya*), the merchants and tradespeople (*vaishya*), and the servants (*shudra*). Both texts asserted that if people ignore their sacred duty the world will fall into chaos, society will crumble, and essential social functions will not be performed. The *Laws of Manu* delineate a system in which people should eventually renounce the world and pursue final liberation, but only after first performing the duties assigned to their social class. In its system of "duties of social classes and stages of life" (*varnashrama-dharma*), there are specific duties for each class, and these should be performed diligently in order to maintain the world. The system assumes that only in an ordered universe will some people have the leisure and resources to pursue liberation.

The ideal life begins with the student stage, in which a man finds a spiritual preceptor (*guru*), who teaches him the lore appropriate to his class. The three highest classes (brahmins, kshatriyas, and vaishyas) are said to be "twice-born" (*dvija*) because they undergo a ceremony (the *upanayana*) that initiates them into adulthood and is considered a "second birth." Only these three classes are permitted to study the Vedas or participate in Vedic rituals (but officiating in Vedic ceremonies is the special duty of brahmins).

After a period of study (which varies in length and content among the four classes), a man should marry, produce male heirs to continue the lineage and perform sacrifices for him and his ancestors after his death, and support the brahmins whose rituals maintain the whole cosmos. According to Manu, after a man has successfully performed his duty, and when he sees his grandson born (assuring that the lineage will continue) and gray hairs on his head, he may withdraw from society (often with his wife) and begin to sever the ties that he cultivated during his life in the world. As a "forest dweller" (*vanaprastha*), he should be celibate and detached from worldly enjoyments, cultivate meditation on ultimate truth, and pursue liberation. When he knows that his attachment to mundane things has ceased, he may take the final step of becoming a "world renouncer" (*samnyasin*), completely devoted to the ultimate goal, wandering from place to place and subsisting on alms, intent on final liberation from cyclic existence.

In this system, everything has its time and place, and while liberation is recognized as the ultimate goal of the religious life, it is not allowed to be pursued in a way that might destabilize society. When the demands of dharma have been met, one may pursue one's own ends, but Manu declares that renouncing the world too soon would lead to a degeneration of the whole society, and the resulting chaos would make the attainment of liberation difficult, if not impossible, for anyone.

The Path of Devotion

Another important path to liberation lies in the "yoga of devotion" (*bhakti-yoga*), in which one finds salvation through completely identifying oneself with God. The yoga of devotion requires that one focus one's attention so completely on God that all thoughts of ego are transcended in a pure experience of union. There are a variety of ways of conceiving devotion: Sometimes it takes the form of a love affair in which the devotee experiences an ecstatic union surpassing any human love; for others devotion takes the form of selfless service to an omnipotent master. Often Hindu devotionalism exhibits elements of both, along with a feeling of an intensely personal relationship between a human being and God.

The selections presented below are arranged in a roughly chronological order and are taken from a wide range of Hindu scriptures. Of necessity many important scriptures have been omitted from this survey, and the ones that have been included were chosen because they exemplify central themes of contemporary and traditional Hindu religious thought.

VEDAS

CREATION OF THE UNIVERSE

The following selections are taken from the Rig Veda, *and are hymns and ritual texts devoted to the worship of the Vedic gods. These verses describe the attributes of the gods, recounting the mythos of each god and his or her particular sacrificial functions and associations. The first hymn depicts the creation of the universe as beginning with the sacrifice of Purusha ("Man"), a giant god whose body formed the raw material for the formation of the stars, the planets, and living things. According to the story, the four social classes* (varna) *of Hinduism were also created through this sacrifice, thus providing a scriptural justification for the stratification of Indian society.*

1. The Man had a thousand heads, a thousand eyes, a thousand feet. He pervaded the earth on all sides and extended beyond it as far as ten fingers.
2. It is the Man who is all this, whatever has been and what ever is to be. He is the ruler of immortality, when he grows beyond everything through food.
3. Such is his greatness, and the Man is yet more than this. All creatures are a quarter of him; three quarters are what is immortal in heaven.
4. With three quarters the Man rose upwards, and one quarter of him still remains here. From this he spread out in all directions, into that which eats and that which does not eat. . . .
6. When the gods spread the sacrifice with the Man as the offering, spring was the clarified butter, summer the fuel, autumn the oblation.
7. They anointed the Man, the sacrifice born at the beginning, upon the sacred grass. With him the gods, Sadhyas, and sages sacrificed.
8. From that sacrifice in which everything was offered, the melted fat was collected, and he made it into those beasts who live in the air, in the forest, and in villages.
9. From that sacrifice in which everything was offered, the verses and chants were born, the metres were born from it, and from it the formulas were born.
10. Horses were born from it, and those other animals that have two rows of teeth; cows were born from it, and from it goats and sheep were born.
11. When they divided the Man, into how many parts did they apportion him? What do they call his mouth, his two arms and thighs and feet?
12. His mouth became the Brahmin; his arms were made into the Warrior (*kshatriya*), his thighs the People (*vaishya*), and from his feet the Servants (*shudra*) were born. . . .
15. The moon was born from his mind; from his eye the sun was born. Indra and Agni came from his mouth, and from his vital breath the Wind was born.
14. From his navel the middle realm of space arose; from his head the sky evolved. From his two feet came the earth, and the quarters of the sky from his ear. Thus they set the worlds in order. . . .
16. With the sacrifice the gods sacrificed to the sacrifice. These were the first ritual laws (*dharma*). These very powers reached the dome of the sky where dwell the Sadhyas, the ancient gods.

Source: *Rig Veda* I0.90: *Purusha-Sukta,* from *The Rig Veda,* tr. Wendy Doniger O'Flaherty (New York: Penguin, 1981), pp. 30–31.

ORIGIN OF THE GODS

This passage offers another view of creation. It indicates that originally existence arose from nonexistence and that the gods later were produced by a goddess "who crouched with legs spread," an image with obvious anthropomorphic overtones. It suggests that the creation of the gods was similar to a human birth, but the position described may also suggest that creation is linked with the practice of yoga, which is believed to produce energy that may be used in the generation of life.

1. Let us now speak with wonder of the births of the gods—so that some one may see them when the hymns are chanted in this later age.
2. The lord of sacred speech, like a smith, fanned them together. In the earliest age of the gods, existence was born from nonexistence.
3. In the first age of the gods, existence was born from nonexistence. After this the quarters of the sky were born from her who crouched with legs spread.
4. The earth was born from her who crouched with legs spread, and from the earth the quarters of the sky were born. From Aditi, Daksha was born, and from Daksha Aditi was born.
5. For Aditi was born as your daughter, O Daksha, and after her were born the blessed gods, the kinsmen of immortality.
6. When you gods took your places there in the water with your hands joined together, a thick cloud of mist arose from you like dust from dancers.
7. When you gods like magicians caused the worlds to swell, you drew forth the sun that was hidden in the ocean.
8. Eight sons are there of Aditi, who were born of her body. With seven she went forth among the gods, but she threw Martanda, the sun, aside.
9. With seven sons Aditi went forth into the earliest age. But she bore Martanda so that he would in turn beget offspring and then soon die.

Source: *Rig Veda* 10.72, from *The Rig Veda*, pp. 38–39.

INDRA, THE PARADIGMATIC WARRIOR

In Vedic mythology, Indra is said to be the king of the gods, and he embodies the warrior virtues valued by the Aryans. He is fearless in battle, always victorious over his enemies and, although he is sometimes portrayed as proud and boastful, these qualities do not detract from his prowess as a warrior. This hymn recounts the greatest of his mighty deeds, the slaying of the demon Vritra, a powerful serpentlike creature that was wreaking havoc throughout the universe, holding back the rain waters that are essential to the prosperity of living things, and obstructing the establishment of cosmic order, which is required for a stable and harmonious world. Wielding his mighty thunderbolt, Indra slays the demon, splits open his body, cuts off his limbs, and thus eliminates the threat he poses.

1. Let me now sing the heroic deeds of Indra, the first that the thunderbolt-wielder performed. He killed the dragon and pierced an opening for the waters; he split open the bellies of mountains.
2. He killed the dragon who lay upon the mountain; Tvashtri fashioned the roaring thunderbolt for him. Like lowing cows, the flowing waters rushed straight down to the sea.
3. Wildly excited like a bull, he took the Soma for himself and drank the extract from the three bowls in the three-day Soma ceremony. Indra the Generous seized his thunderbolt to hurl it as a weapon; he killed the first-born of dragons.
4. Indra, when you killed the first-born of dragons and overcame by your own magic the magic of the magicians, at that very moment you brought forth the sun, the sky, and dawn. Since then you have found no enemy to conquer you.
5. With his great weapon, the thunderbolt, Indra killed the shoulderless Vritra, his greatest enemy. Like the trunk of a tree whose branches have been lopped off by an axe, the dragon lies flat upon the ground.
6. For, muddled by drunkenness like one who is no soldier, Vritra challenged the great hero who had overcome the mighty and who drank Soma to the dregs. Unable to withstand the onslaught of his weapons, he found Indra an enemy to conquer him and was shattered, his nose crushed.
7. Without feet or hands he fought against Indra, who struck him on the nape of the neck with his thunderbolt. The steer who wished to become the equal of the bull bursting with seed, Vritra lay broken in many places.
8. Over him as he lay there like a broken reed the swelling waters flowed for man. Those waters that Vritra had enclosed with his power—the dragon now lay at their feet.
9. The vital energy of Vritra's mother ebbed away, for Indra had hurled his deadly weapon at her. Above was the mother, below was the son; Danu lay down like a cow with her calf.
10. In the midst of the channels of the waters which never stood still or rested, the body was hidden. The waters flow over Vritra's secret place; he who found Indra an enemy to conquer him sank into long darkness.
11. The waters who had the Dasa for their husband, the dragon for their protector, were imprisoned like the cows imprisoned by the Panis. When he killed Vritra he split open the outlet of the waters that had been closed.
12. Indra, you became a hair of a horse's tail when Vritra struck you on the corner of the mouth. You, the one god, the brave one, you won the cows; you won the Soma; you released the seven streams so that they could flow.
13. No use was the lightning and thunder, fog and hail that he had scattered about, when the dragon and Indra fought. Indra the Generous remained victorious for all time to come.

14. What avenger of the dragon did you see, Indra, that fear entered your heart when you had killed him? Then you crossed the ninety-nine streams like the frightened eagle crossing the realms of earth and air.

15. Indra, who wields the thunderbolt in his hand, is the king of that which moves and that which rests, of the tame and of the horned. He rules the people as their king, encircling all this as a rim encircles spokes.

Source: *Rig Veda* 1.3, from *The Rig Veda*, pp. 149–151.

PRAYER TO AGNI, THE GOD OF FIRE

Agni is one of the most important gods of the Vedas. As the god of fire, he transmutes sacrificial offerings into smoke, which is consumed by the gods. Thus he serves as the intermediary between the divine and human realms and is a paradigm for the brahmin priests.

1. I pray to Agni, the household priest who is the god of the sacrifice, the one who chants and invokes and brings most treasure.
2. Agni earned the prayers of the ancient sages, and of those of the present, too; he will bring the gods here.
3. Through Agni one may win wealth, and growth from day to day, glorious and most abounding in heroic sons.
4. Agni, the sacrificial ritual that you encompass on all sides—only that one goes to the gods.
5. Agni, the priest with the sharp sight of a poet, the true and most brilliant, the god will come with the gods.
6. Whatever good you wish to do for the one who worships you, Agni, through you, O Angiras, that comes true.
7. To you, Agni, who shine upon darkness, we come day after day, bringing our thoughts and homage.
8. To you, the king over sacrifices, the shining guardian of the Order, growing in your own house.
9. Be easy for us to reach, like a father to his son. Abide with us, Agni, for our happiness.

Source: *Rig Veda* 1.1, from *The Rig Veda*, p. 99.

BURNING DEAD BODIES

This hymn invokes Agni in his role as transporter of the dead. He is asked to burn the corpse of a dead man and to ensure that he is brought to the land of the dead. The concept of afterlife is rather vague in the early Vedas. There are references to a world of the dead, ruled by Yama, who was the first human to die. He found the way to the land of the dead, and now he brings others there. At the end of the ritual the pyre is soaked so thoroughly with water that a small pool is formed, and plants, frogs, and other living things will grow there, symbolizing the renewal of life from the ashes of death.

[To Agni:] Do not burn him entirely, Agni, or engulf him in your flames. Do not consume his skin or his flesh. When you have cooked him perfectly, O knower of creatures, only then send him forth to the fathers. When you cook him perfectly, O knower of creatures, then give him over to the fathers. When he goes on the path that leads away the vital breath, then he will be led by the will of the gods.

[To the dead man:] May your eye go to the sun, your vital breath to the wind. Go to the sky or to earth, as is your nature; or go to the waters, if that is your fate. Take root in the plants with your limbs.

[To the funeral fire:] The goat is your share; burn him with your heat. Let your brilliant light and flame burn him. With your gentle forms, O knower of creatures, carry this man to the world of those who have done good deeds. Set him free again to go to the fathers, Agni, when he has been offered as an oblation in you and wanders with the sacrificial drink. Let him reach his own descendants, dressing himself in a life-span. O knower of creatures, let him join with a body.

[To the dead man:] Whatever the black bird has pecked out of you, or the ant, the snake, or even a beast of prey, may Agni who eats all things make it whole, and Soma who has entered the Brahmins. Gird yourself with the limbs of the cow as an armor against Agni, and cover yourself with fat and suet, so that he will not embrace you with his impetuous heat in his passionate desire to burn you up.

[To the funeral fire:] O Agni, do not overturn this cup, that is dear to the gods and to those who love Soma, fit for the gods to drink from, a cup in which the immortal gods carouse. I send the flesh-eating fire far away. Let him go to those whose king is Yama, carrying away all impurities. But let that other (form of fire), the knower of creatures, come here and carry the oblation to the gods, since he knows the way in advance.

[To the dead man:] The flesh-eating fire has entered your house, though he sees there the other, the knower of creatures; I take that god away to the sacrifice of the fathers. Let him carry the heated drink to the farthest dwelling place. . . .

[To the new fire:] Joyously would we put you in place, joyously would we kindle you. Joyously carry the joyous fathers here to eat the oblation. Now, Agni, quench and revive the very one you have burnt up. Let water plants grow in this place. O cool one, bringer of coolness; O fresh one, bringer of freshness; unite with the female frog. Delight and inspire this Agni.

Source: *Rig Veda* 10.16, from Wendy Doniger O'Flaherty, *Textual Sources for the Study of Hinduism,* (Chicago: University of Chicago Press, 1988), p. 7.

THE BENEFICIAL EFFECTS OF DRINKING SOMA

Soma is an intoxicating drink that plays a major role in Vedic literature. It was made from a creeping plant that was crushed and strained to make a whitish beverage that apparently produced visions and ecstatic states of mind. The plant used is a matter of current debate, and a number of theories have been proposed, none of which is considered definitive by contemporary scholars. As this passage indicates, those who drank it experienced a feeling of exaltation and expansion of consciousness. The writer of this hymn claims that drinking it has also made him immortal.

1. I have tasted the sweet drink of life, knowing that it inspires good thoughts and joyous expansiveness to the extreme, that all the gods and mortals seek it together, calling it honey.

2. When you penetrate inside, you will know no limits, and you will avert the wrath of the gods. Enjoying Indra's friendship, O drop of Soma, bring riches as a docile cow brings the yoke.

3. We have drunk the Soma; we have become immortal; we have gone to the light; we have found the gods. What can hatred and the malice of a mortal do to us now, O immortal one?

4. When we have drunk you, O drop of Soma, be good to our heart, kind as a father to his son, thoughtful as a friend to a friend. Far-famed Soma, stretch out our lifespan so that we may live.

5. The glorious drops that I have drunk set me free in wide space. You have bound me together in my limbs as thongs bind a chariot. Let the drops protect me from the foot that stumbles and keep lameness away from me.

6. Inflame me like a fire kindled by friction; make us see far; make us richer, better. For when I am intoxicated with you, Soma, I think myself rich. Draw near and make us thrive.

7. We would enjoy you, pressed with a fervent heart, like riches from a father. King Soma, stretch out our lifespans as the sun stretches the spring days.

8. King Soma, have mercy on us for our well-being. Know that we are devoted to your laws. Passion and fury are stirred up. O drop of Soma, do not hand us over to the pleasure of the enemy.

9. For you, Soma, are the guardian of our body; watching over men, you have settled down in every limb. If we break your laws, O god, have mercy on us like a good friend, to make us better.

10. Let me join closely with my compassionate friend [Soma] so that he will not injure me when I have drunk him. O lord of bay horses, for the Soma that is lodged in us I approach Indra to stretch out our lifespan.

11. Weaknesses and diseases have gone; the forces of darkness have fled in terror. Soma has climbed up in us, expanding. We have come to the place where they stretch out lifespans.

12. The drop that we have drunk has entered our hearts, an immortal inside mortals. O fathers, let us serve that Soma with the oblations and abide in his mercy and kindness.

13. Uniting in agreement with the fathers, O drop of Soma, you have extended yourself through sky and earth. Let us serve him with an oblation; let us be masters of riches.

14. You protecting Gods, speak out for us. Do not let sleep or harmful speech seize us. Let us, always dear to Soma, speak as men of power in the sacrificial gathering.
15. Soma, you give us the force of life on every side. Enter into us, finding the sunlight, watching over men. O drop of Soma, summon your helpers and protect us before and after.

Source: *Rig Veda* 8.48, from *The Rig Veda*, pp. 134–136.

SEX AND THE YOGIN

This hymn depicts a struggle between a husband and wife named Agastya and Lopamudra. Lopamudra has just successfully seduced Agastya, who was trying to avoid sexual intercourse in order to store up the vital energy he acquired as a product of yogic exertions. It captures a common theme in classical Indian literature: woman as temptress, whose unrestrained sexual desire and physical charms distract male yogins from their ascetic practice and cause them to dissipate the power they have painstakingly gained through meditation and self-restraint.

1. [Lopamudra:] 'For many autumns past I have toiled, night and day, and each dawn has brought old age closer, age that distorts the glory of bodies. Virile men should go to their wives.
2. For even the men of the past, who acted according to the Law and talked about the Law with the gods, broke off when they did not find the end. Women should unite with virile men.'
3. [Agastya:] 'Not in vain is all this toil, which the gods encourage. We two must always strive against each other, and by this we will win the race that is won by a hundred means, when we merge together as a couple.'
4. [Lopamudra:] 'Desire has come upon me for the bull who roars and is held back, desire engulfing me from this side, that side, all sides.'
5. [The poet:] Lopamudra draws out the virile bull: the foolish woman sucks dry the panting wise man.
6. [Agastya:] 'By this Soma which I have drunk, in my innermost heart I say: Let him forgive us if we have sinned, for a mortal is full of many desires.'
7. Agastya, digging with spades, wishing for children, progeny, and strength, nourished both ways, for he was a powerful sage. He found fulfillment of his real hopes among the gods.

Source: *Rig Veda* 1.179, from *The Rig Veda*, pp. 250–251.

A CLEVER WOMAN

This hymn is spoken by a woman who has managed to eliminate her rivals and emerge victorious over her husband, who now submits to her will.

1. There the sun has risen, and here my good fortune has risen. Being a clever woman, and able to triumph, I have triumphed over my husband.
2. I am the banner; I am the head. I am the formidable one who has the deciding word. My husband will obey my will alone, as I emerge triumphant.
3. My sons kill their enemies and my daughter is an empress, and I am completely victorious. My voice is supreme in my husband's ears.
4. The oblation that Indra made and so became glorious and supreme, this is what I have made for you, O gods. I have become truly without rival wives.
5. Without rival wives, killer of rival wives, victorious and pre-eminent, I have grabbed for myself the attraction of the other women as if it were the wealth of flighty women.
6. I have conquered and become pre-eminent over these rival wives, so that I may rule as empress over this hero and over the people.

Source: *Rig Veda* 10.159, from *The Rig Veda,* p. 291.

THE HORSE SACRIFICE

The horse sacrifice served to establish the dominion of a king by demonstrating how large an area he controlled. For a year prior to the sacrifice, a horse would be set free to wander wherever it wished, indicating the hegemony of the king. To the extent that other rulers were unable to turn the horse away, it served notice of the areas a particular ruler effectively controlled. At the end of the year the horse was offered as a sacrifice to the gods, but although it was killed it is stated in the ritual that it would enjoy a future in heaven.

[To the priests:] The invoker, the officiant, the overseer, the fire-kindler, the holder of the pressing-stones, the cantor, the sacrificial priest—fill your bellies with this well-prepared, well-sacrificed sacrifice. The hewers of the sacrificial stake and those who carry it, and those who carve the knob for the horse's sacrificial stake, and those who gather together the things to cook the charger—let their approval encourage us. The horse with his smooth back went forth into the fields of the gods, just when I made my prayer. The inspired sages exult in him. We have made him a welcome companion at the banquet of the gods.

[To the horse:] The charger's rope and halter, the reins and bridle on the head, and even the grass that has been held up to the mouth—let all that stay with you even among the gods. Whatever of the horse's flesh the fly has eaten, or whatever stays stuck to the stake or the axe, or to the hands or nails of the slaughterer—let all of that stay with you even among the gods. Whatever food remains in the stomach, sending forth gas, or whatever smell there is from the raw flesh—let the slaughterers make that well done; let them cook the sacrificial animal until he is perfectly cooked.

Whatever runs off your body when it has been placed on the spit and roasted by the fire, let it not lie there in the earth or on the grass, but let it be given to the gods who long for it.

[To the priests:] Those (priests) who see that the racehorse is cooked, who say, 'It smells good! Take it away!,' and who wait for the doling out of the flesh of the charger—let their approval encourage us. The testing fork for the cauldron that cooks the flesh, the pots for pouring the broth, the cover of the bowls to keep it warm, the hooks, the dishes—all these attend the horse.

[To the horse:] The place where the horse walks, where he rests, where he rolls, and the fetters on the horse's feet, and what he has drunk and the fodder he has eaten—let all of that stay with you even among the gods. Let not the fire that reeks of smoke darken you, nor the red-hot cauldron split into pieces. The gods receive the horse who has been sacrificed, worshipped, consecrated, and sanctified with the cry of 'Vashat!' The cloth that they spread beneath the horse, the upper covering, the golden trappings on him, the halter and the fetters on his feet—let these things that are his own bind the horse among the gods.

[To the horse:] If someone riding you has struck you too hard with heel or whip when you shied, I make all these things well again for you with prayer, as they do with the ladle for the oblation in sacrifices.

[To the priests:] The axe cuts through the thirty-four ribs of the racehorse who is the companion of the gods. Keep the limbs undamaged and place them in the proper pattern. Cut them apart, calling out piece by piece. One (priest) is the slaughterer of the horse of Tvashtri; two (priests) restrain him. This is the rule.

[To the horse:] As many of your limbs as I set out, according to the rules, so many balls I offer into the fire. Let not your dear soul burn you as you go away. Let not the axe do lasting harm to your body. Let no greedy, clumsy slaughterer hack in the wrong place and damage your limbs with his knife. You do not really die through this, nor are you harmed. You go to the gods on paths pleasant to go on. The two bay stallions, the two roan mares are now your chariot mates. The racehorse has been set in the donkey's yoke.

[To the gods:] Let this racehorse bring us good cattle and good horses, male children and all nourishing wealth. Let Aditi make us free from sin. Let the horse with our offerings achieve sovereign power for us.

Source: *Rig Veda* 1.162, from *Textual Sources for the Study of Hinduism*, pp. 9–10.

TO THE FIRE ALTAR

This hymn is used to help the sacrificer mentally prepare prior to performance of the sacrifice. He visualizes the fire altar as the entire universe and views the sacrifice as a way to attain spiritual knowledge. It is notable in that it shows the increasingly cosmic significance given to the rituals: they were no longer merely localized sacrifices performed for particular ends, but instead microcosmic expressions of macrocosmic forces and processes. The sacrificer meditates on the greater ramifications of the sacrifice about to be performed, its cosmic repercussions, and its transformative effects on the person who performs it. It also shows an expanding view of the cosmos and a corresponding expansion in the religious vision of brahmin priests, who are no longer content simply to perform sacrifices for limited goals, but increasingly interested in the effects they will have beyond this world and in the mind of the sacrificer.

1. The fire altar built here is this world. The stones surrounding it are the waters. Its Yajushmati bricks are humans. Its Sudadohas [a drink of immortality] are cows. Plants and trees are its cement, offerings, and fuel. Agni is its connecting bricks. Thus this constitutes all of Agni. Agni pervades space. Whoever knows this becomes all of Agni, the pervader of space.
2. Moreover, the fire altar is also the air. The horizon is its surrounding circle of bricks. . . .The birds are its Yajushmati bricks. . . .
3. Moreover, the fire altar is also the sky. . . .
4. Moreover, the fire altar is also the sun. . . .
5. Moreover, the fire altar is also the stars. . . .
7. Moreover, the fire altar is also the meters [of verses]. . . .
10. Moreover, the fire altar is also the year. . . .
12. Moreover, the fire altar is also the body. . . .
14. Moreover, the fire altar is also all beings and all gods. All the gods and all beings are the waters, and the constructed fire altar is the same as the waters. . . .
16. Referring to this, the verse states:
   By way of wisdom they ascend to the place where desires disappear.
   Neither sacrificial gifts nor the devoted performers of sacrifices who lack wisdom go there.
   One who is ignorant of this does not go to that world either by sacrificial offerings or devout actions.
   It belongs to those with wisdom.

Source: *Shatapatha Brahmana* 10.5.4.1–16.

WHAT IS THE ORIGIN OF THE WORLD?

This poem represents an early speculative tendency from the Vedic period. The writer of the poem is considering what, if anything, existed before the world as we know it, before creation, and even before the birth of the gods.

There was neither nonexistence nor existence then; there was neither the realm of space nor the sky which is beyond. What stirred? Where? In whose protection? Was there water, bottomlessly deep? There was neither death nor immortality then. There was no distinguishing sign of night nor of day. That one breathed, windless, by its own impulse. Other than that there was nothing beyond. Darkness was hidden by darkness in the beginning; with no distinguishing sign, all this was water. The life force that was covered with emptiness, that one arose through the power of heat.

Desire came upon that one in the beginning; that was the first seed of mind. Poets seeking in their heart with wisdom found the bond of existence in nonexistence. Their cord was extended across. Was there below? Was there above? There were seed-placers; there were powers. There was impulse beneath; there was giving-forth above.

Who really knows? Who will here proclaim it? Whence was it produced? Whence is this creation? The gods came afterwards, with the creation of this universe. Who then knows whence it has arisen? Whence this creation has arisen—perhaps it formed itself, or perhaps it did not—the one who looks down on it, in the highest heaven, only he knows—or perhaps he does not know.

Source: *Rig Veda* 10.129, from *Textual Sources for the Study of Hinduism*, p. 33.

VEDANTA: THE UPANISHADS AND THEIR COMMENTARIES

YAMA'S INSTRUCTIONS TO NACIKETAS

The Katha Upanishad *presents the story of a brahmin boy named Naciketas. His father, Aruni, is performing a sacrifice in which he is required to give away all his possessions, but Naciketas notices that he is not complying with the spirit of the sacrifice. Naciketas asks his father, "To whom will you give me?", to which his father angrily replies, "I give you to Yama [the god of death]." Unfortunately for both Naciketas and his father, words spoken in the context of a sacrifice have great power, and so Naciketas is immediately sent to the palace of Yama.*

Yama, however, is not in the palace when Naciketas arrives and does not return for three days. When Yama returns and sees that Naciketas has been waiting for a long while and has not been given the courtesy due to a brahmin, he apologizes and offers to make restitution by granting Naciketas three wishes. Being a dutiful son, Naciketas first asks that he be able to return to his father and that his father receive him with happiness and love instead of anger.

His next wish is significant: He asks Yama to teach him about the Naciketas fire for which he is named. This is significant because it shows that in this text the traditional values and practices of brahmins are not being questioned. Naciketas does not doubt the efficacy of the sacrifices; instead, he wishes to learn more about them, and only after this does he make his third request, in which he asks Yama to tell him what happens to a human being after death.

Yama responds by testing Naciketas in order to determine his sincerity in asking about this. He offers Naciketas worldly goods instead, things like wealth, land, power, long-lived sons and grandsons, fame, etc., but none of these things interest Naciketas. He understands that such things are transitory and fleeting, and he wishes instead for knowledge of the atman (the self), which is truly valuable. Having tested his resolve, Yama praises him for choosing the good (shreyas) over the pleasant (preyas). Yama then teaches Naciketas about the atman, *the essence of each individual, the eternal, unchanging reality that exists forever, unaffected by the circumstances and events of a person's countless rebirths. The* atman, *he declares, cannot be known through the senses or the intellect: it must be known through direct, intuitive realization. The culmination of the teaching is Yama's revelation that the* atman *is not only a personal essence; it is also said to be identical with the cosmic Ultimate, called* Brahman.

2.1.1. Yama said: "The good is one thing, and the pleasant another. Both of these different goals blind a person. From among the two, it is better for one who chooses the good. A person who chooses the pleasant does not fulfill his goals.

2. "A person receives both the good and the pleasant. Thoroughly examining the two, a wise person distinguishes them. The wise person chooses the good rather than the pleasant. The stupid person, due to grasping, chooses the pleasant. . . ."

14. Naciketas asked Yama: "Tell me what you see beyond righteousness and unrighteousness, beyond what is done and not done, and what is beyond what was and what will be."

15. Yama said: "I will briefly explain to you all that is taught in the Vedas, all that asceticism declares, and that which sages seek through religious practice: It is Om.

16. "This syllable truly is Brahman, it is the supreme syllable. Whoever knows it obtains all wishes.

17. "This is the best support, this is the supreme support. Knowing this support, a person attains happiness in the world of Brahma.

18. "The wise one is not born, does not die; it does not come from anywhere, does not become anything. It is unborn, enduring, permanent; this one is not destroyed when the body is destroyed.

19. "If someone thinks to destroy and if the destroyed thinks of being destroyed, then neither understands. This [atman] neither destroys nor is it destroyed.

20. "The *atman* hidden in the heart of all living beings is smaller than the smallest and greater than the greatest. A person who does not act with desire and is free from sadness sees it and its greatness through the purity of mind and senses. . . .

23. "The self is not gained through study, nor by the intellect, nor by much learning; it is gained only by whomever it chooses: to such a person the self reveals itself.

24. "Not to one who has not renounced wrongdoing, nor by one who is not tranquil, nor to one who is not calm, nor to one whose mind is not at peace: They cannot gain it through intelligence (*prajna*)."

2.3.1. "You should know that the *atman* is like the rider of a chariot, and the body is like the chariot. You should know that the intellect (*buddhi*) is like the chariot driver, and the mind is like the reins. . . .

4. "The senses are said to be the horses, and sense-objects are the area in which they travel. The self, together with senses and mind, are termed 'enjoyer' by the wise.

5. "If one lacks understanding and does not constantly control the mind, then one's senses become uncontrolled like the bad horses of a charioteer.

6. "If one is wise and constantly controls the mind, then one's senses remain controlled like the good horses of a charioteer.

7. "If one lacks understanding, lacks mental control, and is impure, then one can never reach the goal, but continues in cyclic existence (*samsara*).

8. "If one is wise, however, with a fully disciplined mind, then one reaches the goal and will not be reborn again. . . .

13. "The wise should restrain speech and mind, mind should be restrained in the understanding self, understanding should be restrained in the great self, and that should be restrained in the tranquil *atman*.

14. "Arise, awaken, go and attain your wishes; understand them! The poets say that the path is like the sharp edge of a razor, difficult to travel, difficult to obtain.

15. "It is soundless, intangible, formless, inexhaustible. In the same way, it is tasteless, eternal, and odorless, beginningless, endless, beyond the great, unchanging. By understanding it, one escapes the jaws of death."

4.1. Yama said: The Self-Existent opened the senses outward; thus humans look outward, not toward the inner *atman*. But a wise person, seeking immortality, turns in the reverse direction and sees the inner *atman*.

2. "Childish people go after outward pleasures. They walk into the net of death that is spread everywhere. But the wise, knowing immortality, do not seek the permanent among the impermanent.

3. "One knows color, taste, smell, sounds, touches, and sexual pleasures only through this (*atman*). What else remains? This indeed is That.

4. "By recognizing the great, all-pervading *atman*, by which one perceives both sleeping and dream states, the wise overcome sorrow. This indeed is That.

5. "One who knows this experiencer, the living *atman* that is nearest to one, which is lord of the past and the future, is never afraid of it. This indeed is That. . . .

9. "The sun arises from it and sets into it. All gods are based in it, and none ever move beyond it. This indeed is That. . . .

11. "Through it the mind attains [realization]. There is absolutely no difference here. If one perceives difference here, one goes from death to death."

6.1. Yama said: Its root is above, its branches below, this eternal tree. That [root] is the Pure. That is Brahman. That is called the Immortal. All worlds rest on it, and none go beyond it. This, indeed, is That.

2. "The whole world, whatever exists, was created from and moves in life. The great fear, the raised thunderbolt: those who know That become immortal.

3. "From fear of It fire burns, from fear of It the sun gives off heat. From fear of It Indra and Vayu, and Yama the fifth, speed along.

9. "One cannot see its form, and no one ever sees it with the eye. It is framed by the heart, by thought, by the mind: those who know That become immortal.

10. "When one stops the five knowledges [derived from the senses], together with the mind, and the intellect is still, that is said to be the highest path.

11. "This is said to be yoga, the firm restraint of the senses. Then one becomes undistracted. Yoga, truly, is the beginning and the end.

12. "It is not perceived through speech, through mind, nor by sight. How can it be understood other than by saying, 'It is'?"

Source: *Katha Upanishad* selections.

SACRIFICES CANNOT LEAD TO THE ULTIMATE GOAL

This passage expresses a somewhat different opinion of the value of sacrifices: It calls them "unsteady boats" that should not be relied on by a person wishing to leave cyclic existence. It does not, however, urge brahmins to stop performing sacrifices, but instead warns them not to rely on them exclusively and instead advises them to remove themselves from the world and practice asceticism and devotion in the forest in order to work at achieving a tranquil mind that knows truth.

1.2.1. This is the truth: The sacrificial rites that the sages saw in the hymns are variously elaborated in the three [Vedas]. Perform them constantly, O lovers of truth. This is the path to the world of good deeds.

2. When the flame flickers after the offering fire has been kindled, then between the offerings of the two portions of clarified butter one should give one's main oblations—an offering made with faith. . . .

7. These sacrificial rituals, eighteen in number, are, however, unsteady boats, in which only the lesser work is expressed. The fools who delight in this as supreme go again and again to old age and death.

8. Abiding in the midst of ignorance, wise only according to their own estimate, thinking themselves to be learned, but really dense, these deluded men are like blind men led by one who is himself blind.

9. Abiding variously in ignorance, childishly they think, "We have accomplished our aim." Since the performers of actions do not understand because of desire, therefore, they, the wretched ones, sink down [from heaven] when their worlds are exhausted.

10. Regarding sacrifice and merit as most important, the deluded ones do not know of anything better. Having enjoyed themselves only for a

time on top of the heaven won by good deeds, they re-enter this world or a lower one.

11. Those who practice austerities (*tapas*) and devotion in the forest, the tranquil ones, the knowers of truth, living the life of wandering beggars: they depart, freed from desire, through the door of the sun, to where the immortal Person (*purusha*) lives, the imperishable Atman.
12. Having examined the worlds won by actions, a brahmin should arrive at nothing but indifference. The world that was not made is not won by what is done [i.e., by sacrifice]. For the sake of that knowledge, one should go with sacrificial fuel in hand to a spiritual teacher (*guru*) who is well-versed in the scriptures and also firm in the realization of Brahman.
13. Approaching the wise [teacher] properly, one with tranquil thoughts, who has attained peace, is taught this very truth, the knowledge of Brahman by means of which one knows the imperishable Person, the only Reality.

Source: *Mundaka Upanishad,* ch. 1.

INSTRUCTIONS ON RENOUNCING THE WORLD

This passage instructs the aspiring world renouncer (samnyasin) *on the proper motivation for leaving society. It indicates that one should give up performance of the Vedic rituals and leave family, friends, and occupation behind, focusing one's attention on the final goal of realization of the* atman. *In a special ritual, one takes into oneself the sacred fire that one had maintained as a householder, which now becomes identified with the fire of the digestive processes. One discards the sacred thread that one has worn since the initiation* (upanayana) *ceremony, which designates one as a member of one of the three "twice-born" classes. After this one has no caste identity, and can wander anywhere—and take food from anyone—without fear of ritual pollution.*

Aruni went to the realm of Prajapati and, approaching him, said: "Lord, by what means does one completely renounce religious activities?" Prajapati said: "One should forsake sons, brothers, relatives, and so forth; one should give up the topknot, the sacred string, sacrifices, ritual codes, and Vedic recitation. . . . One should have a staff and a garment; and renounce everything else.

"A householder or a student (*brahma-carin*) or a forest hermit should discard his sacred string on the ground or in water. He should place the external fires in the fire of his stomach and the *gayatri* in the fire of his speech. . . ."

"From that point on, he should live without mantras. He should bathe at the start of the three periods of the day and, deeply immersed in meditation, he should realize his union with the Self."

Source: *Aruni Upanishad* 1–2.

SELF-EFFORT AND LIBERATION

The following passage comes from the Crest Jewel of Discrimination, *attributed by Hindu tradition to Shankara, one of the greatest expositors of the thought of the Upanishads and the primary exponent of the nondualist* (advaita) *school of commentary. The author contends that the path to liberation is a solitary one. He states that every person must win salvation alone, and that no one else can help. Even the scriptures are only guideposts, but one who becomes attached to them will remain enmeshed in cyclic existence. They point the way, but the goal is reached only by those who transcend all mundane supports and actualize direct, nonconceptual understanding of the* atman.

Children may free their father from his debts, but no other person can free a man from his bondage: he must do it himself. Others may relieve the suffering caused by a burden that weighs upon the head; but the suffering which comes from hunger and the like can only be relieved by one's self. The sick man who takes medicine and follows the rules of diet is seen to be restored to health—but not through the efforts of another. A clear vision of the Reality may be obtained only through our own eyes, when they have been opened by spiritual insight—never through the eyes of some other seer. Through our own eyes we learn what the moon looks like: how could we learn this through the eyes of others? Those cords that bind us, because of our ignorance, our lustful desires and the fruits of our karma—how could anybody but ourselves untie them, even in the course of innumerable ages? Neither by the practice of Yoga or of Sankhya philosophy, nor by good works, nor by learning, does liberation come; but only through a realization that Atman and Brahman are one—in no other way. . . .

Erudition, well-articulated speech, a wealth of words, and skill in expounding the scriptures—these things give pleasure to the learned, but they do not bring liberation. Study of the scriptures is fruitless as long as Brahman has not been experienced. And when Brahman has been experienced, it is useless to read the scriptures. A network of words is like a dense forest which causes the mind to wander hither and thither. Therefore, those who know this truth should struggle hard to experience Brahman. When a man has been bitten by the snake of ignorance he can only be cured by the realization of Brahman. What use are Vedas or scriptures, charms or herbs? A sickness is not cured by saying the word "medicine." You must take the medicine. Liberation does not come by merely saying the word "Brahman." Brahman must be actually experienced. Until you allow this apparent universe to dissolve from your consciousness—until you have experienced Brahman—how can you find liberation just by saying the word "Brahman?" The result is merely a noise.

Source: *Viveka-chudamani,* from *Shankara's Crest-Jewel of Discrimination,* tr. Swami Prabhavananda and Christopher Isherwood (Hollywood: Vendanta Press, 1975), pp. 40–41]

MAYA

Maya plays a central role in Shankara's interpretation of the Upanishads. The term literally means "magic" or "illusion," and he claims that it is the power by which Brahman hides the truth from ordinary beings. It is a creative power that causes the apparent phenomena of cyclic existence to be superimposed on the unitary Brahman.

Maya, in her potential aspect, is the divine power of the Lord. She has no beginning. She is composed of the three qualities (*guna*), subtle, beyond perception. It is from the effects she produces that her existence is inferred by the wise. It is she who gives birth to the whole universe. She is neither being nor nonbeing, nor a mixture of both. She is neither divided nor undivided, nor a mixture of both. She is neither an indivisible whole, nor composed of parts, nor a mixture of both. She is most strange. Her nature is inexplicable. Just as knowing a rope to be a rope destroys the illusion that it is a snake, so Maya is destroyed by direct experience of Brahman— the pure, the free, the one without a second.

Source: *Viveka-chudamani*, from *Shankara's Crest-Jewel of Discrimination*, p. 49.

THAT IS YOU

The Upanishadic statement "That is you" (tat tvam asi) *is viewed by exponents of nondualist Vedanta as a statement of the nondifference of* atman *and* Brahman. *The following excerpt discusses this statement from the nondualist perspective.*

The scriptures establish the absolute identity of Atman and Brahman by declaring repeatedly: "That is you." The terms "Brahman" and "Atman," in their true meaning, refer to "That" and "you" respectively. In their literal, superficial meaning, "Brahman" and "Atman" have opposite attributes, like the sun and the glow-worm, the king and his servant, the ocean and the well, or Mount Meru and the atom. Their identity is established only when they are understood in their true significance, and not in a superficial sense.

"Brahman" may refer to God, the ruler of Maya and creator of the universe. The "Atman" may refer to the individual soul, associated with the five coverings which are effects of Maya. Thus regarded, they possess opposite attributes. But this apparent opposition is caused by Maya and her effects. It is not real, therefore, but superimposed. These attributes caused by Maya and her effects are superimposed upon God and upon the individual soul. When they have been completely eliminated, neither soul nor God remains. If you take the kingdom from a king and the weapons from a soldier, there is neither soldier nor king. The scriptures repudiate any idea of a duality in Brahman. Let a man seek illumination in the knowledge of Brahman, as the scriptures direct. Then those attributes, which our ignorance has superimposed upon Brahman, will disappear. . . .

Then let him meditate upon the identity of Brahman and Atman, and so realize the truth. Through spiritual discrimination, let him understand the true inner meaning of the terms "Brahman" and "Atman," thus realizing their absolute identity. See the reality in both, and you will find that there is but one. . . .

Just as a clay jar or vessel is understood to be nothing but clay, so this whole universe, born of Brahman, essentially Brahman, is Brahman only—for there is nothing else but Brahman, nothing beyond That. That is the reality. That is our Atman. Therefore, "That is you"—pure, blissful, supreme Brahman, the one without a second.

Source: *Viveka-chudamani*, from *Shankara's Crest-Jewel of Discrimination*, pp. 72–74.

QUALIFIED NONDUALISM: RAMANUJA'S INTERPRETATION

Ramanuja disagress with the nondualist system of Upanishadic interpretation. In this passage, he contends that it is absurd to completely equate the absolute Brahman *with the individual* atman. *As an exponent of devotinalism, Ramanuja rejects the nondualist system, since it would make devotion absurd. If* atman *and* Brahman *were one, there would be no real basis for worship. Ramanuja contends that the Upanishadic statement "That is you" does not mean what nondualists think it does; rather, it indicates that there are two separate entities,* atman *and* Brahman, *and that the former is wholly dependent upon the latter, like a wave in relation to the ocean. The wave appears to stand apart from the ocean, but its substance and being derive from the ocean, although it has at least a qualifiedly separate identity. Similarly, the* atman *derives from* Brahman *but because the history of each atman is distinctly its own, it contradicts reason and actual experience to claim that* atman *is completely identical with* Brahman.

1.1.1. The word "Brahman" refers to the highest Person, in whom all faults are naturally eliminated, who possesses all the most auspicious qualities, is unlimited, unsurpassed, and incalculable. Everywhere the word Brahman is associated with the quality of magnitude. . . . [Brahman] is the "Lord of All.". . .

Our [nondualist Vedantin] opponents say: 'Brahman is only consciousness, is completely opposed to all particularity, and is the highest reality; all difference—such as different types of knowers, objects of knowledge, different knowledge produced by them, and anything beyond that is false when posited of [Brahman].'

[We reply:] Brahman, which is to be understood by means of its distinctive characteristics, has a nature distinguished from all objects other than itself, and those contradictions are eliminated by these three words: The word "truth" excludes anything that is "non-truth," that which is amenable to modification. The word "knowledge" indicates what is excluded from non-sentient things whose illumination depends upon others. And the word "limitless" indicates what is excluded from anything that is circumscribed by space, time or matter. This exclusion is not a positive or negative quality, but [indicates] Brahman itself as distinguished from everything that is other than itself. . . . The ramification of this is that Brahman is self-luminous, with all contradictions excluded. . . .

Those who propound the doctrine of a substance devoid of all difference cannot legitimately assert that there is a proof for such a substance, because all means of valid cognition have for their objects things that are affected by difference. . . . All consciousness implies difference. All states of consciousness have for their objects things that are marked by some difference, as we see in the case of judgements like, "I saw this.". . . It therefore must be admitted that reality is affected with difference, which is well established by valid proofs. . . .

Instead, what all these scriptures deny is only plurality in the sense of contradicting the unity of the world which is utterly dependent on Brahman as an effect and which has Brahman as the inner controlling principle that is its true Self. They do not deny plurality on the part of Brahman in the sense of deciding to become manifold. . . .

Moreover, in texts like the one that states, "That is you" the connection between the constituent parts does not indicate an absolute unity of undifferentiated substance. Instead, the words "that" and "you" indicate that Brahman is distinguished by difference. The word "that" refers to Brahman, which is omniscient and so forth. . . . Moreover, it is impossible that ignorance could belong to Brahman, whose essential nature is knowledge, which is free from all imperfections, omniscient, and contains within itself all auspicious qualities; nor [is it possible that Brahman] could be the basis of the faults and afflictions that arise from ignorance.

Source: Ramanuja, *Sribhasya*, ch. 1.

YOGA

THE MEANING OF YOGA

The following excerpts are taken from the Yoga Aphorisms, *attributed to Patanjali, and an explanatory text entitled the* Yoga Commentary, *attributed to Vyasa. The verses of the Aphorisms are given in boldface, and the Commentary is given in plain text.*

As the text indicates, the term [yoga] may be used to refer to a range of practices for disciplining mind and body. In Patanjali's system the focus is on developing progressively greater control over the agitations and fluctuations of mind and body in order to arrive at a state of perfect equanimity. One accomplishes this by turning the attention inward, away from sense objects, which leads to detachment and wisdom.

A person who becomes detached from external things has no basis for continued existence, and thus becomes liberated from the cycle of birth and death. Unlike the system of the Upanishads, however, Patanjali does not understand liberation as a union of the individual atman with the cosmic ultimate Brahman, but as separation of one's spiritual essence (purusha) *from insentient matter* (prakriti). *In the yoga system, both are considered to be real, and the association of the two is said to be beginningless. Because matter's tendency is to procreate and acquire, and because it is transitory and prone to decay, beings whose spirits are associated with matter necessarily experience suffering. This suffering can, however, be transcended by following the path of the "eight limbs" of physical and mental discipline, which culminate in a state of perfect mental equipoise.*

1. **Here is an instruction on yoga.**
    Yoga is meditative concentration (*samadhi*), and it is a characteristic of the mind pervading all its states. . . . The five states of the mind are: (1) wandering; (2) deluded; (3) distracted; (4) one-pointed; and (5) cut off.

2. **Yoga is the cessation of states of mind.**
    Since the mind has the three functions of perception, movement, and rest, it is constituted by the three qualities of purity (*sattva*), lightness (*rajas*), and heaviness (*tamas*). . . .

3. **Then the seer abides in his own nature.**

5. **The states are of five types, and are afflicted and nonafflicted.**
    The afflicted are those that are based on afflictions like ignorance and so forth and serve as the basis of latencies. The nonafflicted are those that have conceptuality for their object and that oppose the operation of the qualities. . . .

12. **The [states of mind] are restrained by practice and detachment.**
    The stream of mind flows both ways: it flows toward good and it flows toward evil. That which flows on to separation down the plane of discriminative knowledge moves toward happiness. That which leads to rebirth flows down the plane of nondiscrimination and moves toward wrong-doing.

17. **Meditative concentration is attained with the help of conceptual understanding, analytical thought, bliss, and self-awareness.**
    Conceptual understanding is the mind's coarse direct experience when it is directed toward object. Analytical thought is subtle [cognition]. Joy is happiness. Self-awareness is consciousness pertaining to the self. . . . All these states have an object of observation (*alambana*).

30. **Sickness, laxity, doubt, carelessness, laziness, worldliness, wrong views, failure to attain any level [of concentration], instability: these distractions of mind are the obstacles.**

31. **Pain, despair, unsteadiness of the body, inspiration, and expiration are the companions of these distractions.**

32. **In order to prevent them, one should become familiar with one entity.**

33. **By cultivating friendliness, compassion regarding suffering, joy regarding merit, and indifference toward demerit, one [attains] a calm, undisturbed mind.**

Source: *Yoga-sutras* and *Yoga-bhashya*, ch. 1.

YOGIC TECHNIQUES

In section two Patanjali describes the process by which one develops one's powers of concentration through disciplining thoughts, bringing mind and body under control, and weaning oneself from attachment to external objects.

2.1. **Asceticism (*tapas*), study, and devotion to God constitute the yoga of action.**

3. **The afflictions are ignorance, self-cherishing, desire, aversion, and love of life.**

    Ignorance is simply misconception. Self-cherishing and the others are also based on ignorance and, since they cannot exist without it, they are ignorant. Thus when ignorance is destroyed, their destruction also follows.

5. **Ignorance is taking the impermanent, the impure, the painful, and the not-self to be permanent, pure, pleasurable, and the self.**

6. **When one views the appearances of a unitary self through the power of perception, this is self-cherishing.**

7. **Attachment is abiding in pleasure.**

8. **Aversion is abiding in revulsion toward pain.**

9. **Love of life, moving along by its own potency, exists even in the wise.**

11. **Their mental states are destroyed by meditation.**

    As the gross dirt of clothes is at first shaken off, and then the fine dirt is washed off by effort and work, so the coarse essential mental states need only slight counteracting efforts, whereas the subtle mental states need very powerful counteragents.

17. **The conjunction of the knower and the knowable is the cause of what is to be escaped.**

18. **The knowable has the nature of purity, lightness, and heaviness; it consists of the elements and the powers of sensation; its purposes are experience and liberation.**

    Liberation is the ascertainment of the nature of the enjoyer, the self. Beyond the knowledge of these two there is no wisdom.

20. **The perceiver is only perception; even though pure, it perceives by way of conditions.**

    "Only perception": This means that it is nothing other than the power of becoming conscious; that is to say, it is not touched by the qualities. This self cognizes the intellect by reflection. He is neither quite similar nor quite dissimilar to the intellect. "It is not quite similar." Why? The intellect, having for its sphere of action objects known and not yet known, is of course changeable. . . .

"It is not quite dissimilar." Why? . . . Since the self cognizes ideas as the intellect, grasped by consciousness, it is transformed into them; it appears by the act of cognition to be the very self of the intellect, although in reality it is not so. . . .

28. **With the diminution of impurity by the sustained practice of the limbs *(anga)* of yoga, the light of wisdom reaches up to discriminating knowledge.**

29. **Restraint, observance, posture, breath control, withdrawal [of the senses], mental stability, meditation, and meditative concentration are the eight limbs of yoga.**

30. **Of these, the restraints *(yama)* are: non-injury *(ahimsa)*, truthfulness, not stealing, celibacy, and having few possessions.**

32. **The observances *(niyama)* are: cleanliness, contentment, asceticism, study, and devotion to God.**

Of these, cleanliness is brought about by earth and water, etc., and by eating clean things, etc. This is external. It is internal when it involves washing away impurities of the mind. Contentment is absence of desire to get more of the necessities of life than one already possesses. Asceticism involves bearing extreme conditions, hunger, thirst, cold, and heat, standing or sitting . . . or severe penances. Study is reading texts that are concerned with liberation, or the repetition of the sacred syllable *Om.* Devotion to God involves offering one's actions to the supreme Teacher.

33. **When thoughts of wrongdoing bother you, familiarize yourself with their antidotes.**

40. **By cleanliness is meant disgust with one's body and cessation of contact with others.**

46. **Posture is steadily relaxed.**

47. **By relaxation of effort and by limitless absorption.**

Posture is perfected when effort ceases, so that there may be no more agitation of the body. Or, when the mind achieves balance with regard to the infinite, it brings about the perfection of posture.

49. **Breath control *(pranayama)* involves restraining the inhalation and exhalation movements [of breath,] which follows when that [control of posture] has been achieved.**

54. **Withdrawal [of the senses] *(pratyahara)* is that by which the senses do not come into contact with their objects and follow the nature of the mind.**

Source: *Yoga-sutras* and *Yoga-bhashya*, ch. 2.

YOGIC ATTAINMENTS

In this section Patanjali discusses the results of yogic practice, which include unshakable mental stability, equanimity, dispassion, and eventually liberation from the cycle of birth and death.

3.1. Mental stability (*dharana*) is mental steadiness.

Mental stability involves the mind becoming focused on such places as the sphere of the navel, the lotus of the heart, the light in the brain, the tip of the nose, the tip of the tongue, and similar parts of the body; or on any other external object. . . .

49. Only one who fully understands the distinction between purity and the self attains supremacy over all states of being and becomes omniscient.

Omniscience refers to simultaneously discriminating knowledge of the "qualities"—which are of the nature of all phenomena—and showing forth as they do separately the quiescent, the disturbed, and the unpredictable characteristics. This attainment is known as the "sorrowless" (*vishoka*). Reaching this, the yogi moves omniscient and powerful, with all his afflictions ended.

50. When the seed of bondage has been destroyed by desirelessness even for those [attainments], absolute separation (*kaivalya*) results.

Then all the seeds of afflictions pass, together with the mind, into latency. When they have become latent, the self does not then suffer. . . . This state—in which the qualities manifest in the mind as afflictions, actions, and fruitions without having fulfilled their object and come back to action—is the final separation of consciousness from the qualities. This is the state of absolute separation, when the self remains consciousness alone, as in its own nature.

Source: *Yoga-sutras* and *Yoga-bhashya*, ch. 3.

PURANAS AND EPICS

THE FOUR AGES

In contemporary India the Puranas and Epics are among the most widely known of Hindu scriptures. The Puranas recount the mythologies of such popular gods as Shiva, Vishnu, and Devi (the Goddess). Rich in symbolism and containing a wide variety of divergent traditions, they describe the attributes of the gods and indicate how they should be worshiped.

The two great epics of Hinduism, the Ramayana *and the* Mahabharata, *are monumental stories that weave history, myth, and religion into complex, multifaceted tales that recount important historical and mythical events and indicate the lessons that should be drawn from them. The* Ramayana *tells the story of Rama—considered by tradition to be an incarnation (avatara) of Vishnu—who takes birth among humans in order to fight against evil forces and establish dharma in the world. Forced to leave his kingdom with his dutiful wife Sita, he wanders in the wilderness, establishing dharma wherever he goes. In a climactic battle he faces the demon Ravana, who has captured Sita. Rama slays Ravana, thus enabling dharma to be established in the demon's realm.*

The Mahabharata—*which contains the* Bhagavad-gita, *one of the most impor-tant religious texts in contemporary Hinduism—tells the story of a conflict between related clans for supremacy in northern India. Unlike the heroes of the* Ramayana, *the protagonists of the* Mahabharata *(the Pandavas) often make mistakes, question what is the right course of action, and regret wrong decisions.*

In this passage from the Linga Purana, *Indra teaches a human sage about the cyclical nature of time. According to this system, when the universe is first created a golden age begins. During this time beings have long lifespans, beautiful bodies, and great happiness. As time goes on, however, things begin imperceptibly to worsen, and eventually it becomes necessary to divide people according to their predispositions.*

First, you should know, comes the Golden Age, and then the Age of the Trey; and the Age of the Deuce and the Fourth Age come next: these are the four Ages, in brief. The Golden Age is the age of goodness (*sattva*); the Age of the Trey is the age of energy (*rajas*); the Age of the Deuce is a mixture of energy and darkness (*tamas*); and the Dark Age is the age of darkness; each age has its characteristic ways of behaving. Meditation is the main thing in the Golden Age; sacrifice in the Age of the Trey; worship in the Age of Deuce; purity and charity in the Dark Age. The Golden Age lasts for four thousand years, and is followed by a twilight of four hundred years. And the lifespan of living creatures lasts for four thousand human years in the Golden Age.

After the twilight of the Golden Age has passed, one of the four feet of the dharma of the Ages is gone in all of its aspects. The excellent Age of the Trey is one fourth less than the Golden Age; the Age of the Deuce lasts for half the time of the Golden Age, and the Dark Age lasts for one half the time of the Age of the Deuce. The last three twilights last for three hundred, two hundred, and one hundred years; this happens in aeon after aeon, Age after Age. In the first Age, the Golden Age, the eternal dharma walks on four feet; in the Age of Trey, on three feet; in the Age of Deuce, on two feet. In the Fourth Age it lacks three feet and is devoid of the element of goodness.

In (every) Golden Age, people are born in pairs; their livelihood consists in reveling in the taste of what exists right before one's eyes. All creatures are satisfied, always, and take delight in all enjoyments. There is no distinction between the lowest and the highest among them; they are all good, all equal in their lifespan, happiness, and form, in the Golden Age. They have no preferences, nor do they experience the opposing pairs of emotions; they do not hate or get tired. They have no homes or dwelling-places, but live in the mountains and oceans; they have no sorrow, but consist mostly of goodness and generally live alone. They go wherever they wish, constantly rejoicing in their minds; in the Golden Age, people do not engage in any actions, good or bad.

At that time there was no system of separate classes and stages of life, and no mixture (of classes or castes). But in the course of time, in the Age of the Trey, they no longer reveled in the taste (of existence). When that fulfillment was lost, another sort of fulfillment was born. When water reaches its subtle state, it is transformed into clouds; from thundering clouds, rain is emitted. As soon as the surface of the earth was touched by that rain, trees appeared on it, and they became houses for the people, who used those trees for their livelihood and all their enjoyments. People lived off those trees at the beginning of the Age of the Trey.

But then, after a long time, people began to change; the emotions of passion and greed arose, for no apparent cause, as a result of a change in the people that arose out of time. Then all the trees that they regarded as their houses vanished, and when they had vanished, the people who were born in pairs became confused. They began to think about their fulfillment, considering the matter truthfully, and then the trees that they regarded as their houses appeared again. These trees brought forth clothing and fruits and jewelry; and on the very same trees there would grow, in bud after bud, honey made by no bees, powerful honey of superb aroma, color, and taste. People lived on that honey, lived happily all their life long, finding their delight and their nourishment in that perfection, always free from fever.

But then, as another time came, they became greedy. They lopped off the limbs of the trees and took by force the honey that no bees had made. As a result of that crime that they committed in their greed, the magic trees, together with their honey, vanished, first here, then there, and as time exerted its power, very little of that fulfillment was left. As the Age of the Trey came on, the opposing pairs of emotions arose, and people became quite miserable as a result of the sharp cold and rain and heat. Tortured by these opposing pairs, they began to cover themselves; and then they made houses on the mountain to ward off the opposing pairs. Formerly, they had gone wherever they wished, living without fixed dwellings; now they began to live in fixed dwellings according to their need and their pleasure. . . .

Then, by the force of that Age, all the people were so crazy with rage that they seized one another and took their sons, wives, wealth, and so forth, by force. When he realized all this, the lotus-born (Brahma) created the Kshatriyas to protect people from getting wounded (*kshatat-tratum*), in order to establish a firm support for the moral boundaries. Then by means of his own brilliance, the god who is the soul of all established the system of the classes and stages of life, and he himself established the livelihood for each profession to live on. Gradually, the institution of sacrifice evolved in the Age of the Trey, but even then some good people did not perform animal sacrifices. For eventually Vishnu, who sees everything, performed a sacrifice by force, and then as a result of that the Brahmins prescribed the non-violent sacrifice.

But then, in the Age of the Deuce, men began to have differences of opinion, to differ in mind, action, and speech, and to have difficulty making a living. Then, gradually, as a result of the exhaustion of their bodies, all creatures became subject to greed, working for wages, working as merchants, fighting, indecision about basic principles, lack of interest in the schools of the Vedas, confounding of dharmas, destruction of the system of the classes and stages of life, and, finally, lust and hatred. For in the Age of the Deuce, passion, greed, and drunkenness arise.

And in (every) Age of the Deuce, a sage named Vyasa divides the Veda into four. For it is known that there was a single Veda, in four parts, in the Ages of the Trey; but as a result of the shrinking of the lifespan, it was divided up in the Ages of the Deuce. And these divisions were further divided by the sons of the (Rig Vedic) seers, according to their deviant opinions; they transposed the order of the (Rig Vedic) mantras and the Brahmanas, and they changed the accents and the syllables. Wise men compiled the collections of the *Rig Veda, Yajur Veda,* and *Sama Veda;* though they were composed in common, they have been (subsequently) separated by people of various opinions, divided into *Brahmanas, Kalpasutras,* and explications of the mantras. . . .

Drought, death, disease, and other plagues cause sufferings born of speech, mind, and action, and as a result one becomes numb. From this numbness people begin to think about release from suffering. From this thinking there arises detachment, and from detachment they begin to see their faults. As a result of seeing their faults, knowledge arises in the Age of the Deuce. Now, it will be recalled that the behavior characteristic of the Age of the Deuce was a mixture of energy and darkness. But there was dharma in the first age, the Golden Age, and that dharma still functions in the Age of the Trey; in the Age of the Deuce, however, it becomes disturbed, and in the Dark Age it vanishes.

In the Fourth Age, men's senses are disturbed by darkness and they fall prey to illusion and jealousy; they even kill ascetics. In the Dark Age, there is always carelessness, passion, hunger, and fear; the terrible fear of drought pits one country against another. Scripture has no authority, and men take to the violation of dharma; they act without dharma, without morality; they are very angry and not very smart. . . . When scripture is destroyed, and the dharma that is known from the Shastras, then people will kill one another, for they will have no moral boundaries, no check to their violence, no affection, and no shame. When dharma is destroyed, and people attack one another, they will become stunted and live only twenty-five years; their senses will become confused with arguing, and they will abandon their sons and wives. When they are struck by drought, they will abandon agriculture; they will leave their own countries and go to lands beyond their borders, seeking water in rivers, oceans, wells, and mountains.

Suffering greatly, they will live on honey, raw meat, roots, and fruits; they will wear garments of bark, leaves, and antelope skins; they will perform no rituals and have no possessions. They will fall away from the system of classes and stages of life and fall prey to the terrible mingling of classes. Then there will be very few people left, caught up in this calamity. Afflicted by old age, disease, and hunger, their minds will be numbed by suffering. But from this numbness there will arise thought, and thought makes the mind balanced. Understanding comes from a balanced mind, and from understanding comes a dedication to dharma. The people who are left at the end of the Dark Age will have a kind of formless mental peace. Then, in a day and a night, the age will be transformed for them, deluding their wits as if they were dreaming or insane. And then, by the power of the goal of the future, the Golden Age will begin. And when the Golden Age has begun again, the people left over from the Dark Age become the people born in the Golden Age. . . .

Source: *Linga Purana* 1.39.5–34, 48–70; 1.40.1–3, 66cd–76, from *Textual Sources for the Study of Hinduism*, pp. 69–71.

THE LINGAM OF SHIVA

In this passage, Vishnu tells a human sage about the origin of the lingam, *the phallus of Shiva. The* lingam *symbolizes both his procreative force and the energy he stores through asceticism. The story begins with a conversation between Brahma, said to be the creator of the universe in Hindu mythology, and Vishnu, who is the creator of Brahma. Brahma believes himself to be supreme, self-created, and omnipotent, but Vishnu informs him that he is in fact his creature. Both gods are then amazed to see a huge flaming* lingam *that stretches out of sight. They agree to try to find its top and bottom, but after one thousand years flying respectively up and down are unable to fathom its dimensions. At this point they realize that there is a greater power than themselves, which turns out to be Shiva.*

Once upon a time, when the whole triple world was unmanifest, in darkness, swallowed up by me, I lay there alone, with all the creatures in my belly. I had a thousand heads and a thousand eyes, and a thousand feet; I held in my hands the conch shell, discus, and mace, as I lay in the immaculate water. Then, all of a sudden, I saw from afar the four-headed (Brahma), the great yogi, the Person with golden luminosity, infinitely luminous, as bright as a hundred suns, blazing with his own brilliance. The god was wearing a black antelope skin and carrying a water-pot; and in the space of the blinking of an eye, that supreme Person arrived. Then Brahma, to whom all people bow, said to me, 'Who are you? And where do you come from? And why are you staying here? Tell me, sir. I am the maker of the worlds, self-created, facing in all directions.' When Brahma had spoken like that to me, I said to him: 'I am the maker of the worlds, and also the one who destroys them, again and again.' As the two of us were talking together in this way, each wishing to surpass the other, we saw a flame arising in the northern quarter. As we looked at that flame we were amazed, and its brilliance and power made us cup our hands in reverence and bow to that light from Shiva. The flame grew, a surpassing marvel, and Brahma and I hastened to run up to it. It broke through heaven and earth with its halo of flame, and in the middle of the flame we saw a lingam of great lustre, measuring just a handsbreadth, unmanifest and full of supreme light. In the middle, it was neither gold nor stone or silver; it was indescribable, unimaginable, visible and invisible again and again. It had a thousand garlands of flames, amazing, miraculous; it had great brilliance, and kept getting much bigger. It was covered with a halo of flame, terrifying all creatures with its monstrous form, excessive, bursting through heaven and earth.

Then Brahma said to me, 'Quickly, go down and find out the (bottom) end of this noble lingam. I will go up until I see its (top) end.' We agreed to do this, and went up and down. I kept going down for a thousand years, but I did not reach the end of the lingam; and then I became afraid. In the very same way, Brahma did not find its end above, and came back to join me right there in the expanse of water. Then we were amazed and frightened of the noble one; deluded by his power of illusion, we lost our wits and became confused. But then we meditated on the lord who faces in all directions, the origin and resting place of the worlds, the unchanging lord. Cupping our hands in reverence, we paid homage to Shiva, the trident-bearer, who makes the great, terrifying sound, who has a frightening form, and fangs, who is manifest, and great:

'We bow to you, O lord of the gods and people; we bow to you god, noble lord of all creatures. We bow to you, the eternally successful yogi, the support of all the universe, the highest ruler, the highest ultimate reality, the undying, the highest place. You are the eldest, the lovely god, the ruddy one, the jumper, the lord Shiva . . . you are the sacrifice, the vows, and the observances; the Vedas, the worlds, the gods, the true god everywhere. You are the quality of sound in space; you are the origin and dissolution of creatures. You are the perfume in the earth, the fluidity of the waters, the brightness of fire, great lord. You are the touch of the wind, lord of gods, and the form of the moon. You are the knowledge in intelligence, lord of gods, and the seed in nature. You destroy all the worlds; you are Time, the Ender, made of death. You alone maintain the three worlds, and you alone create them, O lord. . . . We bow to you who have the power of a million million suns, who are as white as a thousand moons; we bow to you who hold the thunderbolt and the bow called Pinaka; we bow to you who hold the bow and arrows in your hand. We bow to you whose body is adorned with ashes; we bow to you who destroyed the body of Kama (the god of erotic love); we bow to you, god of the golden embryo, the golden robe, the golden womb, the golden navel, the golden semen, variegated with a thousand eyes; we bow to you, god of the golden color and the golden hair, you the golden hero and the giver of gold; we bow to you, god, master of gold with the sound of gold. We bow to you with the Pinaka bow in your hand, Shankara, the blue-necked.'

When he had been praised like that, he became manifest, the one of great intellect, the god of gods, womb of the universe, shining as bright as a million suns; and filled with pity, the great god, the great light, spoke to us, as if he would swallow up the sky with his thousands of millions of mouths. His neck was shaped like a conch shell; his belly was lovely; he was adorned with various kinds of jewels; his body was variegated with all sorts of gems, and he wore various kinds of garlands and unguents. The lord had the Pinaka bow in his hand and he held the trident; he was fit to be worshipped by the gods. He wore a great serpent for his sacred thread, but he did not frighten the gods.

He sent forth a great laugh, with the noise of the sound of the *dundubhi* drum, like the roar of thunder, a laugh that filled the entire universe. The two of us were terrified by that great sound, but then the great god said, 'I am satisfied with you two, best of the gods. See my great yoga, and lose all your fear. Both of you, eternal, were born from my limbs in the past; Brahma here, the grandfather of all people, is my right arm, and Vishnu is my left arm, always unconquered in battles. I am satisfied with the two of you, and so I will give you a boon, whatever you ask.' Then the two of us were ecstatic, and we bowed to the feet of the lord, and we said to the great god, who was standing there inclined to favor us, 'If you are really satisfied, and if you are going to give us a boon, then let the two of us always have devotion for you, O god, lord of the gods.' The god of gods said, 'So be it, fortunate ones. Create masses of progeny.' And when he had said this, the lord god vanished.

Source: *Brahmanda Purana* 1.2.26.10–61, from *Textual Sources for the Study of Hinduism*, pp. 85–87.

RAMA, A GOD AMONG HUMANS

The opening section of the Ramayana *contains a synopsis of the main events of the story. The following verses tell of how prince Rama was banished from his kingdom through the machinations of his stepmother Kaikeyi, who had been told by his father Dasharatha that she could ask him for anything she wished. Kaikeyi requested that Rama, the rightful ruler, not assume the throne, and that her son Bharata would instead become king. As a righteous king, Dasharatha could not refuse, and so reluctantly he acceded to the request.*

Kaikeyi knew that the people of the kingdom wanted Rama to rule, and so to ensure that Bharata would remain king she asked that Rama be banished in order that popular opinion would not undermine her son's authority. The king agreed, but as a result he died of a broken heart soon after.

Accompanied by his brother Lakshman and Sita, the model of a devout Hindu wife, Rama went off to the forest. During his travels he was beset by a horde of demons (rakshasa), *but he defeated them all. This angered the demon lord Ravana, who captured Sita and imprisoned her in his city of Lanka. Ravana then fell in love with Sita and tried to convince her to renounce Rama and become his queen, but Sita spurned his advances.*

With the help of Hanuman, lord of monkeys, Rama eventually located Sita, slew Ravana, and rescued her. He then returned in triumph to his kingdom, and Bharata eagerly abdicated in Rama's favor, since he had never wished to usurp Rama.

Following Rama's return, however, his subjects began to gossip about Sita, insinuating that while she was in Ravana's castle she may have succumbed to his advances.

Rama knew that Sita was innocent, but reluctantly realized that the gossip could undermine his moral authority, which is closely connected to his wife's conduct. Following the dictates of dharma, Rama was forced to banish Sita from the Kingdom. Rama was heartbroken knowing that her love for him kept her chaste in the castle of Ravana, but his royal duty required him to maintain his reputation for righteousness. The following verses describe how he left the kingdom, joined forces with Hanuman, and then defeated Ravana.

8. There is a famous king named Rama . . . who is self-controlled, very powerful, radiant, resolute, and illustrious.

9. Wise and established in good conduct, he is eloquent and regal. He vanquishes his enemies. He has wide shoulders and powerful arms. . . .

12. He understands dharma and always keeps his promises. He always thinks of his subjects welfare. He is famous, pure, disciplined, and contemplative (*samadhiman*).

13. Protector of all living beings, guardian of dharma, he knows the essence of the Vedas and their subsidiary lore and is equally skilled in the science of combat. . . .

18–19. His generosity is equal to that of Kubera, the provider of wealth, and his devotion to truth is like that of Dharma [the god of righteousness]. Dasharatha, the lord of the earth, loved him and wanted to name Rama, his eldest son, as his successor. . . .

20. As Queen Kaikeyi, the king's wife, watched the coronation preparations, she [decided] to ask for a wish that had been promised long ago. She demanded that Bharata [her son] be crowned instead and that Rama be exiled.

21. Dasharatha was a man who kept his promises, and so, caught in the trap of his own righteousness, he had to exile his beloved son Rama.

22. To please Kaikeyi, the hero Rama honored the promise made by his father and went into the forest. . . .

37–38. Then in battle Rama killed all the *rakshasas*: . . . About fourteen thousand *rakshasas* were killed while he resided in Dandaka.

39–42. Then Ravana, king of *rakshasas*, heard of the massacre of his relatives, and flew into a rage and . . . he lured the king's sons far away. Then he kidnapped Rama's wife. . . .

47. Then [Rama] met the monkey Hanuman on the shores of Lake Pampa. . . .

56. This bull among monkeys wished to find Janaka's daughter [Sita] and sent all the monkeys searching in all directions. . . .

58. When he reached the city of Lanka, which was ruled by Ravana, he saw Sita pensive and sad in a grove of *ashoka* trees. . . .

62. The great monkey burned the city of Lanka, but spared Sita, and then returned to tell Rama the good news. . . .

65. Then the god of the ocean appeared before Rama, and Rama followed his advice by having Nala build a bridge [to Lanka].

66. Using this [bridge], he went to the city of Lanka, and after killing Ravana in battle he crowned Vibhishana as lord of the *rakshasas* in Lanka.

67. One who reads the story of Rama, which brings merit and purity, will be freed from all sin. One who reads it with devotion and faith will ultimately be worshipped, together with his sons, grandsons, and servants after death.

Source: *Ramayana*, ch. 1.

THE *BHAGAVAD-GITA*: ARJUNA'S REFUSAL TO FIGHT

The following passages are taken from the Bhagavad-gita, *one of the most influential of Hindu religious texts. A part of the monumental epic* Mahabharata, *it tells the story of a climactic battle between the Pandavas and the Kauravas, two rival clans contending for supremacy in northern India. As the story opens, the Pandava Arjuna, perhaps the greatest warrior of his generation, decides to scout the opposition. He asks his charioteer Krishna (who, unbeknownst to him, is really an incarnation of the god Vishnu) to drive the chariot in front of the enemy lines. As he rides past the Kauravas, however, he experiences a crisis of conscience: He recognizes that many of his opponents are relatives, friends, and teachers, and that killing them would result in a great deal of negative karma.*

It is important to note that Arjuna is not concerned with killing per se; as a warrior he has killed many people in the past, but these particular people are linked to him by close karmic bonds, and so he perceives a contradiction between the demands of his warrior's duty (dharma) *and the dictates of the law of karma. He decides that the only solution is to opt out of the conflict altogether and become a world renouncer.*

In response, Krishna lectures him on the necessity of correctly performing dharma and indicates that Arjuna will receive more negative karma by dereliction of duty than by killing. Furthermore, Krishna asserts, his opponents have already assured their own destruction by their evil deeds, and so Arjuna is merely the instrument through which God will exact punishment. Then Krishna gives Arjuna a solution to the problem he faces, which involves a mental reorientation. Arjuna's problem, as explained by Krishna, is that he sees himself as an agent and is attached to the results of his actions. If, however, he learns the technique of "disciplined action" (karma-yoga), *he can develop the ability to act without involving the false sense of ego. Arjuna is told to act selflessly, perceiving himself as an impersonal agent of dharma who is simply following God's will. If he offers all of his actions to God as an act of devotion and cultivates complete detachment, then Arjuna may act without acquiring any negative karma. Moreover, Krishna tells him, such a mental perspective is the mind-set of the true world renouncer, and this alone leads to liberation from cyclic existence.*

20. Arjuna, his war flag a rampant monkey, saw Dhritarashtra's sons assembled as weapons were ready to clash, and he lifted his bow.

21. He told his charioteer: "Krishna, halt my chariot between the armies! . . ."
26. Arjuna saw them standing there: fathers, grandfathers, teachers, uncles, brothers, sons, grandsons, and friends.
27. He surveyed his elders and companions in both armies, all his kinsmen assembled together.
28. Dejected, filled with strange pity, he said this: "Krishna, I see my kinsmen gathered here, wanting war.
29. "My limbs sink, my mouth is parched, my body trembles, the hair bristles on my flesh.
30. "The magic bow slips from my hand, my skin burns, I cannot stand still, my mind reels.
31. "I see omens of chaos, Krishna; I see no good in killing my kinsmen in battle.
32. "Krishna, I seek no victory, or kingship or pleasures. What use to us are kingship, delights, or life itself? . . .
36. "What joy is there for us, Krishna, in killing Dhritarashtra's sons? Evil will haunt us if we kill them, though their bows are drawn to kill.
37. "Honor forbids us to kill our cousins, Dhritarashtra's sons; how can we know happiness if we kill our own kinsmen? . . .
40. "When the family is ruined, the timeless laws of family duty perish; and when duty is lost, chaos overwhelms the family.
41. "In overwhelming chaos, Krishna, women of the family are corrupted; and when women are corrupted, disorder is born in society. . . .
44. "Krishna, we have heard that a place in hell is reserved for men who undermine family duties. . . .
46. "If Dhritarashtra's armed sons kill me in battle when I am unarmed and offer no resistance, it will be my reward."
47. Saying this in the time of war, Arjuna slumped into the chariot and laid down his bow and arrows, his mind tormented by grief.

2.2. [Krishna:] "Why this cowardice in time of crisis, Arjuna? The coward is ignoble, shameful, foreign to the ways of heaven.
3. "Don't yield to impotence! It is unnatural to you! Banish this petty weakness from your heart. Rise to the fight, Arjuna! . . .
11. "You grieve for those beyond grief, and you speak words of insight; but learned men do not grieve for the dead or the living.
12. "Never have I not existed, nor you, nor these kings; and never in the future shall we cease to exist. . . .
16. "Nothing of nonbeing comes to be, nor does being cease to exist; the boundary between these two is seen by men who see reality.
17. "Indestructible is the presence that pervades all this; no one can destroy this unchanging reality.
18. "Our bodies are known to end, but the embodied self is enduring, indestructible, and immeasurable; therefore, Arjuna, fight the battle!

19. "He who thinks this self a killer and he who thinks it killed, both fail to understand; it does not kill, nor is it killed.

20. "It is not born, it does not die; having been, it will never not be; unborn, enduring, constant, and primordial, it is not killed when the body is killed. . . .

22. "Just as a man discards worn-out clothes to put on new and different ones, so the embodied self discards its worn-out bodies to take on other new ones. . . .

30. "The self embodied in the body of every being is indestructible; you have no cause to grieve for all these creatures, Arjuna!

31. "Look to your own duty; do not tremble before it; nothing is better for a warrior than a battle of sacred duty.

32. "The doors of heaven open for warriors who rejoice to have a battle like this thrust on them by chance.

33. "If you fail to wage this war of sacred duty, you will abandon your own duty and fame only to gain evil.

34. "People will tell of your undying shame, and for a man of honor shame is worse than death.

35. "The great chariot warriors will think you deserted in fear of battle; you will be despised by those who held you in esteem.

36. "Your enemies will slander you, scorning your skill in so many unspeakable ways—could any suffering be worse?

37. "If you are killed, you win heaven; if you triumph, you enjoy the earth; therefore, Arjuna, stand up and resolve to fight the battle!

38. "Impartial to joy and suffering, gain and loss, victory and defeat, arm yourself for the battle, lest you fall into evil. . . .

47. "Be intent on action, not on the fruits of action; avoid attraction to the fruits and attachment to inaction!

48. "Perform actions, firm in discipline (*yoga*), relinquishing attachment; be impartial to failure and success—this equanimity is called discipline. . . .

50. "Wise men disciplined by understanding relinquish the fruit born of action; freed from these bonds of rebirth, they reach a place beyond decay. . . .

55. "When he gives up desires in his mind, is content with the self within himself, then he is said to be a man whose insight is sure, Arjuna.

56. "When suffering does not disturb his mind, when his craving for pleasures has vanished, when attraction, fear, and anger are gone, he is called a sage whose thought is sure. . . .

61. "Controlling all [the senses], with discipline he should focus on me; when his senses are under control, his insight is sure. . . .

71. "When he renounces all desires and acts without craving, possessiveness, or individuality, he finds peace.

72. "This is the place of the infinite spirit (Brahman); achieving it, one is freed from delusion; abiding in it even at the time of death, one finds the pure calm of infinity. . . .

4.6. "Though myself unborn, undying, the lord of creatures, I fashion nature, which is mine, and I come into being through my own magic.

7. "Whenever sacred duty decays and chaos prevails, then I create myself, Arjuna. . . .

13. "I created mankind in four classes, different in their qualities and actions; though unchanging, I am the agent of this, the actor who never acts!

14. "I desire no fruit of actions, and actions do not defile me; one who knows this about me is not bound by actions. . . .

6.2. "Know that discipline, Arjuna, is what men call renunciation; no man is disciplined without renouncing willful intent. . . .

4. "He is said to be mature in discipline when he has renounced all intention and is detached from sense objects and actions. . . .

20. "When his thought ceases, checked by the exercise of discipline, he is content within the self, seeing the self through himself.

21. "Absolute joy beyond the senses can only be grasped by understanding; when one knows it, he abides there and never wanders from this reality. . . .

9.27. "Whatever you do—what you take, what you offer, what you give, what penances you perform—do as an offering to me, Arjuna!

28. "You will be freed from the bonds of action, armed with the discipline of renunciation, your self liberated, you will join me."

Source: *Bhagavad-gita* selections, from *The Bhagavad-gita: Krishna's Counsel in Time of War,* tr. Barbara Stoler Miller (New York: Columbia University Press, 1986), pp. 23–27, 29, 31–34, 36, 37, 39, 50, 52, 86.

DEVOTIONAL LITERATURE

PRAISE OF THE GODDESS

This passage declares that the goddess is the real source of all creation. All the male deities of Hinduism—as well as all that exists—has its origin in her. It also indicates how she should be worshiped: with all one's heart, as the Divine Mother who protects her devotees as a mother protects her children.

This blessed goddess Mahamaya, having forcibly seized the minds even of men of knowledge, leads them to delusion.
Through her is created the entire three-tiered universe, that which both does and does not move.
Just she is the gracious giver of boons to men, for the sake of (their) release.
From bondage to mundane life; she is indeed the queen (governing) all who have power. . . .
Brahma said:
By you is everything supported, by you the world created;

By you is it protected, O Goddess, and you always consume (it) at the end (of time). . . .
Terrible with your sword and spear, likewise with cudgel and discus,
With conch and bow, having arrows, sling, and iron mace as your weapons,
Gentle, more gentle than other gentle ones, exceedingly beautiful,
You are superior to the high and low, the supreme queen.
Whatever and whenever anything exists, whether it be real or unreal, O you have everything as your very soul,
Of all that, you are the power; how then can you be adequately praised?

Source: *Devi-Mahatmya* I.42–I.63, from *Encountering the Goddess*, tr. Thomas B. Coburn (Albany: State University of New York Press, 1991), pp. 35–37.

PRAYER FOR IDENTITY WITH THE GODDESS

The Goddess is described as both fearful and benevolent, indicating that she is connected with both the pleasant and unpleasant aspects of existence. This poem, traditionally attributed to Shankara, asks for her help in attaining perfect identification with her in a state of perfect devotion in which notions of separateness and personality are transcended.

If Shiva is united with Shakti, he is able to exert his powers as lord; if not, the god is not able to stir.
Hence to you, who must be propitiated by Hari [Vishnu], Hara [Shiva], Virarnchi [Brahma], and the other [gods],
How can one who has not acquired merit be fit to offer reverence and praise? . . .

For the ignorant you are the island city of the sun, for the mentally stagnant you are a waterfall of streams of nectar [flowing] from a bouquet of intelligence,
For the poor you are a rosary of wishing-jewels; for those who in the ocean of birth are submerged, you are the tusk of that boar who was the enemy of Mura, O Lady.

Banded with a tinkling girdle, heavy with breasts like the frontal lobes of young elephants,
Slender of waist, with face like the full moon of autumn, bearing on the palms of her hands bow, arrows, noose, and goad,
Let there be seated before us the pride of him who shook the cities [Shiva]. . . .

May you, O Blessed Lady, extend to me, your slave, a compassionate glance!
When one desiring to praise you utters the words "you, O Lady" [which also mean, "May I be you"],
At that moment you grant him a state of identity with you.
With your feet illuminated by the crests of Mukunda, Brahma, and Indra.

Source: *Saundaryalahari*, attributed to Shankara, tr. W. N. Brown (Cambridge: Harvard University Press, 1958), pp. 48, 50, 56.

MIRABAI'S MYSTICAL MARRIAGE TO KRISHNA

Mirabai remains one of the most popular devotional poets of medieval India. She was probably born around 1550 and is said to have been the wife of a Rajput prince who was the son of the ruler (Rana) of Mewar. According to legend, before her marriage she had fallen in love with Krishna and refused to consummate her marriage to the prince because her relationship with the Lord took precedence. One story that is told of her relates that one time she was exchanging words of love to a visitor on the other side of a locked door. Her father-in-law, the ruler, overheard her and, outraged by the shame she had brought on his family, threatened to kill her. She told him that the person to whom she was speaking was the Lord Krishna, and not a human lover, and her life was spared. In this poem she alludes to an incident in which the Rana tries to poison her, but she believes that she was saved by Krishna. She indicates that her devotion to the Lord has caused her to leave behind her family, friends, and the privileged life she led in the palace, and to seek the company of fellow devotees.

> My love is reserved for Gopal, the Mountain Lifter
> and for no one else.
> O saints and ascetics,
> I have seen the world and its ways.
> I left my brothers and relatives
> And all my possessions.
> Abandoning worldly shame,
> I came to sit with ascetics.
> Together with devotees [of Krishna,] I was happy.
> [But] when I looked at the world, I wept.
> I planted the vine of love
> And watered it with my tears.
> I churned curds
> And extracted the ghee;
> I threw out the buttermilk.
> The King sent me a cup of poison,
> And I gladly drank it all.
> Mira's love is deeply rooted;
> She accepts whatever comes to her.

Source: Poem from *Mirabai ki Padavali.*

CHEATING ON HER HUSBAND

Mahadeviyakka was an important poet of the iconoclastic Virashaiva tradition. In her poetry, her devotion to Shiva was often expressed in sexual terms. This led to conflicts with traditional mores and values, particularly those regarding the proper conduct of women. In the following verses, she indicates that her intense devotion to Shiva prevented her from the devotion to her husband required of a traditional Hindu wife. She compares her apparently loveless marriage with her husband to her devotion to Shiva

and indicates how little she values the former relationship in comparison with her
devotional love affair with the Lord.

> I have Maya for mother-in-law; the world for father-in-law;
> three brothers-in-law, like tigers;
> And the husband's thoughts are full of laughing women: no god, this man.
> And I cannot cross the sister-in-law.
> But I will give this wench the slip and go cuckold my husband with Hara, my
> Lord.
> My mind is my maid: by her kindness, I join my Lord, my utterly beautiful
> Lord from the mountain-peaks, my lord white as jasmine,
> and I will make Him my good husband.

Source: poem by Mahadeviyakka, from *Speaking of Siva,* tr. A. K. Ramanujan
(Baltimore: Penguin Books, 1973), p. 141.]

TREATISES ON DHARMA

ACTIONS AND THEIR RESULTS

The Laws of Manu *codify the hierarchy of medieval Indian society and outline the*
duties of the four primary social groups: (1) brahmins, *the priests; (2)* kshatriyas, *the*
warriors and rulers; (3) vaishyas, *tradespeople and merchants, and (4)* shudras, *or*
servants. Each of them is said to have a role to play in creating a stable and ordered
society. Manu also outlines the duties for four stages of life: the student, the house-
holder, the forest-dweller, and the world renouncer. According to this scheme, libera-
tion is recognized as the supreme goal of the religious life, but its pursuit should be
postponed until the proper time, which is said to be when one has seen a grandson born
(indicating that one's lineage will continue) and gray hairs have appeared on one's head
(indicating that one has lived long enough to fulfill the requirements of dharma).

4.97. It is better (to discharge) one's own (appointed) duty (*dharma*) incom-
pletely than to perform completely that of another; for he who lives
according to the law of another (caste) is instantly excluded from his
own. . . .

12.3. Action, which springs from the mind, from speech, and from the
body, produces either good or evil results; by actions are caused (the
various) conditions of men, the highest, middling, and the lowest.

4. Know that the mind is the instigator here below, even for [actions]
that are connected with the body. . . .

40. Those endowed with Goodness (*sattva*) reach the state of gods, those
endowed with Activity (*rajas*) the state of men, and those endowed
with Darkness (*tamas*) always sink to the condition of beasts; that is
the threefold course of transmigrations. . . .

95. All those traditions (*smriti*) and all those despicable systems of philosophy, which are not based on the Veda, produce no reward after
death; for they are declared to be founded on darkness. . . .

104. Austerity and sacred learning are the best means by which a brahmin gains supreme happiness; by austerity he destroys guilt, by sacred learning he obtains the cessation of (births and) deaths. . . .
173. If (the punishment falls) not on (the offender) himself, (it falls) on his sons, if not on the sons, (at least) on his grandsons; but an iniquity (once) committed never fails to produce consequences for him who wrought it.
174. He prospers for a while through unrighteousness, then he gains great good fortune, next he conquers his enemies, but (at last) he perishes (branch and) root. . . .
240. Single is each being born; single it dies; single it enjoys (the reward of its) virtue; single (it suffers the punishment of its) sin. . . .
31. For the sake of the prosperity of the worlds, he (the Lord) caused the brahmin, the kshatriya, the vaishya, and the shudra to proceed from his mouth, his arms, his thighs, and his feet. . . .
87. But in order to protect this universe He, the most glorious one, assigned separate (duties and) occupations to those who came from his mouth, arms, thighs, and feet. . . .
10.1. The three twice-born castes, carrying out their (prescribed) duties, study (the Veda); but among them the brahmin (alone) shall teach it, and not the other two; this is an established rule. . . .
3. On account of his pre-eminence, on account of the superiority of his origin, on account of his observance of restrictive rules, and on account of his particular sanctification, the brahmin is the lord of (all) castes.
4. The brahmin, the kshatriya, and the vaishya castes are the twice-born ones, but the fourth, the shudra, has one birth only; there is no fifth (caste).
5. In all castes those (children) only which are begotten in the direct order on wedded wives, equal (in caste and married as) virgins, are to be considered to belong to the same caste (as the fathers). . . .
45. All those tribes in this world, which are excluded from the (community of) those born from the mouth, the arms, the thighs, and the feet (of Brahman), are called Dasyus ["slaves"], whether they speak the language of the barbarians (*mleccha*) or that of the Aryans. . . .

Source: *The Laws of Manu*, chs. 4, 12, 10.

The Four Stages of Life

6.87. The student, the householder, the forest dweller, and the world renouncer: these constitute the four separate orders. . . .
89. And in accordance with the precepts of the Veda and of the traditional texts, the householder is declared to be superior to all of them, because he supports the other three. . . .
7.352. Men who commit adultery with the wives of others, the king shall cause to be marked by punishments which cause terror, and afterwards banish.

353. For by (adultery) is caused a mixture of the castes among men; from that (follows) sin, which cuts up even the roots and causes the destruction of everything. . . .

2.36. In the eighth year after conception, one should perform the initiation (*upanayana*) of a brahmin, in the eleventh (year) after conception (that) of a kshatriya, but in the twelfth that of a vaishya. . . .

69. Having performed the (rite of) initiation, the teacher must first instruct the (pupil) in (the rules of) personal purification, conduct, of the fire sacrifice, and of the twilight (morning and evening) devotions. . . .

176. Every day, having bathed and being purified, he must offer libations of water to the gods, sages . . . worship the gods, and place fuel (on the sacred fire).

177. He should abstain from honey, meat, perfumes, garlands, substances (used for) flavoring (food), women, all substances turned acid, and from doing injury to living creatures, . . .

179. From gambling, idle disputes, backbiting, and lying, looking at and touching women, and from hurting others. . . .

199. Let him not pronounce the mere name of his teacher (without adding an honorific title), behind his back even, and let him not mimic his gait, speech, and deportment. . . .

201. By censuring (his teacher), though justly, he will become a donkey (in his next birth); by falsely defaming him, a dog; he who lives on his teacher's substance will become a worm, and he who is envious (of his merit), a (larger) insect. . . .

3.1. The vow (of studying) the three Vedas under a teacher must be kept for thirty-six years, or for half that time, or for a quarter, until the (student) has perfectly learned them.

3.2. (A student) who has studied in due order the three Vedas, or two, or even one only, without breaking the (rules of) studentship, shall enter the order of the householders. . . .

4. Having bathed, with the permission of his teacher, and performed according to the rule the rite on homecoming, a twice-born man shall marry a wife of equal caste who is endowed with auspicious (bodily) marks. . . .

75. Let (every man) in this (second order, at least) daily apply himself to the private recitation of the Veda, and also to the performance of the offering to the gods; for he who is diligent in the performance of sacrifices supports both the movable and the immovable creation. . . .

78. Because men of the three (other) orders are daily supported by the householder with (gifts of) sacred knowledge and food, therefore (the stage of) householder is the most excellent stage. . . .

2. A brahmin must seek a means of subsistence which either causes no, or at least little, pain (to others), and live (by that) except in times of distress.

3. For the purpose of gaining bare subsistence, let him accumulate property by (following those) irreproachable occupations (which are prescribed for) his (caste), without (unduly) fatiguing his body. . . .

11. Let him never, for the sake of subsistence, follow the ways of the world; let him live the pure, straightforward, honest life of a brahmin. . . .

Source: *The Laws of Manu*, chs. 6, 7, 3.

Leaving Home Life

6.1. A twice-born *snataka*, who has thus lived according to the law in the order of householders, may, taking a firm resolution and keeping his organs in subjection, live in the forest, duly [observing the rules given below].

2. When a householder sees his (skin) wrinkled, and (his hair) white, and the sons of his sons, then he may resort to the forest.

3. Abandoning all food raised by cultivation, and all his belongings, he may depart into the forest, either committing his wife to his sons, or accompanied by her. . . .

8. Let him be always industrious in privately reciting the Veda; let him be patient in hardships, friendly, of collected mind, ever liberal, and never a receiver of gifts, and compassionate towards all living creatures. . . .

26. Making no effort (to procure) things that give pleasure, chaste, sleeping on the bare ground, not caring for any shelter, dwelling at the roots of trees. . . .

33. Having thus passed the third part of his life in the forest, he may live as an ascetic during the fourth part of his existence, after abandoning all attachment to worldly objects.

34. He who after passing from order to order, after offering sacrifices and subduing the senses, becomes, tired with (giving) alms and offerings of food, an ascetic, gains bliss after death. . . .

36. Having studied the Vedas in accordance with the rule, having begat sons in accordance with the sacred law, and having offered sacrifices according to his ability, he may direct his mind to (the attainment of) final liberation.

37. A twice-born man who seeks final liberation, without having studied the Vedas, without having begotten sons, and without having offered sacrifices, sinks downwards.

38. Having performed the *Ishti*, sacred to the Lord of Creatures, where (he gives) all his property as a sacrificial fee, having deposited the sacred fires in himself, a brahmin may depart from his house (as an ascetic). . . .

41. Departing from his house fully provided with the means of purification, let him wander about absolutely silent, and caring nothing for enjoyments that may be offered (to him). . . .

45. Let him not desire to die, let him not desire to live; let him wait for (his appointed) time, as a servant (waits) for the payment of his wages. . . .

49. Delighting in what refers to the Self, sitting (in yogic meditation), independent (of external help), entirely abstaining from sensual enjoyments, with himself for his only companion, he shall live in this world, desiring the bliss (of final liberation). . . .

65. By deep meditation let him recognize the subtle nature of the Supreme Self, and its presence in all organisms. . . .

85. A twice-born man who becomes an ascetic, after the successive performance of the above-mentioned acts, shakes off sin here below and reaches the highest Brahman.

Source: *The Laws of Manu*, ch. 6.

Duties of the Four Social Classes

i. The Brahmin

4.74. Brahmins who are intent on the means (of gaining union with) Brahman and firm in [discharging] their duties shall live by correctly performing the following six acts in their (proper) order.

75. Teaching, studying, sacrificing for oneself, sacrificing for others, making gifts and receiving them are the six acts of a brahmin. . . .

79. To carry arms for striking and for throwing (is prescribed) for kshatriyas as a means of subsistence; to trade, (to raise) cattle, and agriculture for vaishyas; but their duties are liberality, study of the Vedas, and performance of sacrifices.

80. Among the several occupations, the most commendable are: teaching the Veda for a brahmin, protecting (the people) for kshatriya, and trade for a vaishya.

81. But a brahmin, unable to subsist by his peculiar occupations just mentioned, may live according to the law applicable to kshatriyas, for the latter is next to him in rank.

82. If it is asked, "What should he do if he cannot maintain himself by either (of these occupations," the answer is), he may adopt the vaishya's mode of life, employing himself in agriculture and raising cattle.

83. But a brahmin, or a kshatriya, living by a vaishya's mode of subsistence, shall carefully avoid agriculture, (which causes) injury to many beings and depends on others. . . .

92. By (selling) flesh, salt, and lac a brahmin at once becomes an outcaste; by selling milk he becomes (equal to) a shudra in three days.

93. But by willingly selling in this world other (forbidden) commodities, a brahmin assumes after seven nights the character of vaishya. . . .

95. A kshatriya who has fallen into distress may subsist by all these (means); but he must never arrogantly adopt the mode of life of his betters. . . .

102. A brahmin who has fallen into distress may accept (gifts) from anybody; because according to the law it is not possible that anything pure can be sullied.

ii. The Kshatriya

18. Punishment alone governs all created beings, punishment alone protects them, punishment watches over them while they sleep; the wise declare punishment to be the law (*dharma*).
19. If (punishment) is properly inflicted after consideration it makes all people happy; but inflicted without consideration, it destroys everything.
20. If the king did not, without tiring, inflict punishment on those worthy to be punished, the stronger would roast the weaker, like fish on a spit. . . .
22. The whole world is kept in order by punishment, for a guiltless man is hard to find; through fear of punishment the whole world yields enjoyments. . . .
88. Not to turn back in battle, to protect the people, to honor the brahmins is the best means for a king to secure happiness.
89. Those kings who, seeking to slay each other in battle, fight with the utmost exertion and do not turn back, go to heaven. . . .
144. The highest duty of a kshatriya is to protect his subjects, for the king who enjoys the rewards just mentioned is required to do that duty. . . .
198. He should, (however), try to conquer his foes by conciliation by (well-applied) gifts and by creating dissension, used either separately or conjointly, never by fighting (if it can be avoided).
199. For when two (princes) fight, victory and defeat in the battle are, as experience teaches, uncertain; he should therefore avoid an engagement.

iii. The Vaishya

9.326. After a vaishya has received the sacraments and has taken a wife, he shall be always attentive to the business whereby he may subsist and to (that of) cattle.
327. For when the Lord of Creatures created cattle, he gave them to vaishyas; to the brahmins and to the king he entrusted all created beings.
328. A vaishya must never wish, "I will not keep cattle"; and if a vaishya is willing (to keep them), they must never be kept by other (castes).
329. (A vaishya) must know the respective value of gems, of pearls, of coral, of metals, of (cloth) made of thread, of perfumes, and of spices.
330. He must know how to plant seeds and the good and bad qualities of fields, and he must perfectly know all measures and weights. . . .
333. Let him exert himself to the utmost in order to increase his property in a righteous manner, and he should zealously give food to all created beings.

iv. The Shudra

8.334. Serving brahmins who are learned in the Vedas, who are householders, and who are famous (for virtue) is the highest duty of a shudra,
which leads to beatitude.

335. [A shudra who is] pure, the servant of his betters, gentle in his speech,
free from pride, and who always seeks a refuge with brahmins, attains
(in his next life) a higher caste. . . .

413. But a shudra, whether bought or unbought, he may compel to do
servile work; for he was created by the Self-existent to be the slave of
brahmins.

414. A shudra, even though emancipated by his master, is not released
from servitude; since that is innate in him, who can set him free from
it? . . .

128. The more a (shudra), keeping himself free from envy, imitates the
behavior of the virtuous, the more he gains . . . in this world and the
next.

Source: *The Laws of Manu,* chs. 4, 9, 8.

How Women Should Live

3.55. Women must be honored and adorned by their fathers, brothers, husbands, and brothers-in-law, who desire (their own) welfare.

56. Where women are honored, there the gods are pleased; but where
they are not honored, no sacred rite yields rewards.

57. Where the female relations live in grief, the family soon wholly perishes; but that family where they are not unhappy ever prospers.

58. The houses on which female relations, not being duly honored, pronounce a curse, perish completely, as if destroyed by magic. . . .

60. In that family where the husband is pleased with his wife and the wife
with her husband, happiness will assuredly be lasting. . . .

67. The nuptial ceremony is stated to be the Vedic sacrament for women
(and to be equal to the initiation), serving the husband is (equivalent
to) the residence in (the house of the) teacher, and household duties
are (the same) as the (daily) worship of the sacred fire. . . .

5.147. By a girl, by a young woman, or even by an aged one, nothing must
be done independently, even in her own house.

148. In childhood a female must be subject to her father, in youth to her
husband, when her lord is dead to her sons; a woman must never be
independent. . . .

150. She must always be cheerful, clever in household affairs, careful in
cleaning her utensils, and economical in expenditure.

151. Him to whom her father may give her, or her brother with her father's
permission, she shall obey as long as he lives, and when he is dead,
she must not insult (his memory). . . .

154. Though destitute of virtue, or seeking pleasure (elsewhere), or devoid of good qualities, a husband must be constantly worshipped as a god by a faithful wife.

155. No sacrifice, no vow, no fast must be performed by women apart (from their husbands); if a wife obeys her husband, she will be exalted for that (reason alone) in heaven.

156. A faithful wife, who desires to dwell (after death) with her husband, must never do anything that might displease him who took her hand, whether he be alive or dead.

157. At her pleasure let her emaciate her body by (living on) pure flowers, roots, and fruit; but she must never even mention the name of another man after her husband has died. . . .

160. A virtuous wife who after the death of her husband constantly remains chaste, even if she has no sons, reaches heaven, just like those chaste men. . . .

164. By violating her duty towards her husband, a wife is disgraced in this world; (after death) she enters the womb of a jackal, and is tormented by diseases for her sin.

165. She who, controlling her thoughts, words, and deeds, never fights her lord, lives (after death) with her husband (in heaven) and is called virtuous. . . .

167. A twice-born man, versed in the sacred law, shall burn a wife of equal caste who conducts herself thus and dies before him with (the sacred fires used for) the Agnihotra and with the sacrificial implements.

168. Having thus, at the funeral, given the sacred fires to his wife who dies before him, he may marry again, and again kindle (the fires).

Source: *The Laws of Manu*, chs. 3, 5.

MANU'S INSTRUCTIONS
ON FINDING THE RIGHT MATE

Marriage is a matter of great concern in classical Hindu texts, since stable marriages are thought to be essential to the proper ordering of society. According to Manu, marriage should occur only within one's caste, and he provides a number of other criteria for men to consider when looking for a wife.

When, with the permission of his teacher, he has bathed and performed the ritual for homecoming (at the end of his studies) according to the ritual rules, a twice-born man should take a wife who is of the same class and has the right marks. A woman who does not come from the same blood line on her mother's side, nor belong to the same ritual line on her father's side, is considered proper as a wife and a sexual partner for a twice-born man. When it comes to relations with a woman, a man should avoid the ten following families, even if they are great or prosperous with cattle, rich in sheep, or possessing other wealth: a family that has abandoned the rituals, one that does not have boys, or a family that does not chant the Veda; and those families in which they have hairy bodies, piles, consumption, weak digestion, bad memories, and families with white leprosy, or black leprosy. A man should not marry a maiden who is a redhead or has an extra limb or is sickly or who is bald or too hairy or talks too much or is sallow or who is named after a constellation, a tree, or a river, who has a low caste name, who is named after a mountain, a bird, a snake, or has a slave name, or who has a fearsome name. He should have nothing to do with a woman who is too fat or too thin, too tall or too dwarfish, who is past her prime or lacks a limb, or who is fond of quarreling.

He should take a woman whose limbs are complete and who has a pleasant name, who walks like a swan or an elephant, whose body hair and hair on the head are fine and whose teeth are not big, with delicate limbs. A wise man, out of concern for the dharma of daughters, will not marry a woman who has no brother or whose father is unknown.

Taking a woman of the same class is recommended to twice-born men for the first marriage; but for men in whom sexual desire has arisen, these should be the choices, listed in order: according to the tradition, only a Shudra woman can be the wife of a Shudra; she and one of his own class can be the wife of a Vaishya; these two and one of his own class for a Kshatriya; and these three and one of his own class for the high-born (Brahmin). A Shudra woman is not mentioned as the wife of a Brahmin or a Kshatriya even when they are under duress, even in a story. Twice-born men who are so infatuated as to take as wives women of low caste quickly reduce their families, including the children, to the status of Shudras. . . . A Brahmin who beds a Shudra woman goes to hell; if he begets a child on her, he forsakes the status of Brahmin. The ancestors and the gods do not eat the offerings to the gods, to the ancestors, and to guests made by such a man, and so he does not go to heaven. No expiation is ordained for a (twice-born) man who drinks the froth from the lips of a Shudra woman or who is tainted by her breath or who begets a son on her.

Now listen to the summary of these eight marriage rituals for the four classes, that are both for good and for ill, in this life and after death. Now, the eight are the marriages named after Brahma, the gods, the sages, Prajapati, the demons, the Gandharvas, the ogres, and the ghouls. I will tell you all about which one is within the dharma of each class, and the faults and qualities of each, and their merits and demerits when it comes to offspring. It should be understood that the first six as they are listed above are within the dharma of a Brahmin, the last four are for a Kshatriya, and these same four, with the exception of the ogre marriage, are for a Vaishya or a Shudra. . . .

A marriage is known as following the dharma of a Brahma marriage when a man dresses his daughter and adorns her and summons a man who knows the Vedas and is moral, and himself gives her to him as a gift.

They say a marriage is in the dharma of the gods when a man adorns his daughter and gives her as a gift to a sacrificial priest, in the course of a properly performed sacrifice. . . .

It is called a demonic dharma when the maiden is given to a man because he desires her himself, when he has given as much wealth as he can to her relatives and to the maiden herself. The ritual is known as a Gandharva marriage when the bride and her groom unite with one another because they want to, as a result of the desire for sexual intercourse. The wedding is called the rule of the ogres when a man forcibly carries off a maiden out of her house, screaming and weeping, after he has killed, wounded, or beaten (her and/or her relatives). The lowest and most evil of marriages, known as that of the ghouls, takes place when a man secretly seduces a girl who is asleep, drunk, or out of her mind. . . .

A man should approach his wife sexually during her fertile period, and always find his sexual pleasure in his own wife; and when he desires sexual pleasure he may go to her to whom he is vowed, except on the days at the junctures. The natural fertile season of a woman lasts for sixteen nights, according to the tradition. . . . On the even nights, sons are conceived, and on the uneven nights, daughters; therefore, a man who wants sons should unite with his wife during her fertile season on the even nights. A male child is born when the seed of the man is greater (than that of the woman), and a female child when the seed of the woman is greater (than that of the man); if both are equal, a hermaphrodite is born, or a boy and a girl; and if the seed is weak or scanty, there will be a miscarriage.

Source: *The Laws of Manu*, ch. 3, from *Textual Sources for the Study of Hinduism*, pp. 101–103.

GLOSSARY

Agni   God of fire in the Vedas, who transmutes sacrificial offerings into food for the gods.

Aryan   The European tribes that settled in India in the second millennium B.C.E.

Atman   "Soul," the divine essence of every individual.

Avidya   "Ignorance," the primary factor that enmeshes living beings in the cycle of birth, death, and rebirth.

Bhagavad-gita   "*Song of God*," a section of the epic *Mahabharata* that describes the ethical dilemma of Arjuna, who is torn between the demands of karma and dharma.

Bhakti   Selfless devotion to God.

Brahman   The ultimate reality described in the Upanishads.

Brahmin   The priestly caste of traditional Hinduism.

Deva   The gods of Hinduism.

Devi   The Goddess, who manifests in various female forms.

Dharma   "Duty," "Law," the occupational, social, and religious roles required of individuals as a result of their places in society.

Dravidian   Term coined by Western scholars for the indigenous inhabitants of India, who were displaced and conquered by the Aryans.

Harijan   "Children of God," a term coined by Mahatma Gandhi for groups of Hindus traditionally viewed as being outside the caste system (commonly referred to as "untouchables").

Hindu   An adherent of Hinduism.

Indra   King of the gods in the Vedic stories, and the paradigmatic warrior.

Karma   "Actions," which bring about concordant results.

Kshatriya   The caste whose members were traditionally warriors and rulers.

Loka-samgraha   "Upholding the World," the goal of the sacrifices enjoined by the Vedas.

Maya   "Magic" or "illusion," the creative power of Brahman that manifests as the phenomena of the world.

Moksha   "Release" from the cycle of birth, death, and rebirth.

Ramayana   Epic story of the heroic deeds of Rama, believed by tradition to be an incarnation of the god Vishnu.

Rishi   "Seers" who revealed the Vedas.

Rita   Cosmic order, which is maintained by the gods.

Samnyasin   One who renounces the world in order to seek liberation from cyclic existence.

Samsara   "Cyclic Existence," the beginningless cycle of birth, death, and rebirth in which ignorant beings are trapped.

Sanatana-dharma   "Universal Truth," a term for Hinduism, implying that it is able to embrace the limited "truths" of other religions and philosophies.

Shankara   Most influential of traditional commentators on the Upanishads.

Shiva   God who exemplifies yogic practice, who will destroy the world at the end of the present cosmic cycle.

Shudra   The caste whose traditional duty was to serve the castes above them.

Upanishads   Mystical texts that speculate on the nature of human existence and the ultimate reality.

Vaishya   The caste whose members traditionally were merchants and skilled artisans.

Varna   The four main social groupings of traditional Indian society (brahmins, kshatriyas, vaishyas, and shudras).

Veda   The four early sacred texts of Hinduism, which describe the gods and rituals connected with them.

Vedanta   Tradition of commentary on the Upanishads.

Vishnu   God whose traditional role is to protect dharma.

Yoga   System of meditative cultivation involving physical and mental discipline.

FURTHER READINGS

AVALON, ARTHUR (Sir John Woodroffe). *Shakti and Shakta.* New York: Dover, 1978.

BASHAM, A. L. *The Wonder That Was India.* London: Sidgwick & Jackson, 1967.

DANIÉLOU, ALAIN. *The Myths and Gods of India.* Rochester, VT: Inner Traditions International, 1985.

DASGUPTA, SURENDRANATH. *A History of Indian Philosophy.* 5 vols. Delhi: Motilal Banarsidass, 1975.

ELIADE, MIRCEA. *Yoga: Immortality and Freedom.* Princeton: Princeton University Press, 1969.

HIRIYANA, M. *Essentials of Indian Philosophy.* London: Unwin, 1949.

HOPKINS, THOMAS J. *The Hindu Religious Tradition.* Belmont, CA: Wadsworth, 1971.

KAELBER, WALTER O. *Tapta Marga: Asceticism and Initiation in Vedic India.* New York: State University of New York Press, 1989.

KINSLEY, DAVID R. *Hindu Goddesses: Visions of the Divine Feminine in the Hindu Religious Tradition.* Delhi: Motilal Banarsidass, 1987.

——. *Hinduism: A Cultural Perspective.* Englewood Cliffs, NJ: Prentice-Hall, 1982.

MINOR, ROBERT. *Modern Indian Interpreters of the Bhagavad Gita.* Albany: State University of New York Press, 1986.

POTTER, KARL H. *Encyclopedia of Indian Philosophies, Vol I: Bibliography.* Princeton: Princeton University Press, 1983.

——. *Encyclopedia of Indian Philosophies, Vol. III: Advaita Vedānta up to Śaṃkara and His Pupils.* Delhi: Motilal Banarsidass, 1981.

——. *Presuppositions of India's Philosophies.* Delhi: Motilal Banarsidass, n.d.

RAMANUJAN, A. K. *Speaking of Śiva.* Baltimore: Penguin, 1973.

SIVARAMAN, KRISHNA. *Saivism in Philosophical Perspective: A Study of the Formative Concepts, Problems and Methods of Śaiva Siddhānta.* Delhi: Motilal Banarsidass, 1973.

ZAEHNER, R. C. *Hindu and Muslim Mysticism.* New York: Schocken, 1969.

ZIMMER, HEINRICH. *Philosophies of India.* Princeton: Princeton University Press, 1951.

Jainism

INTRODUCTION

The contemporary Jaina tradition traces itself back to Vardhamana Jnatriputra, an ascetic who was born in the northern part of modern-day Bihar in the sixth century B.C.E. This was also the area in which the Buddha lived, and the two religious leaders were said to have been familiar with each other's reputations and teachings. Both traditions rejected key elements of the dominant brahamanical system, including the sacrifices enjoined by the Vedas and the caste system, and both emphasized the goal of final liberation from cyclic existence, although they differed significantly in their paths.

Jainism's founder, referred to by his followers as Mahavira ("Great Hero"), advocated a path of strict asceticism and noninjury (*ahimsa*) to all living things as the keys to liberation (*moksha*). By controlling desires, restraining the wandering of the senses, and limiting consumption to the minimum needed to sustain life, Mahavira eliminated all attachments to material enjoyments, wandered naked from place to place (symbolizing his dispassion toward mundane norms and possessions), and through rigorous spiritual discipline eventually overcame any possibility of return to cyclic existence. In recognition of his hard-won victory over the temptations of the world, his followers commonly refer to him as Jina, meaning "Victor." The term *Jaina* means "Followers of the Victor."

Mahavira did not claim to be a religious innovator or to have discovered a new path to salvation; rather, he asserted that he was one of many who have discovered the way. According to Jaina tradition, he was the twenty-fourth Tirthankara, or "Ford-Maker," a name given by Jainas to the great ascetics who not only find the path to liberation, but also show it to others.

The most distinctive features of Jainism are its extreme asceticism, together with its emphasis on personal effort, and its strict adherence to the doctrine of noninjury. The Jaina path to liberation involves renunciation of material things, coupled with ascetic practices aimed at purifying the soul (*jiva*), cleansing it of the karmic accretions that have colored it and bound it to matter (*ajiva*). In this process, one can depend only upon oneself and one's own effort. In Jainism there is no creator God and no higher power that can aid one in reaching salvation, which in Jainism is attained by first ridding oneself of all karma, both good and bad, and by attaining "liberating wisdom" (*kevala-jnana*), which allows one to separate oneself from matter.

Jain metaphysics divides the universe into two main categories, *jiva* and *ajiva*. *Jiva* refers to the life-principle that is found in all things, while *ajiva* is insentient matter, along with the categories of time and space. It is the main impediment to the release of individual *jivas*. According to Jainism, all things, even material entities, have a life force. *Jiva* is an eternal substance that adjusts in size and shape to the physical body it inhabits. Matter is nonsentient, and because of its connection with the life force, living beings inevitably suffer as a result of the fact that matter is prone to change and decay.

The *jiva's* natural purview is universal—it is omniscient, but the senses place restrictions on it. To bring the soul to its natural omniscience, one needs to overcome the limitations imposed upon it by matter, to let the soul perceive without the constraints placed on it by the senses, which serve as blinders for the naturally omniscient *jiva*. This leads to full and direct knowledge of all things in all aspects.

God is unnecessary in Jainism, because the soul by itself is capable of knowing everything and accomplishing the highest goal of liberation. Furthermore, karma operates according to its own laws and does not require or permit the intervention of a higher power that can alleviate or erase its effects. Each being must suffer the results of his or her actions, and no god can change this. It is up to the individual to work out his or her own salvation.

In Jain metaphysics, the universe is filled with life—everything possesses a soul, even plants and such apparently unliving things as stones, which are at such a low level of sentience, and so oppressed by matter, that they appear to be devoid of life. The soul is considered to be permeable, and all of one's actions lead to influxes of karma, which is seen as subtle matter that pervades the soul (as opposed to merely covering or obscuring it). Karmic matter varies in color in accordance with the relative goodness or evil of the act committed. For instance, killing a living being, even inadvertently, leads to an influx of very dark karma (this is why many Jaina monks wear masks over their noses and mouths and carry brooms to sweep in front of themselves, in order to avoid inadvertently killing living beings). Beings who engage in occupations that involve a great deal of killing, such as butchers, have jet black *jivas,* which can be cleansed only through prodigious amounts of asceticism and physical mortification. Because of this, Jainas are strictly prohibited from engaging in occupations that involve the taking of life, which has kept them from being, for instance, hunters and fishermen.

Jainas also hold that each *jiva* has eternally been associated with *ajiva,* and there has never been a time when they were separated, and no "fall" through which *jiva* became associated with *ajiva*. *Jiva's* association with *ajiva* is beginningless, but it is possible to terminate it. In addition, there is no creator deity that made the world as it is—it has always been as it is and always will be, although it does go through cycles of relative degeneration and regeneration.

All actions lead to karmic influx, but evil actions color the *jiva* with very dark karma that is difficult to eliminate, while good or meritorious actions color the *jiva* with light karma that is easily cleansed. Elimination of karma occurs naturally, and in every moment beings are working off the effects of past actions. Most beings, however, are simultaneously creating new karma, and so the process is self-perpetuating.

The only way to burn off more karma than one creates is to dedicate oneself to a program of asceticism and meditation. The karma accumulated in the *jiva* will burn off naturally, but this is a slow process. It can be aided through fasting, celibacy, and various types of ascetic practices aimed at developing *tapas* (literally "heat," the energy one acquires through self-restraint and asceticism). This may be used to burn off karma.

The first step of the Jaina path to liberation involves halting the influx of new karma (*samvara*), which is followed by a program of cleansing the karma one has already acquired (*nirjara*). When this process is completed one attains liberation (*moksha*).

Because of past karma that has not yet been eradicated, one may still have a physical body, but this too will pass away when its past karma is exhausted. At this point, the soul is freed of its bondage to matter, and is luminous, omniscient, and completely free. It then rises toward the top of the universe (which in traditional Jaina cosmology is pictured as a giant human), and comes to rest at the base of the cranium of the universe in a realm called "World of Saints" (*siddha-loka*), where it dwells forever with the other perfected beings, completely beyond any future suffering and eternally removed from the world.

No outside force or power can aid the individual in this process. Only one's own effort can cleanse one's *jiva* of the effects of accumulated karma. Gods and other human beings are unable to help the individual, since they are similarly enmeshed in the process. Even the Tirthankaras are unable to help (beyond providing instruction and guidance during their lifetimes), since their liberation has removed them from any concern with the world, and so they are beyond the reach of prayers and supplications.

Liberation is only possible in the realm in which humans live, which is said to be a small disk in the middle of the universe. Below this realm are various painful destinies, such as hells, and above it are the realms of demigods and gods. Humans are in a position superior to that of the gods, who live a long and blissful existence, and thus are unaware that when their good karma is exhausted they will inevitably sink back to the lower levels of rebirth.

Jaina Scriptures

Jainism today has two main sects, the Digambaras ("Sky Clad") and the Shvetambaras ("White Clad"). The former group believes that liberation requires renunciation of all possessions, including clothes. Digambara monks, following Mahavira's example, are expected to be completely naked, their only permitted possession a small broom used to whisk away insects before they sit or lie down.

The Shvetambaras agree that Mahavira wore no clothes, but assert that the present time is one of degeneration, and so nudity is inappropriate today. Their monks and nuns wear simple white robes, but this practice is denounced by Digambaras as indicating that they have attachments to worldly things. As a result, Digambaras hold that Shvetambara monastics are actually no more advanced spiritually than laypeople who follow the Jaina precepts.

These differences in monastic discipline parallel the divergences in their respective scriptural traditions. Each school has its own canon, and for the most part they do not accept the authority of the other's scriptures (although the doctrinal contents of the their texts are generally in accord). One reason for the disagreement is the fact that the first Jaina synod was held about two centuries after Mahavira's death. The canon that resulted from this forms the core of the Digambara canon, but since it was held well after the death of the founder many texts had become lost or forgotten, and there were differing recensions of many works. In the fifth century the Shvetambaras held a council that resulted in their authoritative texts being written down and distributed to the Jaina community.

The oldest texts of the Jaina canon were written in Prakrits, languages that were related to Sanskrit but that contained numerous grammatical forms and vocabulary from local dialects. In later times Jaina writers began composing texts in local vernaculars, and sometimes in Sanskrit. The most widely accepted scriptures are named "Early Texts" (*Purva*), but these are no longer extant. Jaina scholars contend that elements of these texts are incorporated into the present canons. The Digambaras, for example, contend that one of the branches of their canon, the twelfth "Limb" (*Anga*), contains portions of the Early Texts.

The Shvetambara canon is referred to as "Tradition" (*Agama*) or "Doctrine" (*Siddhanta*), and contains 45 texts that are arranged into six divisions: (1) the Limbs; (2) Sub-Limbs (*Upanga*); (3) Miscellaneous Texts (*Prakirnaka*); (4) Treatises on Cutting (*Chedasutra*), which mostly focus on matters of discipline; (5) Appendices (*Culikasutras*); and (6) Basic Texts (*Mulasutras*). This canon contains a variety of texts of different ages and in different languages, and some texts contain material in different dialects.

The primary texts for Digambaras are scholastic works written by authors who lived around the first century C.E., the most important of whom are Vattakera, author of the *Basic Conduct* (*Mulacara*), Kundakunda, author of the *Essence of Doctrine* (*Samayasara*), and Shivarya, who wrote the *Accomplishment* (*Aradhana*). Both Digambaras and Shvetambaras accept the authority of the *Treatise on Attaining the Meaning of the Principles* (*Tattvarthadhigama Sutra*), a text that summarizes the key points of Jaina doctrine in 350 stanzas. In addition, both schools have extensive collections of didactic and expository works called *Supplements* (*Anuyoga*), which cover a wide range of subjects, including rules for right living and dialectical debate, poetry, uplifting stories, and hymns.

The following passages are drawn from texts of the two main sects of Jainism and touch on most of the important themes of Jaina religious practice and the path to liberation. They stress the total responsibility of the individual for his or her own actions and indicate that salvation is won or lost by oneself alone. The Jaina path begins with renunciation of worldly things, conjoined with avoidance of any action that injures another living being. These practices are also linked to yogic meditation, which allows a person to discipline the senses and emotions and to eliminate desire. They also allow one to generate *tapas*, a spiritual energy that can burn up karma and thus cleanse the *jiva*.

JAINA SCRIPTURES

MAHAVIRA, THE ASCETIC PARADIGM

Jaina scriptures contain a number of descriptions of the life and liberation of Mahavira. These emphasize his extreme asceticism, his self-control, his unshakable patience and equanimity, and his final victory. Due to his years of fighting the desires of the flesh, he gradually weaned himself of all physical desires and separated his spiritual essence from the bonds of material existence.

Even in places crowded with ordinary people, Mahavira remained in profound concentration. Even when people spoke to him, he would not answer, but would quietly move away. In all situations he remained undisturbed. . . . He did not pay any attention to harsh words or vicious insults, but remained immersed in religious pursuits. He had no interest in stories, plays, songs, fights, or other entertainments. . . . He did not do any harm to any living beings, nor did he cause others to do so. . . . He did not own any clothes, nor did he accept any from anyone else. . . . He knew exactly how much food and drink was needed [to sustain life], and he had no interest in delicious food. He did not even care what sort of food [he ate]. He did not even wipe his eyes, nor did he scratch his body when it itched. When he walked, he moved in silence, not looking to the side, nor backwards. He only spoke when spoken to, and even then only very little. Always fully aware of the dangers of harming living beings, his gaze was fixed on the path ahead of him. He had forsworn the use of clothing, and in winter would walk with his hands outspread, rather than [warming himself by] folding his arms under his shoulders. . . . He endured many terrible hardships when he stopped. He might be bitten by a snake, a mongoose, or a dog; he was sometimes attacked by ants who made his flesh bleed, and he was often tormented by flies, mosquitoes, bees, and wasps. . . . Mahavira endured all of the many hardships and difficulties caused by humans and other beings. . . . Even in times of bitter cold, he did not even consider [finding shelter], but would stand near a shed and bear the cold with equanimity. When the night grew cold, he would go outside for a while, and in this way he endured the torments of cold with perfect calm and correct conduct. . . . Indifferent to all sensual delights, he cheerfully wandered from place to place, speaking very little. In the winter he would meditate in the shade, and in summer he would expose himself to the blazing heat of the sun. . . . Thoroughly purifying himself, disciplining his mind, body, and speech, Mahavira became completely calm and equanimical. During the time [he practiced meditation], he remained in perfect equipoise and peace.

Source: *Acaranga-sutra* and *Kalpa-sutra* selections.

WOMEN CANNOT ATTAIN LIBERATION

Digambara and Shvetambara texts disagree on the spiritual aptitude of women. The Digambaras contend that women should not be permitted to go without clothing, and that since nudity is a precondition for liberation, women are unable to attain the supreme religious goal. A woman's best hope is to follow the precepts and work toward a future rebirth as a man.

The Shvetambaras reject this idea and assert that women are able to attain liberation. Nudity, while commendable during Mahavira's time, is inappropriate today, and the wearing of simple clothes is no hindrance to liberation. Interestingly, both sects agree on the point that women should not be permitted to renounce clothing, since a woman's body is inherently sexual, and a naked woman would attract unwanted sexual desire.

The following passage is perhaps the earliest example of the Digambara doctrine that women are unable to attain liberation because of their gender. They cannot renounce clothing, they are fickle and emotional, their bodies are breeding grounds for small organisms, and their bodily processes lead to the destruction of these creatures, which is a violation of the dictates of noninjury.

10. [Going] without clothes and [using] the hands as a bowl for receiving alms have been taught by the supreme lords of the Jinas [as] the sole path to liberation (moksha); all other [ways of mendicant behavior] are not [valid] paths.
19. [Worldly behavior,] the outward sign of which is the accepting of possessions—be they small or great—is condemned in the teaching of the Jinas; [only] one without possessions is free from household life.
20. One endowed with the five great vows (*mahavrata*) and the three protections (*gupti*) is restrained [i.e. is a mendicant]. He [alone] is on the path to liberation free from bonds and is worthy of praise.
21. The second outward sign is said to be that of the higher and lower "listeners" [i.e. lay people: the lower, holding] the bowl, wanders for alms silently, with well controlled movement and speech.
22. The [third] outward sign is that of women: a nun eats food only once per day and wears one piece of cloth [while a female novice who wears two pieces of clothing] eats wearing [only] one.
23. In the teaching of the Jina no person who wears clothes attains [liberation], even if he is a Tirthankara. The path to liberation is that of nakedness, and all other [paths] are wrong paths.
24. It is taught [in the scriptures] that in the genital organs of women, in the area between their breasts, and in their navels and armpits are

extremely small (sukshma) living beings, so how can women be ordained [since their bodies make them unable to keep the first vow of non-violence]?

25. If there is purity because of right-view, then she too is said to be associated with the path. [However, even if] she has practiced severe [ascetic] practices it is said in the teaching that there is no ordination for women.

26. Women do not have purity of mind, and by nature their minds are slack, women get their period each month, [and therefore] they have no meditation free from anxiety.

Source: Kundakunda, *Sutraprabrita;* tr. Royce Wiles.

WOMEN CAN ATTAIN LIBERATION

2. There is liberation for women, because women possess all the causes [necessary for liberation]. The cause of liberation is fulfillment of the three jewels (*ratna-traya*), and this is not incompatible [with womanhood].

   [Commentary:] The cause of liberation from the sickness of cyclic existence is the non-deficiency of the [three jewels:] correct view, knowledge, and conduct. There is liberation from cyclic existence for those who perfect them. Furthermore, because women do not lack the causes of nirvana, it is not reasonable [to assert] that any of the three jewels are incompatible with womanhood, and so it is not the case that there is no liberation for women. . . .

4. Nuns are able to understand the Jina's words, have faith in them, and practice them faultlessly.

   [Commentary:] Correct knowledge is the proper understanding of the Jina's words. Correct view is faith in [the Jina's words]. . . . Correct conduct involves applying them appropriately. And this is just what the three jewels are said to be. Release [from cyclic existence] is characterized by complete freedom from all karmas, [which occurs when the three jewels] are perfected. . . . All of these are found in women.

   [A Digambara opponent] might assert that women cannot attain release because they have clothes. People like householders, who are bound by possessions, cannot attain release. If it were not the case [that people who own clothes have possessions], then even male [monks] could wear clothes, and renouncing them would be irrelevant [to the attainment of release]. . . .

   If [as the opponent claims] liberation cannot be attained by those who [wear] clothes, and if one could attain liberation by renouncing them, then certainly it would be acceptable for [women] to renounce [clothing]. Clothes are not necessary for life, and since even life itself may be abandoned [in order to attain liberation], then it goes without saying that [one may renounce] mere clothes! If release were attained simply due to the absence of those [clothes], then what fool seeking release would lose it just through wearing clothes?

The Lord Arhats, the guides for the path to release, taught that women must wear clothes and prohibited them from renouncing clothes, and so it follows that clothes are necessary for release, like a whisk broom [that is used to sweep away small creatures]. . . .

If women were to give up clothing, this would result in their abandoning the whole corpus of monastic rules. As is well known, women are overpowered by [men who] are excited due to seeing their naked bodies and limbs, in the same way that mares—who naturally have clothing—are overpowered by stallions. . . . Furthermore, women from good families are naturally very shy, and if they [were required to] abandon clothing [in order to become nuns], then they would refuse to do so. Clothes are a possession, and so there is some demerit in wearing them, but still by this all of the monastic rules are maintained. Therefore, having ascertained that there is greater benefit and lesser demerit in wearing clothes, rather than renouncing them, the holy Arhats declared that nuns must wear clothes and prohibited them from abandoning them.

Source: *Strinirvana-pariccheda;* tr. Royce Wiles.

BONDAGE AND LIBERATION

This passage states some of the most important themes of Jaina philosophy and religious practice: the importance of overcoming desire for worldly things, the importance of noninjury, and how negative actions result in negative consequences.

One should understand the causes of the soul's bondage [to cyclic existence], and through knowing them, one should overcome them. . . .

A person who owns even a little property—of either living or nonliving things—or who acquiesces to others' owning it, will not be released from suffering. Those who kill living beings, or who cause others to kill them, or who consent to their being killed, will have increasing demerit.

A person who is emotionally attached to relatives or friends is a fool who will suffer greatly, because the numbers of those to whom one is attached always increase. Wealth and relatives cannot protect one [from suffering]. Only by understanding this and [the nature of] life will a person overcome karma.

Source: *Sutrakritanga* 1.1.1.

THE WORTHLESSNESS OF POSSESSIONS, FRIENDS, AND RELATIVES

This passage looks at the things that most people value—possessions, friends, family, etc.—and dismisses them as transitory things that ultimately lead to suffering. In addition, it warns people not to put off religious practice until a future time: the best time to begin is right now, since one's faculties will diminish over time. Thus, a wise person will recognize the tenuousness of the things of the world and renounce them in order to pursue a life of religious practice and asceticism, which alone can lead to salvation.

1.2.2 Oppressed by great suffering and deluded, worldly people [think,] "My mother, father, sister, wife, sons, daughters, daughters-in-law, friends, relatives, and associates, my things, transactions, food, and clothes [are all important]." Infatuated by strong attachments to these things, they are immersed in them.

[Such people] live constantly tormented by greed. In season and out of season, they strive [to amass wealth]; desiring money and fortune, they become thieves who rob and steal. Their minds are always engrossed [in accumulating wealth], and they repeatedly become killers.

In this [world], some lives are short, and their hearing, sight, sense of smell, sense of touch, and tactile sense degenerate [and so they die young and unfulfilled]. Realizing that life is moving [toward its end, they become depressed]. Then eventually they are overcome by senility.

Then, at a certain time, the members of their families begin to grumble at them, and then they begin to grumble [at their families]. They will be unable to protect or give refuge [to their aging relative], and [the old person] will be unable to protect them or give them refuge. An old person is not fit for laughter, nor play, nor sexual intercourse, nor adornment. Thus, one should make effort in asceticism. Having considered the opportunity [that the present life presents for those intent on liberation], the wise will not relax in their efforts, even for a short while. The years are passing by, and youth is fading away.

Source: *Acarangasutra* 1.2.1–12.

THE IMPORTANCE OF EQUANIMITY

In Jaina practice, asceticism serves to discipline body and mind and is also used to burn off one's karma. Since in Jainism karma has a physical manifestation, it is not enough simply to gain knowledge: A person must also perform physical austerities in order to eradicate the physical effects of karma. In practicing monastic discipline, self-control is important, and a monk should gain firm control over his emotions and never lose his temper. No matter what others do to him—whether they speak harshly to him, injure him, or disturb him—he should never become angry at them and should always remain in control, because a moment of anger can destroy hard-won self-discipline and can lead to negative mental states and harmful actions.

If someone abuses a monk, he should not become angry. Losing one's temper is foolish, and so a monk does not become heated [with anger]. When [a monk] hears cruel and harsh words that prick his senses like thorns, he remains perfectly silent and does not take them to heart.

When he is beaten, he does not become angry, nor does he have malicious thoughts. Understanding that patience is the supreme good, a monk should meditate on dharma. If someone hurts a restrained and equanimical monk, he should think, "The soul (*jiva*) is eternal," and bear his torment with a smile. . . .

A monk should seek a bit of food after a householder has finished cooking but, whether or not he receives food, he does not care in either case, [thinking,] "I received no food today, but tomorrow I may get some." For a monk who thinks thus, success and failure are equal.

Realizing that he had encountered suffering, if he is oppressed by pain, he should steady his mind cheerfully and bear all the ills that afflict him. . . . Though the monk is physically oppressed by sweat or dust, or the rays of the summer sun, he does not yearn for comfort. A monk who desires liberation bears [all this, practicing] the unsurpassed, noble dharma, bearing untold filth on his body until the body expires.

Source: *Uttaradhyayanasutra* 2.24–37.

THE WORLD IS FULL OF SUFFERING

This passage is spoken by a prince named Mrigaputra to his parents. He wishes to convince them to allow him to renounce household life and become a monk. He tells them that since according to the Jaina doctrine of transmigration he has been reborn an infinite number of times, he has suffered excruciating torments in many lives. He recounts various painful types of physical suffering and death and concludes that he no longer wishes to be a part of the cycle of birth and death.

From clubs and knives, stakes and maces, breaking my limbs,
An infinite number of times I have suffered without hope.
By sharp-edged razors, by knives and shears,
Many times I have been drawn and quartered, torn apart and skinned.
Helpless in snares and traps, a deer,
I have been caught and bound and fastened, and often I have been killed.
A helpless fish, I have been caught with hooks and nets;
An infinite number of times I have been killed and scraped, split and gutted.
A bird, I have been caught by hawks or trapped in nets,
Or trapped by birdlime, and I have been killed an infinite number of times.
A tree, with axes and saws by the carpenters
An infinite number of times I have been felled, stripped of my bark, cut up, and sawn into planks.
As iron, with hammer and tongs by blacksmiths an infinite number of times I have been struck and beaten, split and filed. . . .
Ever afraid, trembling, in pain and suffering, I have felt the greatest sorrow and agony. . . .
In every kind of existence I have suffered pains that have known no reprieve for a moment.

Source: *Uttaradhyayanasutra* 19.61–67, 71, 74: *Sources of Indian Tradition*, ed. Ainslie Embree (New York: Columbia University Press, 1988), pp. 62–63.

FASTING UNTO DEATH

This passage speaks of the Jaina practice of itvara *or* sallekhana, *in which an advanced practitioner may voluntarily starve to death. This practice is said to eliminate large amounts of negative karma and may even lead to final liberation. According to legend, Mahavira himself did this, since he knew that he would be released at the end of his life and that the fast unto death would be an effective means of eliminating the last subtle vestiges of his karma. Generally a monk will prepare for this practice through a gradu-ated program of fasting that may last for 12 years, but if he is sick he can begin the fast without this previous training. In this passage, it is described as a difficult discipline, but the end reward is seen as a glorious culmination of one's spiritual training.*

If a monk thinks, "Illness is causing my body to wither, and I am not able to perform my religious duties," he should gradually reduce his diet, and through this reduction should pare away his desires. . . . He should enter a village . . . and beg for straw. After receiving it, he should retire into seclusion somewhere outside [the village]. After thoroughly examin-ing and clearing the ground—where there are no eggs [of insects], nor insects, nor seeds, nor sprouts, nor dew, nor water, nor ants, nor mildew, nor marsh, nor cobwebs—he should spread the straw on it. Then he should observe [the religious fast until death] called *itvara*. . . .

The *itvara* is proper. The monk, remaining true [to his vows], devoid of desires, successfully crosses over the ocean of cyclic existence, never doubting his ability to fulfill the fast, happily accomplishing [his goal], unaffected by circumstances, understanding that the body is mortal, over-coming various hardships and troubles, understanding that body and soul are separate, accomplishing the formidable (*bhairava*) task [of *itvara*]. This is not a miserable or untimely death. It may even lead to attainment of final liberation. Such a death is a peaceful haven for all monks who are completely free from craving for life. It is beneficial and leads to happi-ness; it is proper, salutary, and meritorious.

Source: *Acarangasutra* 1.7.105.

THERE IS NO CREATOR GOD

This passage considers various arguments for the existence of a creator of the universe and rejects them. This reflects a fundamental Jaina emphasis on the individual: There is no other power that is able to help the individual escape from cyclic existence—we are on our own, and every person's present position is the result of his or her own past actions. No outside power can change the results of one's karma, nor can anyone other than oneself effect one's salvation. The law of karma is absolute and operates according to its own laws, and no deity can abrogate the workings of karma.

Some foolish men declare that a Creator made the world.
The doctrine that the world was created is ill-advised, and should be rejected.
If God created the world, where was he before creation?

If you say he was transcendent then, and needed no support, where is he now?

No single being had the skill to make this world—

For how can an immaterial god create that which is material?

How could God have made the world without any raw material?

If you say he made this first, and then the world, you are faced with an endless regression.

If you say that this raw material arose naturally you fall into another fallacy,

For the whole universe might thus have been its own creator and have arisen naturally in the same way.

If God created the world by an act of his own will, without any raw material,

Then it is just his will and nothing else—and who will believe this nonsense?

If he is ever perfect and complete, how could the will to create have arisen in him?

If, on the other hand, he is not perfect, he could no more create the universe than a potter could.

If he is formless, actionless, and all-embracing, how could he have created the world?

Such a soul, devoid of all modality, would have no desire to create anything.

If he is perfect, he does not strive for the three aims of humanity,

So what advantage would be gained by creating the universe?

If you say that he created for no purpose, because it was his nature to do so, then God is pointless.

If he created in some kind of sport, it was the sport of a foolish child, leading to trouble. . . .

If out of love for living things and need of them he made the world,

Why did he not make creation wholly blissful, free from misfortune?

If he were transcendent he would not create, for he would be free;

Nor if involved in transmigration, for then he would not be almighty.

So the doctrine that the world was created by God makes no sense at all.

And God commits great sin in killing the children that he himself created.

If you say that he kills only to destroy evil beings, why did he create such beings in the first place? . . .

Good men should combat the believer in divine creation, maddened by an evil doctrine.

Know that the world is uncreated, as time itself is, without beginning and end. . . .

Uncreated and indestructible, it endures through the compulsion of its own nature,

Divided into three sections—hell, earth, and heaven.

Source: *Mahapurana* 4.16–31, 38–40: *Sources of Indian Tradition*, pp. 80–82.

EXCERPTS FROM *THE SUTRA ON UNDERSTANDING THE MEANING OF THE CATEGORIES*

This text is accepted as canonical by both Shvetambaras and Digambaras. It contains a concise overview of the primary categories of the Jaina philosophical system and a summary of the path to liberation.

1.1. Right belief, [right] knowledge, [right] conduct: these [together constitute] the path to liberation.

2. Belief or conviction in things ascertained as they are [is] right belief.

3. This is attained by insight or understanding.

4. The categories (*tattva*) are: (1) soul (*jiva*); (2) non-soul (*ajiva*); (3) inflow [of karmic matter into the soul: *asrava*]; (4) bondage (*bandha*); (5) stopping [inflow of karmic matter: *samvara*]; (6) elimination [of karmic matter: *nirjara*]; and (7) liberation (*moksha*) [of the soul from matter]. . . .

2.7. The soul's [essence] is life, the capacity to be liberated, and the incapacity to be liberated.

8. The distinctive characteristic of the soul is attention. . . .

10. Souls are [of two kinds]: worldly and liberated.

11. [Worldly souls] are [of two kinds]: with mind and without mind.

12. Worldly souls are again [of two kinds]: moving and unmoving. . . .

14. Moving souls have two senses, etc.

15. There are five senses. . . .

23. Worms, ants, bumblebees, and humans each have one more than the one preceding. . . .

5.16. Due to expansion or contraction of its enclosure, [the soul occupies space] in the same way that light from a lamp does. . . .

18. [The function] of space is to give place [to all the other substances].

19. [The function] of matter is [to form the basis of] bodies, speech, mind, and breath.

20. [The function] of matter is also to make possible worldly enjoyment, pain, life, and death.

21. [The function] of souls is to support each other.

22. And [the function] of time is [to explain] continued existence, change, movement, and long or short duration. . . .

6.1. Yoga is activity of body, speech, and mind.

2. It [is concerned with] inflow [of karmic matter].

3. [Inflow is of two kinds]: good, which is [inflow] of meritorious [karmas]; and bad, which is [inflow] of negative [karmas]. . . .

12. Compassion for living beings, compassion for those who have taken vows, charity, self-control with some attachment, etc., yoga, patience, and contentment: these are [the causes of inflow] of pleasant karmic matter. . . .

7.1. The vows involve avoidance of harming (*himsa*), lying, stealing, non-celibacy, and attachment. . . .

3. In order to establish these [in the mind], there are five meditations for each.

4. The five [meditations for the vow against harming] are carefulness of speech, carefulness of mind, care in walking, care in lifting and laying down things, and thoroughly seeing to one's food and drink.

5. And the five [meditations for the vow against lying] are avoiding anger, greed, cowardice and frivolity, and speaking in accordance with scriptural injunctions.

6. The five [meditations for the vow against stealing] are living in a solitary place, living in a deserted place, living in a place where one is not likely to be interfered with by others and where one is not likely to interfere with others, purity of alms, and not disputing with followers of the true doctrine [as to "mine" and "yours"].

7. The five [meditations for the vow against non-celibacy] are renunciation of hearing stories inciting desire for women, renunciation of seeing their beautiful bodies, renunciation of remembrance of past enjoyments, renunciation of aphrodisiacs, and renunciation of beautifying one's own body.

8. The five [meditations for the vow against worldly desire] are giving up love and hatred for the pleasing and displeasing objects of the senses. . . .

12. In order [to develop] detachment toward the tribulations [of the world, one should consider] the nature of the world and the body. . . .

8.1. The causes of bondage are wrong belief, non-renunciation, carelessness, passions, and union [of the soul with the mind, body, and speech].

2. The soul, due to its having passion, assimilates matter which is fit to form karmas. This is bondage. . . .

9.1. Stopping [of karmic inflows] is destruction of inflows.

2. It is [brought about by] discipline, carefulness, observances, meditation, overcoming suffering, and good conduct.

3. Due to asceticism, one eliminates [karmic matter].

4. Discipline is proper control [over mind, speech, and body].

5. Carefulness is [taking proper care] when walking, speaking, eating, lifting and laying down, and in excreting.

6. Observances are: forgiveness, humility, honesty, contentment, truth, restraint, asceticism, renunciation, non-attachment and celibacy, all to the highest degree.

7. The meditations are: impermanence, vulnerability, cyclic existence, aloneness, separateness, inflow, stopping [of inflows], elimination [of inflows], [the nature of] the world, the difficulty of attaining enlightenment, and the nature of the true doctrine. . . .

19. External austerities are: fasting, eating less than one's fill, taking a vow to accept food from a householder, renunciation of delicacies, sleeping in a lonely place, and mortification of the body.

20. The others, that is, internal austerities, are: expiation, discipline, service, study, giving up attachment, and concentration. . . .

10.1. Separation [results from] destruction of delusion and by simultaneous destruction of what obscures wisdom and perception.

2. Liberation is complete freedom from all karma due to the non-existence of the causes of bondage and to the eradication [of karmic matter].

4. After [attainment of] separation, there remain perfect correct wisdom, perfect correct perception, and the state of ultimate accomplishhment (*siddhatva*).

Source: *Tattvarthadhigama-sutra* selections.

GLOSSARY

Ajiva   Lifeless, insentient matter.

Digambara   "Sky-Clad," one of the two sects of contemporary Jainism, whose monks abjure the wearing of clothes.

Jaina   "Follower of the Conqueror (Mahavira)."

Jina   "Victor," an epithet of Mahavira, symbolizing his victory over ignorance.

Jiva   "Soul," the life force that inheres in all beings.

Karma   "Actions," which bring about concordant results.

Kevala-jnana   "Liberating Wisdom," which breaks the bonds of ignorance and leads to release from the cycle of birth, death, and rebirth.

Mahavira   "Great Hero," title of the founder of Jainism.

Moksha   "Release" from the cycle of birth, death, and rebirth.

Samsara   "Cyclic Existence," the beginningless cycle of birth, death, and rebirth in which ignorant beings are trapped.

Shvetambara   "White-Clad," one of the two sects of contemporary Jainism, whose monks and nuns wear simple white robes.

Siddha-loka   Supramundane realm in which liberated souls reside.

Tapas   "Heat," the energy generated by ascetic practices, which burns up accumulated karma.

Tirthankara   "Ford Maker," an epithet of Mahavira and his legendary predecessors, who are said to have found the path to liberation and taught it to others.

FURTHER READINGS

ALSDORF, LUDWIG. "What Are the Contents of the Drstavāda?" *German Scholars on India.* Varanasi: Chowkambha Sanskrit Series, 1973, vol. 1, pp. 1–5.

BHARGAVA, DAYANAND. *Jaina Ethics.* Delhi: Motilal Banarsidass, 1968.

BRONKHORST, JOHANNES. "On the Chronology of the *Tattvārtha Sūtra* and Some Early Commentaries." *Archiv für Indische Philosophie*, 29 (1985), pp. 155–184.

BUHLER, GEORG. "On the Authenticity of the Jaina Tradition." *Wiener Zeitschrift für die Kunde des Morganlandes*, 1 (1887), pp. 165–180.

———. *The Indian Sect of the Jainas.* Calcutta: Gupta [India] Private Ltd., 1963.

BURCH, GEORGE BOSWORTH. "Seven-Valued Logic in Jain Philosophy." *International Philosophical Quarterly*, 3 (1964), pp. 68–93.

CHATTERJEE, A. K. *A Comprehensive History of Jainism.* 2 vols. Calcutta: Firma KLM, 1978–84.

CORT, JOHN. "Models of and for the Study of the Jains." *Method of Theory in the Study of Religion*, 2 (1990), pp. 42–71.

FISHER, EBERHARD, AND JAIN, JYOTINDRA. *Art and Rituals: 2500 Years of Jainism in India.* New Delhi: Sterling, 1877.

FOLKERT, KENDALL W. *Scripture and Community: Collected Essays on the Jains.* Atlanta: Scholars Press, 1993.

GLASENAPP, HELMUTH VON. *The Doctrine of Karman in Jain Philosophy* (tr. Barry Gifford). Bombay: Bai Vijbai, 1942.

JAINI, PADMANABH S. *Gender and Salvation: Jaina Debates on the Spiritual Liberation of Women.* Berkeley: University of California Press, 1991.

——. *The Jaina Path of Purification.* Berkeley: University of California Press, 1979.

MEHTA, MOHAN LAL. *Jaina Philosophy.* Varanasi: P.V. Research Institute, 1971.

SANGAVE, VILAS ADINATH. *Jaina Community: A Social Survey.* Bombay: Popular Prakashan, 1980.

TALIB, G. S., ed. *Jainism.* Patiala: Punjabi University, 1975.

TATIA, NATHMAL. *Studies in Jaina Philosophy.* Banaras: Jain Cultural Research Society, 1951.

ZYDENBOS, ROBERT I. *Mokṣa in Jainism, According to Umāsvāti.* Wiesbaden: Franz Steiner Verlag, 1983.

Buddhism

INTRODUCTION

Nearly 2,500 years ago, according to Buddhist tradition, a young man sat under a tree in northern India, determined to find a way to transcend the sufferings that he recognized as being endemic to the world. Born a prince named Siddhartha Gautama in a small kingdom in what is today southern Nepal, he had renounced his royal heritage in order to escape the cycle of birth, death, and rebirth that inevitably leads to suffering, loss, and pain. As he sat under the tree, he recognized that all of the world's problems begin with a fundamental ignorance (*avidya*) that causes beings to misunderstand the true nature of reality. Because of this, they engage in actions that lead to their own suffering and fail to recognize what leads to happiness.

Siddhartha remained in meditation throughout the night, and during this time the veils of ignorance lifted from his perception. He came to understand how the lives of all beings in the world are constantly influenced by the effects of their own actions (*karma*), and that seeking happiness within the changing phenomena of the mundane world is a fundamental mistake. He saw everything in the world as impermanent (*anitya*) and understood that because of the fact of constant change even things that seem to provide happiness—such as wealth, fame, power, sex, relationships—are in fact sources of suffering (*duhkha*).

In addition, he perceived that everything comes into being in dependence upon causes and conditions—a doctrine referred to in Buddhism as "dependent arising" (*pratitya-samutpada*)—and he understood that because phenomena are in a constant state of flux there is no enduring essence underlying them. Nor is there a supreme being who oversees the process of change and decides the fates of beings. Rather, every being is responsible for its own destiny, and the entire system of universal interdependent causation is driven by its own internal forces. Individual beings are what they are because of the actions they performed in the past.

Moreover, beings lack an enduring self or soul. This doctrine is referred to in Buddhist literature as "selflessness" (*anatman*), which is a denial of the sort of permanent, partless, and immortal entity that is called "*atman*" (literally "I" or "self") in Hinduism and "soul" in Christianity. This doctrine is connected with the idea that all phenomena lack substantial entities, and are characterized by an "emptiness" (*shunyata*) of inherent existence (*svabhava*, literally "own-being").

At dawn of the following morning, full awareness arose in him, and all traces of ignorance disappeared. He had become a *"buddha,"* a term derived from the Sanskrit root word *budh,* meaning to wake up or to regain consciousness. Thus he was now fully awakened from the sleep of ignorance in which most beings spend life after life. At first he thought to remain under the tree and pass away without revealing what he had understood, since he knew that the teachings of an awakened being are subtle and difficult for ordinary beings to comprehend. As he sat there in blissful contemplation, however, the Indian god Brahma came to him, bowed down before him, and begged him to teach others. Brahma pointed out that there would be some intelligent people who would derive benefit from his teachings and that many people would find true happiness by following the path that he had discovered.

Feeling a sense of profound compassion for suffering beings, Buddha agreed to share his wisdom with them, and so embarked on a teaching career that would last for about 40 years. He traveled around India, teaching all who wished to listen, and many people recognized the truth of his words and became his disciples. According to Buddhist tradition, he was an accomplished teacher who was able to perceive the proclivities and mind-sets of his listeners and who could skillfully adapt his teachings for each person and group while still retaining the essential message. He had many lay disciples, but he emphasized the centrality of a monastic lifestyle for those who were intent on liberation. According to his biography, he died in a grove of trees near the town of Vaishali at the age of 80.

Shortly after his death his followers convened a council to codify the teachings of the Buddha. According to tradition, the council met in Rajagriha, a place in which Buddha had delivered many discourses. The participants were five hundred of his closest disciples who had become *arhats* (meaning that they had eradicated mental afflictions and transcended all attachment to mundane things). Such people, it was believed, would not be afflicted by faulty memories or biased by sectarian considerations.

The members of the assembly recounted what they had heard Buddha say on specific occasions, and they prefaced their remarks with the phrase, "Thus have I heard: At one time the Exalted One was residing in. . . ." This formula indicated that the speaker had been a member of the audience, and it provided the context and background of the discourse. Other members would certify the veracity of the account or correct minor details, and at the end of the council all present were satisfied that the Buddha's words had been definitively recorded. The canon of Buddhism was declared closed, and the council issued a pronouncement that henceforth no new teachings would be admitted as the "word of the Buddha" (*buddha-vacana*).

Despite the intentions of the council, however, new teachings and doctrines continued to appear in the following centuries, and the Buddhist community developed numerous divisions. The most significant of these was the split into two schools termed "Hinayana," or "Lesser Vehicle" and "Mahayana," or "Greater Vehicle." These names were obviously coined by the latter group, which considered itself to be superior to its rivals because it propounded a goal of universal salvation, while the Hinayana emphasized the importance of working primarily for one's own emancipation. The Hinayana ideal is the *arhat,* a being who overcomes all ties to the phenomenal world and so attains *nirvana,* which is said to be a state beyond birth and death. It is also described as perfect bliss.

Their Mahayana rivals condemned this as a selfish and limited goal. The Mahayana ideal is the *bodhisattva* (a being—*sattva*—whose goal is awakening—*bodhi*), who seeks to attain the state of buddhahood in order to help others to find the path to final happiness. This form of Buddhism later predominated in Central and East Asia—countries such as Tibet, Mongolia, Korea, Japan, Vietnam, and China—while Hinayana schools took hold in Southeast Asia—in such countries as Sri Lanka, Thailand, Burma, Cambodia, and Laos.

Buddhists in these countries do not accept the designation of their tradition as a "Lesser Vehicle." Rather, they contend that the dominant Theravada tradition (the only one of the numerous schools collectively designated by the term "Hinayana" that survives today) is in fact the true teaching of Buddha. They further believe that the Mahayana *sutras* (discourses believed by Mahayanists to have been spoken by the historical Buddha) are in fact forgeries that proclaim practices and doctrines that the Buddha never taught, but which were actually falsely propounded by others long after his death.

The oldest distinctively Mahayana literature is a group of texts that discuss the "perfection of wisdom" (*prajna-paramita*). The earliest of these is probably the *Perfection of Wisdom in 8,000 Lines, the* oldest version of which may have been composed as early as the first century B.C.E. The Perfection of Wisdom texts do not make their appearance until several centuries after the death of the Buddha, but they claim to have been spoken by him during his lifetime. Mahayana tradition explains the chronological discrepancy by contending that they were indeed taught by the Buddha to advanced disciples, but that he ordered that they be hidden in the underwater realm of *nagas* (beings with snakelike bodies and human heads) until the time was right for their propagation.

The legend further reports that the second-century philosopher Nagarjuna (fl. ca. 150 C.E.) was the person preordained by Buddha to recover and explicate the Perfection of Wisdom texts. After one of his lectures, some *nagas* approached him and told him of the texts hidden in their kingdom, and so Nagarjuna traveled there and returned with the sutras to India. He is credited with founding the Madhyamaka (Middle Way) school of Buddhist philosophy, which emphasized the centrality of the doctrine of emptiness. Nagarjuna and his commentators (the most influential of whom was Candrakirti, ca. 550–600) developed the philosophical ramifications of this doctrine, which is closely connected with the notion of dependent arising. Since all phenomena come into being as a result of causes and conditions, abide due to causes and conditions, and pass away due to causes and conditions, everything in the universe is empty of a substantial entity. Ordinary beings, however, perceive them as existing in the way that they appear—that is, as real, substantial things that inherently possess certain qualities. Nagarjuna declared that a failure to understand emptiness correctly leads to mistaken perceptions of things, and that erroneous philosophical views are the reifications of such notions.

The Madhyamaka philosophers applied this insight not only to mistaken perceptions but also to the doctrines of rival schools, which they contended were founded on self-contradictory assumptions. Through a process of dialectical reasoning, Madhyamaka thinkers exposed both Buddhist and non-Buddhist systems of thought to a rigorous critique, the goal of which was to lead people to recognize the ultimate futility of attempting to encapsulate truth in philosophical propositions.

Approximately two centuries after Nagarjuna, a new Mahayana school arose in India, which is commonly known as the Yogic Practice School (*Yogacara*). The main scriptural source for this school is the *Sutra Explaining the Thought* (*Samdhinirmocana-sutra*), which consists of a series of questions put to the Buddha by a group of bodhisattvas.

The name "Yogic Practice School" may have been derived from an important treatise by Asanga (ca. 310–390) entitled the *Levels of Yogic Practice* (*Yogacara-bhumi*). Along with his brother Vasubandhu (ca. 320–400), Asanga is credited with founding this school and developing its central doctrines. Yogacara emphasizes the importance of meditative practice, and several passages in Yogacara texts indicate that the founders of the school perceived other Mahayana Buddhists as being overly concerned with dialectical debate while neglecting meditation.

The Yogacara school is commonly referred to in Tibet as "Mind Only" (*sems tsam*; Sanskrit: *citta-matra*) because of an idea found in some Yogacara texts that all the phenomena of the world are "cognition-only" (*vijnapti-matra*), implying that everything we perceive is conditioned by consciousness.

In the following centuries, a number of syncretic schools developed. They tended to mingle Madhyamaka and Yogacara doctrines. The greatest examples of this syncretic period are the philosophers Shantarakshita (ca. 680–740) and Kamalashila (ca. 740–790), who are among the last significant Buddhist philosophers in India.

In addition to these developments in philosophy, sometime around the sixth or seventh century a new trend in practice developed in India, which was written down in texts called *tantras*. These texts purported to have been spoken by the historical Buddha (or sometimes by other buddhas), and while they incorporated the traditional Mahayana ideal of the bodhisattva who seeks buddhahood for the benefit of all beings, they also proposed some radically new practices and paradigms. The central practices of *tantra* include visualizations intended to foster cognitive reorientation, the use of prayers (*mantra*) to buddhas that are intended to facilitate the transformation of the meditator into a fully enlightened buddha, and often elaborate rituals.

In the tantric practice of deity yoga (*devata-yoga*), meditators first visualize buddhas in front of themselves (this is referred to as the "generation stage," *utpanna-krama*), and then they invite the buddhas to merge with them, a process that symbolically transforms them into buddhas (this is referred to as the "completion stage," *nishpanna-krama*). The practice of deity yoga is intended to help meditators to become familiar with having the body, speech, and mind of buddhas, and with performing the compassionate activities of buddhas. Because meditators train in the desired effect of buddhahood, the path of tantra is said by its adherents to be much shorter than that of traditional Mahayana, which was said to require a minimum of three "countless eons" (*asamkhyeya-kalpa*) to complete. With the special practices of tantra, it is said to be possible to become a buddha in as little as one human lifetime.

Following this last flowering of Buddhist thought in India, Buddhism began to decline. It became increasingly a tradition of elite scholar-monks who studied in great monastic universities like Nalanda and Vikramashila in northern India. Buddhism failed to adapt to changing social and political circumstances, and apparently lacked a wide base of support. Thus, when a series of invasions by Turkish Muslims descended on India in the 9th through 12th centuries, after the invaders had sacked the great north Indian monastic universities and killed many prominent monks, Buddhism was dealt a death blow from which it never recovered.

The Spread of Buddhism Outside of India

During the third century B.C.E. the spread of Buddhism was furthered by Ashoka (270–232), the third of the Mauryan kings who created the first pan-Indian empire. Ashoka was converted to Buddhism by a Theravada monk and, after a bloody war of conquest against the neighboring state of Kalinga, he recognized that such aggression violated the principles of Buddhism. From this point on he renounced war as an instrument of foreign policy. He began to implement Buddhist principles in the administration of the kingdom and, in order to inform the populace of his political and ruling philosophy, he had edicts inscribed on stone pillars and placed throughout his kingdom. A number of them still survive today. His reign is considered by Buddhists to have been a model of good government, one that was informed by Buddhist principles of righteousness and respect for life.

His advocacy of Buddhism was one of the primary reasons for the spread of the tradition into Southeast Asia. He sent teams of missionaries all over the Indian subcontinent, and to Sri Lanka, Burma, and other neighboring areas. Due to Ashoka's influence and personal power, the missionaries were generally well received in the countries they visited, and they were often successful in convincing people to convert to Buddhism. One of the most successful of the missions he sponsored was led by his son Mahinda, who traveled to Sri Lanka along with four other monks and a novice. According to Buddhist tradition, the mission was so successful that the king of Sri Lanka became a Buddhist, and Mahinda then supervised the translation of the Theravada canon (written in the Pali language) into Sinhala. He also helped to found a monastery that was named the Mahavihara, which became the main bastion of Theravada orthodoxy on Sri Lanka for over 1,000 years.

It is unclear exactly when Buddhism first arrived in East Asia. China was the first country in the region to record contact with Buddhism: A royal edict issued in 65 C.E. reports that a prince in what is now northern Kiangsu Province performed Buddhist sacrifices and entertained Buddhist monks and laypeople. The earliest Buddhists in China were probably from Central Asia, and for centuries Buddhism was widely perceived as a religion of foreigners.

In 148 C.E. a monk named An Shigao, from the Central Asian kingdom of Kusha, began translating Indian Buddhist texts into Chinese in Loyang, which was to become the capital of the later Han dynasty. An Shigao and a number of other monks (mostly from Central Asia) translated about 30 Buddhist texts during the next three decades. The early translators used a translation system termed "matching concepts" (*keyi*), which was to have important ramifications for the development of Chinese Buddhism. Realizing that China had a highly developed culture and that Chinese tended to view people from other countries as uncouth barbarians, the early translators used indigenous terminology—particularly Daoist terminology—to translate Sanskrit technical terms. One result of this practice was that it made many foreign ideas more palatable to Chinese readers, but it also inevitably colored the translations to such an extent that for the first few centuries after Buddhism's arrival in China, many Chinese believed it to be another version of Daoism.

In later centuries, Chinese Buddhism developed its own identity, and from China Buddhism was passed on to Korea and Japan. In 552, according to the *Nihonshoki,* the Korean state of Paekche sent Buddhist texts and images to Japan, hoping to persuade the Japanese emperor to become an ally in its war with the neighboring state of Silla. Some members of the Soga clan wanted to worship the buddha as a powerful foreign god (*kami*), hoping by this to gain influence by associating themselves with what they believed to be a deity of the powerful Chinese empire. The early Japanese interest in Buddhism was mostly connected with purported magical powers of buddhas and Buddhist monks, but after the emperor Yomei (r. 585–587) converted to Buddhism, Japanese began to travel to China in order to study with Buddhist teachers there, and indigenous Buddhist schools developed in Japan.

Yomei's son Prince Shotoku (574–622) enthusiastically propagated Buddhism. He is credited with building numerous Buddhist temples and with sponsoring Japanese monks to travel to China for study. He is also the author of commentaries on three Buddhist texts. In later times he was viewed in Japan as an incarnation of the bodhisattva Avalokiteshvara.

During the reign of the Tibetan king Trisong Detsen (740–798), the Indian scholar Shantarakshita traveled to Tibet, but opposition from some of the king's ministers forced him to leave. Before departing, he urged the king to invite the tantric adept Padmasambhava. Upon his arrival in Tibet, Padmasambhava claimed that Shantarakshita's efforts had been frustrated by the country's demons. Padmasambhava then challenged the demons to personal combat, and none were able to defeat him. This so impressed the king and his court that Shantarakshita was invited back at Padmasambhava's urging, and the first monastery in Tibet was built at Samye. This marked the beginning of the "first dissemination" of Buddhism to Tibet, which ended when the devout Buddhist king Relbachen (815–836) was assassinated.

His death in 836 marked the beginning of an interregnum period for Tibetan Buddhism, which ended in 1042 when Atisha (982–1054), one of the directors of the monastic university of Nalanda, traveled to Tibet. This is considered by Tibetan historians to mark the beginning of the "second dissemination" of Buddhism to Tibet. Atisha was so successful in bringing the dharma to Tibet that Buddhism quickly became the dominant religious tradition in the country.

Today Buddhism continues to flourish in Asia, despite such setbacks as the suppression of religion in China since the inauguration of the People's Republic of China. The current government follows Karl Marx's notion that religion is "the opiate of the masses" and an impediment to social development. In recent years government persecution of Buddhism has eased somewhat, and currently it is enjoying increased support from the Chinese populace. The government is also allowing young people to become ordained as Buddhist monks and nuns.

Buddhism is becoming increasingly popular in Western countries, and a number of prominent Buddhist teachers have established successful centers in Europe and North America. The Dalai Lama, Thich Nhat Hanh, Sogyal Rinpoche, a number of Zen masters (*roshi*), and Theravada meditation teachers have attracted substantial followings outside of Asia, and books and articles about Buddhism are appearing with increasing frequency in Western countries.

Buddhist Scriptures

The early Buddhist canon is traditionally referred to as the "Three Baskets" (*tripitaka*; Pali: *tipitaka*), consisting of (1) *vinaya*: rules of conduct, which are mainly concerned with the regulation of the monastic order; (2) *sutras*: discourses purportedly spoken by the Buddha, and sometimes by his immediate disciples; and (3) *abhidharma*, which includes scholastic treatises that codify and interpret the teachings attributed to the Buddha. According to Buddhist tradition, this division was instituted at the first council. This canon was written in a language called Pali, which is believed to have been derived from a dialect used in the region of Magadha. A second council introduced some modifications to the rules of monastic discipline, and later councils added other texts to the canon.

At first the canon was transmitted orally, but after a time of political and social turmoil King Vattagamani of Sri Lanka ordered that it be committed to writing. This was accomplished between 35 and 32 B.C.E. The *sutras* and *vinaya* were written in Pali, but some of the commentaries were in Sinhala. The Sinhala texts were translated into Pali in the fifth century C.E.

The *Vinaya* section of the Pali canon consists of rules of conduct, most of which are aimed at monks and nuns. Many of these are derived from specific cases in which the Buddha was asked for a ruling on the conduct of particular members of the order, and the general rules he promulgated still serve as the basis for monastic conduct.

The *Sutra* (Pali: *Sutta*) section of the Pali canon is traditionally divided into five "groupings" (*nikaya*): (1) the "long" (*digha*) discourses; (2) the "medium length" (*majjhima*) discourses; (3) the "grouped" (*samyutta*) discourses; (4) the "enumerated" (*anguttara*) discourses, which are arranged according to the enumerations of their topics; and (5) the "minor" (*khuddaka*) discourses, which constitute the largest section of the canon and the one that contains the widest variety of materials. It includes stories of the Buddha's former births (*Jataka*), which report how he gradually perfected the exalted qualities of a buddha; accounts of the lives of the great disciples (*apadana*); didactic verses (*gatha*); an influential work entitled the *Path of Truth* (*Dhammapada*); and a number of other important texts.

The *Abhidharma* (Pali: *abhidhamma*) section includes seven treatises, which organize the doctrines of particular classes of Buddha's discourses. The *Abhidharma* writers attempted to systematize the profusion of teachings attributed to Buddha into a coherent philosophy. Their texts classify experience in terms of impermanent groupings of factors referred to as *dharma* (Pali: *dhamma*), which in aggregations are the focus of the doctrine (*dharma*) taught by Buddha. They are simple real things, indivisible into something more basic. Collections of *dharmas* are the phenomena of experience. Everything in the world—people, animals, plants, inanimate objects—consists of impermanent groupings of *dharmas.* Thus nothing possesses an underlying soul or essence. The collections of *dharmas* are changing in every moment, and so all of reality is viewed as a vast interconnected network of change and interlinking causes and conditions.

Other early schools developed their own distinctive canons, many of which have very different collections of texts, although the doctrines and practices they contain are similar. Some schools, such as the Sarvastivadins, used Sanskrit for their canons, but today only fragments of these collections exist, mostly in Chinese translations. Although Mahayana schools developed an impressive literature, there does not seem to have been an attempt to create a Mahayana canon in India. The surviving Mahayana canons were all compiled in other countries.

Canons compiled in Mahayana countries contain much of the material of the Pali canon, but they also include Mahayana sutras and other texts not found in the Pali canon. The Tibetan canon, for example, contains a wealth of Mahayana sutras translated from Sanskrit, treatises (*shastra*) by important Indian Buddhist thinkers, *tantras* and tantric commentaries, and miscellaneous writings that were deemed important enough to include in the canon. The Chinese canon also contains Mahayana sutras, Indian philosophical treatises, and a variety of other texts, but its compilation was much less systematic than that of the Tibetan canon. The Tibetan translators had access to a much wider range of literature, due to the fact that the canon was collected in Tibet many centuries after the Chinese one. In addition, Buddhist literature came to China in a rather haphazard way. The transmission of Buddhist texts to China occurred over the course of several centuries, and during this time the tradition in India was developing and creating new schools and doctrines.

The Chinese canon was transmitted to Korea and Japan. Tibet and Mongolia both follow the Tibetan canon, which according to tradition was redacted and codified by Pudön (1290–1364). The Theravada countries of Southeast Asia follow the Pali canon and generally consider the texts of Mahayana to be heterodox.

In addition to this canonical literature, each school of Buddhism has created literature that it considers to be authoritative. In the selections below we provide examples of such texts from a wide range of schools and periods of Buddhist literature, but the vast scope of canonical and extracanonical literature prevents us from including many important works. The selections are intended to present a representative sampling of early texts that contain central doctrines or that recount important events in the history of Buddhism, along with statements by Buddhist thinkers of later times that represent influential developments in Buddhist thought and practice.

PALI CANON

THE LIFE OF THE BUDDIIA

According to traditional accounts, the Buddha was born a prince named Siddhartha Gautama in a small kingdom in what is today southern Nepal. His final incarnation was a culmination of a training program that spanned countless lifetimes, during which he gradually perfected the exalted qualities that would mark him as a buddha. Shortly after his birth, his father consulted a number of astrologers, all of whom declared that the newborn prince would become a great king and that he would rule the whole world with truth and righteousness. One astrologer, however, declared that if the prince were to see a sick person, an old person, a corpse, and a world-renouncing ascetic, he would become dissatisfied with his life and become a wandering mendicant in order to seek final peace. These four things became known in Buddhism as the "four sights." The first three epitomize the problems inherent in the world, while the fourth points to the way out of the endless cycle of birth, death, and rebirth, which is characterized by suffering and loss.

According to the Extensive Sport Sutra (Lalitavistara-sutra), *Siddhartha's father, king Shuddhodana, decided to prevent his son from encountering any of the four sights and surrounded him with pleasant diversions during his early years. The prince, however, eventually convinced his father to let him visit a part of the city that lay outside the palace gates.*

Before allowing the prince to ride out in his chariot, Shuddhodana first ordered that the streets be cleared of all sick and old people, and that the prince not be allowed to see any corpses or world renouncers. Despite the king's efforts, however, at one point the path of the royal chariot was blocked by a sick man. Siddhartha had never before encountered serious illness, and he turned to Candaka, his charioteer, and asked,

> O charioteer, who is this man, weak and powerless?
> His flesh, blood, and skin withered, his veins protruding,
> With whitened hair, few teeth, his body emaciated,
> Walking painfully and leaning on a staff?

Candaka informed the prince that the man had grown old and that such afflictions were the inevitable result of age. He added,

> O prince, this man is oppressed by age
> His organs are weak; he is in pain, and his strength and vigor are gone.
> Abandoned by his friends, he is helpless and unable to work,
> Like wood abandoned in a forest. . . .
> Lord, this is not unique to his race or his country.
> Age exhausts youth and the entire world.
> Even you will be separated from the company
> Of your mother and father, friends and relatives.
> There is no other fate for living beings.

Siddhartha was amazed to find that most people see such sights every day but persist in shortsighted pursuits and mundane affairs, apparently unconcerned that they will inevitably become sick, grow old, and die.

In three subsequent journeys outside the palace, Siddhartha saw an old man and a corpse, and when he learned that eventually his young, healthy body would become weak and decrepit he fell into a profound depression. On a fourth trip, Siddhartha saw a world renouncer, a man who stood apart from the crowd, who owned nothing and was unaffected by the petty concerns of the masses, and who radiated calm, serenity, and a profound inner peace. This sight lifted Siddhartha's spirits, since it revealed to him that there is a way to transcend the vicissitudes of mundane existence and find true happiness. Intrigued by the ascetic, Siddhartha asked Candaka what sort of man he was, and the charioteer replied,

> Lord, this man is one of the order of bhikshus [mendicants].
> Having abandoned sensual desires,
> He has disciplined conduct.
> He has become a wandering mendicant.
> Who views himself and the external world with the same regard.
> Devoid of attachment or emnity, he lives by begging.

Realizing the folly of remaining in the palace, Siddhartha resolved to renounce the world and find inner peace.

> Candaka, for countless ages I have enjoyed sensual objects
> Of sight, sound, color, flavor, and touch, in all their varieties;
> But they have not made me happy. . . .
> Realizing this, I will embark on the raft of dharma, which is steadfast,
> Endowed with the range of austerities, good conduct,
> Equanimity, effort, strength, and generosity,
> Which is sturdy, made of the firmness of effort, and strongly held together.

Siddhartha then declared his desire to become awakened in order to show other suffering beings a way to end suffering:

> I desire and wish that,
> After attaining the level of awakening,
> Which is beyond decay and death,
> I will save the world.
> The time for that has arrived.

Siddhartha left the palace and subsequently practiced meditation with several teachers, but none could show him a path leading to the cessation of suffering. At one point he fell in with five spiritual seekers who told him that the way to salvation lies in severe asceticism. He followed their practices, and eventually was eating only a single grain of rice per day. After swooning due to weakness, however, Siddhartha realized that extreme asceticism is just as much a trap as the hedonistic indulgence of his early years.

Thus he left his ascetic companions behind and resolved to find a path leading to the cessation of suffering. He recognized that he would have to discover the truth for himself. Before embarking on his final quest for truth Siddhartha made a solemn vow,

> As I sit here, my body may wither away,
> My skin, bones, and flesh may decay,
> But until I have attained awakening—
> Which is difficult to gain even during many ages—
> I will not move from this place.

Siddhartha stood in a spot that is now known as "the Circle of Awakening," located in modern-day Bodhgaya. Sitting under a tree, during the night Siddhartha entered into progressively deeper meditative states, in which the patterns of the world fell into place for him, and thus he came to understand the causes and effects of actions, why beings suffer, and how to transcend all the pains and sorrows of the world.

By the dawn of the next morning he had completely awakened from the misconceptions of ordinary people, and at this point Buddhist texts refer to him as "buddha," indicating that he was now fully awake and aware of the true nature of all things. Scanning the world with his heightened perception, the Buddha recognized that his realization was too profound to be understood by the vast majority of beings in the world, and so initially he decided to remain under the tree in profound equanimity, and to pass away without teaching what he had learned.

> Profound, peaceful, perfectly pure,
> Luminous, uncompounded, ambrosial
> Is the dharma I have attained.
> Even if I were to teach it,
> Others could not understand
> Thus, I should remain silent in the forest.

After the Buddha had made this statement, however, the Indian god Brahma appeared before him and begged him to teach what he had learned for the benefit of those few beings who could understand and profit from his wisdom. Moved by compassion for the sufferings of beings caught up in the round of cyclic existence, the Buddha agreed, and for the next 40 years he traveled around India, teaching all who cared to listen.

Source: *Lalita-vistara* selections.

THE FIRST SERMON

Shortly after making the decision to teach, Buddha surveyed the world in order to choose a place to begin his teaching career. He decided to travel to Sarnath, where his five former companions were still practicing pointless austerities, hoping in this way to find happiness.

The following excerpt purports to be Buddha's first public teaching. It is referred to as the "Sutra Turning the Wheel of Doctrine" because it set in motion the Buddha's teaching career. In this passage, he lays out some of the themes that would be central to his later teachings, such as the importance of following a "middle way" that avoids the extremes of sensual indulgence and extreme asceticism, and the "four noble truths": (1) that all mundane existence involves suffering; (2) that suffering is caused by desire; (3) that there can be a cessation of suffering; and (4) the eightfold noble path that leads to this cessation.

Thus have I heard: At one time, the Exalted One was living near Varanasi, at Isipatana near the Deer Park. Then the Exalted One spoke to the group of five monks: These two extremes, O monks, should not be practiced by one who has gone forth [from the household life]. What are the two? That which is linked with sensual desires, which is low, vulgar, common, unworthy, and useless, and that which is linked with self-torture, which is painful, unworthy, and useless. By avoiding these two extremes the Tathagata [Buddha] has gained the knowledge of the middle path which gives vision and knowledge, and leads to calm, to clair-voyances, to enlightenment, to nirvana.

O monks, what is the middle path, which gives vision. . . ? It is the noble eightfold path: right views, right intention, right speech, right action, right livelihood, right effort, right mindfulness, right concentration. This, O monks, is the middle path, which gives vision. . . .

1. Now this, O monks, is the noble truth of suffering: birth is suffering, old age is suffering, death is suffering, sorrow, grieving, dejection, and despair are suffering. Contact with unpleasant things is suffering, not getting what you want is also suffering. In short, the five aggregates of grasping are suffering.
2. Now this, O monks, is the noble truth of the arising of suffering: that craving which leads to rebirth, combined with longing and lust for this and that—craving for sensual pleasure, craving for rebirth, craving for cessation of birth. . . .
3. Now this, O monks, is the noble truth of the cessation of suffering: It is the complete cessation without remainder of that craving, the abandonment, release from, and non-attachment to it.
4. Now this, O monks, is the noble truth of the path that leads to the cessation of suffering: This is the noble eightfold path. . . .

Now monks, as long as my threefold knowledge and insight regarding these noble truths . . . were not well purified, so long, O monks, I was not sure that in this world . . . I had attained the highest complete awakening.

But when my threefold knowledge and insight in these noble truths with their twelve divisions were well purified, then, O monks, I was sure that in this world . . . I had attained the highest complete awakening. Now knowledge and insight have arisen in me, so that I know: My mind's liberation is assured; this is my last existence; for me there is no rebirth.

Source: *Samyutta-nikaya* 5.420–423.

THE BUDDHA'S GOOD QUALITIES

From a Buddhist perspective, the Buddha is not only important as a person who taught a corpus of texts. The events of his life serve as an inspiration to devout Buddhists, who see him as the supreme example of how meditative realization should be put into practice in daily life. The following passage describes how he lived and related to people and things around him.

Renouncing the killing of living beings, the ascetic Gotama abstains from killing. He has put down the club and the sword, and he lives modestly, full of mercy, desiring in his compassion the welfare of all living beings.

Having renounced the taking of what is not given, the ascetic Gotama abstains from grasping after what does not belong to him. He accepts what is given to him and waits for it to be given; and he lives in honesty and purity of heart. . . .

Having renounced unchastity, the ascetic Gotama is celibate and aloof and has lost all desire for sexual intercourse, which is vulgar.

Having renounced false speech, the ascetic Gotama abstains from lying, he speaks the truth, holds to the truth, is trustworthy, and does not break his word in the world. . . .

Having renounced slander, the ascetic Gotama abstains from libel. When he hears something in one place he will not repeat it in another in order to cause strife . . . but he unites those who are divided by strife and encourages those who are friends. His pleasure is in peace, he loves peace and delights in it, and when he speaks he speaks words that make for peace. . . .

Having renounced harsh speech, the ascetic Gotama avoids abusive speech. He speaks only words that are blameless, pleasing to the ear, touching the heart, cultured, pleasing to people, loved by people. . . .

Having renounced frivolous talk, the ascetic Gotama avoids gossip. He speaks at the right time, in accordance with the facts, with meaningful words, speaking of the truth (*dhamma*), of the discipline (*vinaya*). His speech is memorable, timely, well illustrated, measured, and to the point.

The ascetic Gotama has renounced doing harm to seeds or plants. He takes only one meal per day, not eating at night, nor at the wrong time. He abstains from watching shows or attending fairs with song, dance, and music. He has renounced the wearing of ornaments and does not adorn himself with garlands, scents, or cosmetics. He abstains from using a large or high bed. He abstains from accepting silver or gold, raw grain or raw meat. He abstains from accepting women or girls, male or female slaves, sheep or goats, birds or pigs, elephants or cows, horses or mares, fields or property. He abstains from acting as a go-between or messenger, from buying and selling, from falsifying with scales, weights, or measures. He abstains from crookedness and bribery, from cheating and fraud. He abstains from injury, murder, binding with bonds, stealing, and acts of violence.

Source: *Digha-nikaya* 1.4–10.

CRITERIA FOR ASSESSING
VALID TEACHINGS AND TEACHERS

Although there are many passages in Buddhist literature in which faith is extolled as an important virtue, this faith should ideally be based on evidence and valid reasoning. In addition, there are several places in Buddhist literature in which Buddha exhorts his listeners to examine teachers and teachings closely before putting trust in them. In the following passage, Buddha addresses a group of people collectively referred to as Kalamas, who are confused by the conflicting claims of the religious systems of their day. Buddha advises them to verify all claims themselves by examining which doctrines lead to positive results, and which lead to negative ones. The former should be adopted, and the latter rejected.

Do not be [convinced] by reports, tradition, or hearsay; nor by skill in the scriptural collections, argumentation, or reasoning; nor after examining conditions or considering theories; nor because [a theory] fits appearances, nor because of respect for an ascetic [who holds a particular view]. Rather, Kalamas, when you know for yourselves: These doctrines are non-virtuous; these doctrines are erroneous; these doctrines are rejected by the wise, these doctrines, when performed and undertaken, lead to loss and suffering—then you should reject them, Kalamas.

Source: *Anguttara-nikaya* 1.189.

NIRVANA

Nirvana is said to be the final cessation of suffering, a state beyond the cycle of birth and death. As such, it could be said to be the ultimate goal of the path taught by the Buddha, whose quest was motivated by a concern with the unsatisfactoriness of cyclic existence and a wish to find a way out of the round of suffering that characterizes the mundane world. Despite its importance, however, there are few descriptions of nirvana in Buddhist literature. The selection below is one of the most detailed analyses of what nirvana is and how one attains it.

Monks, there exists something in which there is neither earth nor water, fire nor air. It is not the sphere of infinite space, nor the sphere of infinite consciousness, nor the sphere of nothingness, nor the sphere of neither perception nor non-perception. It is neither this world nor another world, nor both, neither sun nor moon.

Monks, I do not state that it comes nor that it goes. It neither abides nor passes away. It is not caused, established, arisen, supported. It is the end of suffering. . . .

What I call the selfless is difficult to perceive, for it is not easy to perceive the truth. But one who knows it cuts through craving, and for one who knows it, there is nothing to hold onto. . . .

Monks, there exists something that is unborn, unmade, uncreated, unconditioned. Monks, if there were not an unborn, unmade, uncreated, unconditioned, then there would be no way to indicate how to escape from the born, made, created, and conditioned. However, monks, since there exists something that is unborn, unmade, uncreated, and unconditioned, it is known that there is an escape from that which is born, made, created, and conditioned. . . .

There is wandering for those who are attached, but there is no wandering for those who are unattached. There is serenity when there is no wandering, and when there is serenity, there is no desire. When there is no desire, there is neither coming nor going, and when there is no coming nor going there is neither death nor rebirth. When there is neither death nor rebirth, there is neither this life nor the next life, nor anything in between. It is the end of suffering.

Source: *Udana*, ch. 8.80.

DEPENDENT ARISING

After attaining awakening, the Buddha indicated that he had come to realize that all the phenomena of the universe are interconnected by relationships of mutual causality. Things come into being in dependence upon causes and conditions, abide due to causes and conditions, and eventually pass away due to causes and conditions. Thus, the world is viewed by Buddhists as a dynamic and ever-changing system. The following passage describes the process of causation in relation to human existence, which is said to proceed in a cyclical fashion. Because of a basic misunderstanding of the workings of reality (referred to as "ignorance"), people falsely imagine that some worldly things can bring them happiness, and thus they generate desire and try to acquire these things. Such attitudes provide the basis for the arising of negative mental states, and these states in turn provide a basis for beings to return to the world in a future birth. This next life will begin with the conditioning of the last, and so the entire cycle will repeat itself unless a person recognizes the folly of conventional wisdom and chooses to follow the Buddhist path, which is designed to provide a way out of the trap of cyclic existence.

[Ananda, quoting Buddha, said:] 'Kaccana, on two things the world generally bases its view: existence and non-existence. Kaccana, one who perceives with correct insight the arising of the world as it really is does not think of the non-existence of the world. Kaccana, one who perceives with correct insight the cessation of the world as it really is does not think of the existence of the world. Kaccana, the world in general seizes on systems and is imprisoned by dogmas. One who does not seek after, seize on, or fixate on this seizing on systems, this dogma, this mental bias does not say, "This is my self." One who thinks, "Whatever arises is only suffering; whatever ceases is suffering" has no doubts or qualms. In this sense, knowledge not borrowed from others comes to one. This, Kaccana, is right view.

'Kaccana, "Everything exists" is one extreme; Kaccana, "Nothing exists" is the other extreme. Not approaching either extreme, Kaccana, the Tathagata teaches you a doctrine in terms of a middle path: ignorance depends on action; action depends on consciousness; consciousness depends on name and form; name and form depend on the six sense spheres; the six sense spheres depend on contact; contact depends on feeling; feeling depends on attachment; attachment depends on grasping; grasping depends on existence; existence depends on birth; birth depends on aging and death. Suffering, despair, misery, grief, and sorrow depend on aging and death. In this way, the whole mass of suffering arises. But due to the complete eradication and cessation of ignorance comes a cessation of karmas and so forth. This is the cessation of this whole mass of suffering.

Source: *Samyutta-nikaya* 3.90.

QUESTIONS THAT SHOULD BE AVOIDED

The following passage contains a series of questions about metaphysical topics posed to the Buddha by a wandering ascetic named Vacchagotta. The Buddha's response is interesting: He does not even try to provide answers, nor does he indicate that he does not answer because of ignorance on his part. Rather, he tells Vacchagotta that there is no point in answering the questions, since they are irrelevant to the goal of salvation. He indicates that people who spend their time pondering such questions and arguing about philosophical conundrums are unlikely to find release from suffering, and so the wisest course of action is to avoid such questions as a waste of time.

Thus have I heard: At one time the Exalted One was staying near Savatthi in the Jeta Grove in Anathapindika's hermitage. . . . Then the wanderer Vacchagotta approached the Exalted One . . . and said, 'Gotama, does the reverend Gotama have this view: "The world is eternal; this is the truth, and all else is falsehood"?'

'Vaccha, I do not have this view. . . .'

'Then, Gotama, does the reverend Gotama have this view: "The world is not eternal; this is the truth, and all else is falsehood"?'

'Vaccha, I do not have this view. . . .'

'Now, Gotama, does the reverend Gotama have this view: "The world is finite; this is the truth, and all else is falsehood"?'

'Vaccha, I do not have this view. . . .'

'Then, Gotama, does the reverend Gotama have this view: "The world is not finite; this is the truth, and all else is falsehood"?'

'Vaccha, I do not have this view. . . .'

'Now, Gotama, does the reverend Gotama have this view: "The soul (*jiva*) and the body are the same; this is the truth, and all else is falsehood"?'

'Vaccha, I do not have this view. . . .'

'Then, Gotama, does the reverend Gotama have this view: "The soul is one thing and the body is another; this is the truth, and all else is falsehood"?'

'Vaccha, I do not have this view. . . .'

'Now, Gotama, does the reverend Gotama have this view: "After death, the Tathagata exists; this is the truth, and all else is falsehood"?'

'Vaccha, I do not have this view. . . .'

'Then, Gotama, does the reverend Gotama have this view: "After death, the Tathagata does not exist; this is the truth, and all else is falsehood"?'

'Vaccha, I do not have this view. . . .'

'Now, Gotama, does the reverend Gotama have this view: "After death, the Tathagata both exists and does not exist; this is the truth, and all else is falsehood"?'

'Vaccha, I do not have this view. . . .'

'Then, Gotama, does the reverend Gotama have this view: "After death, the Tathagata neither exists nor does not exist; this is the truth, and all else is falsehood"?'

'Vaccha, I do not have this view. . . .'

'Gotama, what is the danger that the reverend Gotama sees that he does not hold any of these views?'

'Vaccha, thinking that "the world is eternal" is going to a [wrong] view, holding a view, the wilderness of views, the writhing of views, the scuffling of views, the bonds of views; it is accompanied by anguish, distress, misery, fever; it does not lead to turning away from [the world], to dispassion, cessation, calm, clairvoyances, awakening, nor to nirvana. . . . Vaccha, contending that this is dangerous, I do not approach any of these views.'

'But does Gotama have any views?'

'Vaccha, holding to any view has been eliminated by the Tathagata . . . so I say that through destruction, dispassion, cessation, abandoning, getting rid of all imaginings, all supposings, all latent pride that "I am the doer, mine is the deed," a Tathagata is released without desire.'

'But Gotama, where is a monk whose mind is thus released reborn?'

'Vaccha, the term "reborn" does not apply.'

'Then, Gotama, is he not reborn?'

'Vaccha, the term "not reborn" does not apply.'

'Then, Gotama, is he both reborn and not reborn?'

'Vaccha, "both reborn and not reborn" does not apply.'

'Then, Gotama, is he neither reborn nor not reborn?'

'Vaccha, "neither reborn nor not reborn" does not apply.' . . .

'I am confused at this point, Gotama; I am bewildered, and I have lost all the satisfaction from the earlier conversation I had with Gotama.'

'You should be confused, Vaccha, you should be bewildered. Vaccha, this doctrine *(dhamma)* is profound, difficult to see, difficult to understand, peaceful, wonderful, beyond argumentation, subtle, understood by the wise; but it is difficult for you, who hold another view, another allegiance, another goal, having different practices and a different teacher. Well, then, Vaccha, I will now question you in return. . . . If a fire were burning in front of you, would you know, "This fire is burning in front of me'?"

'Gotama . . . I would know.' . . .

'Vaccha, if the fire in front of you were put out, would you know, "This fire that was in front of me has been put out"?'

'Gotama . . . I would know.'

'But, Vaccha, if someone were to ask you—"Regarding that fire that was in front of you and that has been put out, in which direction has the fire gone from here: to the east, west, north, or south"—what would you reply to this question, Vaccha?'

'Gotama, it does not apply. Gotama, the fire burned because of a supply of grass and sticks, but due to having totally consumed this and due to a lack of other fuel, it is said to be put out since it is without fuel.'

'Vaccha, in the same way, the form by which one recognizing the Tathagata would recognize him has been eliminated by the Tathagata, uprooted, made like a stump of a palm tree that has become non-existent and will not arise again in the future. Vaccha, the Tathagata is released from designation by form, he is profound, immeasurable, unfathomable like the great ocean. "Reborn" does not apply; "not reborn" does not apply. The feelings . . . discriminations . . . compositional factors . . . consciousness by which one recognizing the Tathagata might recognize him have been eliminated by the Tathagata, uprooted . . . and will not arise again in the future. Vaccha, the Tathagata is released from all designation by consciousness; he is profound, immeasurable, unfathomable as the great ocean. "Reborn" does not apply; "not reborn" does not apply; "both reborn and not reborn" does not apply; "neither reborn nor not reborn" does not apply.'

Source: *Majjhima-nikaya* 3.72.

SELFLESSNESS

Buddhism denies that there is anything corresponding to the common idea of a soul or self. Instead, the Buddha taught that the soul is a false notion imputed to a collection of constantly changing parts. These are referred to as the five "aggregates" (skandha): form, feelings, discriminations, consciousness, and compositional factors. Form refers

to one's physical form, and feelings are our emotional responses to the things we experience. Discriminations are classifications of these experiences into pleasant, unpleasant,
and neutral. Consciousness refers to the functioning of the mind, and compositional
factors are other aspects connected with the false sense of self, such as one's karmas.

[Buddha:] 'Monks, form is selflessness. Monks, if form were the self,
then form would not be involved with sickness, and one could say of the
body: "Let my form be thus; let my form not be thus." Monks, because
form is selfless, it is involved with sickness, and one cannot say of form:
"Let my form be thus; let my form not be thus."

'Feeling is selfless . . . discrimination is selfless . . . the aggregates
are selfless . . . compositional factors are selfless . . . consciousness is
selfless. Monks, if consciousness were the self, then consciousness would
not be involved with sickness, and one could say of consciousness: "Let
my consciousness be thus; let my consciousness not be thus. . . ."

'What do you think monks: Is form permanent or impermanent?'
'Impermanent, sir.'
'And is the impermanent suffering or happiness?'
'Suffering, sir.'
'And with respect to what is impermanent, suffering, naturally unsta-
ble, is it proper to perceive it in this way: "This is mine; I am this; this is
my self?"'
'Definitely not, sir.'
'It is the same way with feelings, discriminations, compositional fac-
tors, and consciousness. Therefore, monks, every single form—past,
future, or present; internal or external; gross or subtle; low or high; near or
far—should be viewed in this way, as it really is, with correct insight:
"This is not mine; this is not I; this is not my self."'
'Every single feeling, every single discrimination, every single compositional factor . . . every single consciousness [should be viewed in this way].
'Perceiving [these] in this way, monks, the well-taught, wise disciple
feels disgust for form, feels disgust for feeling, feels disgust for discrimination, feels disgust for compositional factors, and feels disgust for consciousness. Feeling disgust in this way, one becomes averse; becoming averse,
one is liberated. Awareness that the liberated person is liberated arises, so
that one knows: "Birth is destroyed; the virtuous life has been lived; my
work is done; for such a life there is nothing beyond [this world]."'

Source: *Samyutta-nikaya* 3.59.

INSTRUCTIONS ON MEDITATION

*Following the example of the Buddha, Buddhism emphasizes the importance of medita-
tion as a means for attaining clarity of perception, eliminating mental afflictions, and
escaping from cyclic existence. The following passage, attributed to Ashvaghosha*

(ca. second century C.E.*), is believed to contain instructions given by Buddha to his half-brother Nanda.*

Now after having closed the windows of the senses with the shutters of mindfulness, you should know the proper measure of food in order to meditate properly and maintain good health. For too much food impedes the intake of breath, makes one lethargic and sleepy, and saps one's strength. Furthermore, just as too much food leads to distraction, eating too little makes one weak. . . . Thus as a practitioner of yoga you should feed your body simply in order to overcome hunger, and not out of desire for food or love of it.

After spending the day in self-controlled mental concentration, you should shake off sleepiness and spend the night engaged in the discipline of yoga. And do not think that your awareness is properly aware when drowsiness manifests itself in your heart. When you are overcome by sleepiness, you should apply your attention to exertion and steadfastness, strength and courage. You should clearly recite the texts you have been taught, and you should teach them to others and ponder them yourself. In order to remain awake, splash water on your face, look around in all directions, and look at the stars. . . .

During the first three watches of the night, you should practice [meditation], but after that you should lie down and rest on your right side, remaining awake in your heart, your mind at peace, keeping your attention on the idea of light. In the third watch, you should get up and, either walking or sitting, continue to practice yoga, with a pure mind and controlled senses. . . .

Sit cross-legged in a solitary place, keep your back straight, and direct your mindfulness in front of you, [focusing] on the tip of the nose, the forehead, or the space between the eyebrows. Keep the wandering mind focused completely on one thing. If a mental affliction—a desirous thought—arises, you should not hold to it, but should brush it off like dust on your clothes. Even if you have eliminated desires from your mind, there is still an innate tendency toward them, like a fire smoldering in ashes. My friend, this should be extinguished by meditation, in the way that fire is extinguished by water. Unless you do this, desire will arise again from the innate tendency, as plants arise from a seed. Only by destroying [the tendencies] will they finally be eradicated, like plants whose roots have been destroyed. . . .

When one washes dirt from gold, one first gets rid of the largest pieces of dirt, and then the smaller ones, and having cleaned it one is left with pieces of pure gold. In the same way, in order to attain liberation, one should discipline the mind, first washing away the coarser faults, and then the smaller ones, until one is left with pure pieces of dharma.

Source: *Saundarananda* chs. 14, 15.

ORDINATION OF WOMEN

When Buddha began his teaching career, his first disciples were monks, but eventually some women became followers and began to desire ordination as nuns. The woman who put the request to Buddha was Mahapajapati Gotami, who had raised him after his mother died. Buddha first refused her request, but after she obtained the support of Ananda, Buddha's personal assistant, he eventually agreed, but added that the decision to admit nuns into the order would shorten the period of "true dharma" by 500 years. It seems clear from the passage, however, that this is not due to any inherent inferiority on the part of women, since Buddha asserts that women are capable of following the spiritual path and attaining the fruits of meditative training. Some commentators speculate that the reason for his refusal may have been that his early followers were homeless wanderers, and so there were no adequate facilities for separating men and women. Because of the pervasiveness and strength of sexual desire, groups of men and women in close proximity inevitably develop attractions and tensions, which lead to conflict. Whatever the reasons for his initial reluctance, Buddha did eventually ordain women, but he added the condition that nuns must observe eight additional rules.

Then Mahapajapati Gotami approached the Lord and, having paid obeisance to him, stood to one side. And Mahapajapati Gotami said this to the Lord:

"Lord, it would be good if women could be initiated into the order, in the doctrine and discipline taught by the Tathagata."

[Buddha replied:] "Gotami, do not request the initiation of women into the order. . . ."

She made her request two more times, but after being refused she despondently concluded that Buddha would not allow the ordination of women.

Then Mahapajapati Gotami, having cut off her hair, putting on saffron robes, went to Vesali . . . and when she arrived, her feet were swollen, her body covered with dust, tears covered her face, as she stood outside the grove [where Buddha was staying].

When the venerable Ananda saw Mahapajapati Gotami standing there . . . he asked, "Gotami, why are you standing there, your feet swollen, your body covered with dust, and crying?"

"Venerable Ananda, it is because the Lord does not allow women to be initiated into the order, in the doctrine and discipline taught by the Tathagata."

On hearing this, Ananda offered to intercede on her behalf and approached the Buddha, asking why he had refused her.

Then the venerable Ananda approached the Lord and, having paid obeisance to him, stood to one side. . . . And he said this to the Lord:

"Lord, Mahapajapati Gotami is standing outside the grove, her feet swollen, her body covered with dust, tears on her face, and crying, and she says that the Lord will not allow women to be initiated into the order, in the doctrine and discipline taught by the Tathagata. Lord, it would be good if women were to be initiated into the order. . . ."

"Ananda, do not request the initiation of women into the order, in the doctrine and discipline taught by the Tathagata."

Then the venerable Ananda thought, "The Lord does not allow the initiation of women into the order . . . but perhaps I can ask in another way. . . ." Then the venerable Ananda said to the Lord: "Lord, are women who have been initiated into the order, in the doctrine and discipline taught by the Tathagata, able to attain the fruit of a stream-enterer, or the fruit of a once-returner, or the fruit of a non-returner, or arhathood?"

"Ananda, women who have been initiated into the order . . . are able to attain the fruit of a stream-enterer, or the fruit of a once-returner, or the fruit of a non-returner, or arhathood."

"So, Lord, women who have been initiated into the order are able to attain [these fruits], and Mahapajapati Gotami was very helpful to the Lord: she was the Lord's aunt, foster mother, and nurse, she suckled him when his mother died [and he should repay her kindness]."

[Hearing this, Buddha said:] "Ananda, if Mahapajapati Gotami accepts eight cardinal rules she may receive initiation into the order. . . ." Then Ananda . . . went to Mahapajapati Gotami and said, "Gotami, if you will accept eight cardinal rules, you may receive initiation into the order. . . ." [She replied:] "Honored Ananda, I accept these eight cardinal rules and will never transgress them during my entire life."

Ananda then informed Buddha that Mahapajapati had accepted these rules, to which he replied:

"Ananda, if women had not been given the opportunity to receive initiation into the order, in the doctrine and discipline taught by the Tathagata, then, Ananda, the monastic system would have lasted longer, and the true doctrine would have endured for one thousand years. But, Ananda, since women may now receive ordination . . . the monastic system will only endure for five hundred years."

Source: *Vinaya-pitaka, Cullavagga*, ch. 10, from the *Rules of Discipline for Nuns* (*Bhiksuni Vinaya*): tr. John Strong, *The Experience of Buddhism* (Belmont, CA: Wadsworth, 1995), pp. 52–56.

THE CESSATION OF SUFFERING

After the Buddha agreed to create an order of nuns, a number of women took monastic vows, and some were eventually recognized as advanced meditators. The verses below were written by the nun Patacara after she became an arhati (a female arhat). Her early biography is recounted in the Songs of the Nuns (Therigatha), *and it graphically illustrates the problems of cyclic existence. Her entire family is killed one by one under tragic circumstances, and she is driven to the brink of madness. In a state of utter despair, she meets the Buddha, who counsels her and allows her to become a nun.*

After years of meditative practice, she severs all attachments to worldly things, recognizing them as a source of suffering.

> Ploughing their fields, sowing seeds in the ground,
> Men care for their wives and children and prosper.
> Why is it that I, endowed with morality and adhering to the teachings,
> Do not attain nirvana? I am neither lazy nor conceited.
> After washing my feet, I observed the water; watching the water flow downwards,
> I focused my mind as one [trains] a noble thoroughbred horse.
> Then I took a lamp and entered my cell. After observing the bed, I sat on the couch.
> Holding a pin, I pulled out the wick.
> The lamp goes out: nirvana. My mind is free!

Source: *Therigatha*, psalm 47.

MY TEACHER

The Songs of the Nuns *collection contains a wealth of information on the religious lives of the early Buddhist nuns. Their biographies describe their struggles and tribulations, and many indicate that they saw monastic ordination as a way to escape the drudgery of household work and loveless marriages. The following passage was written by an anonymous nun who celebrates her liberation from sorrow, and it praises her teacher, a fellow nun who showed her the path.*

> Four or five times I went from my cell
> Without having attained peace of mind or control over my mind.
> I approached a nun whom I could trust, and she taught me about the doctrine,
> The aggregates, the sense spheres, and the elements.
> Having listened to her doctrinal instructions, I sat cross legged for seven days,
> Possessed of joy and bliss.
> On the eighth day I stretched out my feet,
> Having eliminated the mass of darkness (of ignorance).

Source: *Therigatha*, psalm 38.

THE JOY OF RELEASE

The following poem was written by the mother of Sumangala (a monk who became an arhat). She was the wife of a poor umbrella maker who left her home and became a nun. Later she attained the level of arhathood, which she celebrates in these verses.

> Free, I am free!
> I am completely free from my kitchen pestle!
> [I am free from] my worthless husband and even his sun umbrella!
> And my pot that smells like a water snake!
> I have eliminated all desire and hatred,

Going to the base of a tree, [I think,] 'What happiness!'
And contemplate this happiness.

Source: *Therigatha,* psalm 22.

THE BUDDHA'S LAST DAYS
AND FINAL INSTRUCTIONS

After a long and successful teaching career, Buddha's body had become old and wracked with constant pain. Realizing that his mission had been accomplished, Buddha decided to enter final nirvana (parinirvana). He first asked his disciples if they had any final questions, and then told them that they should rely on the teachings they had already received. Buddha further informed them that he had told them everything of the path and the true doctrine that could be put into words, holding nothing back, and so it was now up to them to put these teachings into practice.

[Buddha:] 'Ananda, I have taught the doctrine without distinguishing "inner" and "outer." As to this, the Tathagata is not a "closed-fisted teacher" with reference to the doctrine [i.e., he does not hold anything back]. If anyone thinks, "I should watch over the order," or "The order should refer to me," then let him promulgate something about the order. The Tathagata does not think in such terms. Thus the Tathagata does not promulgate something about the order. . . .

Ananda, I am now aged, old, an elder, my time has gone, I have arrived at the age of eighty years. Just as an old cart is made to go by tying it together with straps, so the Tathagata's body is made to go by strapping it together. Ananda, during periods when the Tathagata, by withdrawing his attention from all signs, by the cessation of some emotions, enters into the signless concentration of thought and stays in it, on such occasions the Tathagata's body is made comfortable.

'Therefore, Ananda . . . you should live with yourselves as islands, with yourselves as refuges, with no one else as refuge; with the doctrine as an island, with the doctrine as a refuge, with no one else as refuge. . . .

'It might be that you will think, Ananda, "The Teacher's word has ceased, now we have no teacher!" You should not perceive things in this way. The doctrine and discipline that I have taught and described will be the teacher after I pass away.'

He then told Ananda that after his death it would be permissible for monks to abolish the minor rules of monastic discipline, but Ananda neglected to ask him which these were. Buddha again exhorted his followers to rely on the teachings he had already taught them, and Ananda informed him that none of the monks present had any doubts about the doctrine, the path, or monastic discipline. Buddha then delivered his final teaching to his disciples:

'Monks, all compounded things are subject to decay and disintegration. Work out your own salvations with diligence.' These were the Tathagata's last words.

Source: *Digha-nikaya, Mahaparinibbana-sutta.*

THE QUESTIONS OF KING MILINDA

According to Buddhist tradition, the Bactrian king Menander (Pali: Milinda) engaged the Buddhist sage Nagasena in a series of philosophical discussions in which Nagasena convinced him of the truth of Buddha's teachings. The following dialogue concerns the Buddhist doctrine of selflessness, which holds that there is no enduring self, no soul, no truly existent personal identity. The king at first expresses disbelief, pointing out that he is clearly speaking to Nagasena, who seems to be a concretely existing person. Nagasena convinces the king by using the analogy of a chariot, which is composed of parts that separately are incapable of performing the functions of a chariot, but which when assembled are given the conventional designation "chariot." Similarly, human beings (and all other phenomena) are merely collections of parts that are given conventional designations, but they lack any enduring entity.

Then King Milinda said to the venerable Nagasena: 'What is your reverence called? What is your name, reverend sir?'

'Sire, I am known as Nagasena; my fellow religious practitioners, sir, address me as Nagasena. But although [my] parents gave [me] the name of Nagasena . . . still it is only a designation, a name, a denotation, a conventional expression, since Nagasena is only a name because there is no person here to be found. . . .'

'If, reverend Nagasena, there is no person to be found, who is it that gives you necessities like robe material, food, lodging, and medicines for the sick, who is it that uses them, who is it that keeps the precepts, practices meditation, actualizes the paths, the fruits, nirvana; who kills living beings, takes what is not given, commits immoral acts, tells lies, drinks intoxicants, and commits the five types of immediate karmas? In that case, there is no virtue; there is no non-virtue; there is no one who does or who makes another do things that are virtuous or non-virtuous; there is no fruit or ripening of good or bad karma. Reverend Nagasena, if someone kills you, there will be no demerit. Also, reverend Nagasena, you have no teacher, no preceptor, no ordination. . . .'

'Is form Nagasena?'

'No, sire.'

'Is feeling Nagasena?'

'No, sire.'

'Is discrimination Nagasena?'

'No, sire.'

'Are compositional factors Nagasena?'

'No, sire.'

'Is consciousness Nagasena?'

'No, sire.'

'Then, reverend sir, are form, feelings, discriminations, compositional factors, and consciousness together Nagasena?'

'No, sire.'

'Then, reverend sir, is there something other than form, feelings, discriminations, compositional factors, and consciousness that is Nagasena?'

'No, sire.'

'Reverend sir, although I question you closely, I fail to find any Nagasena. Nagasena is only a sound, sir. Who is Nagasena? Reverend sir, you are speaking a lie, a falsehood: there is no Nagasena.'

Then the venerable Nagasena said to king Milinda: '. . . Your majesty, did you come here on foot, or riding?'

'Reverend sir, I did not come on foot; I came in a chariot.'

'Sire, if you came in a chariot, show me the chariot. Is the pole the chariot, sire?'

'No, reverend sir.'

'Is the axle the chariot?'

'No, reverend sir.'

'Are the wheels . . . the frame . . . the banner-staff . . . the yoke . . . the reins . . . the goad the chariot?'

'No, reverend sir.'

'Then, sire, are pole, axle, wheels, frame, banner-staff, yoke, reins, goad together the chariot?'

'No, reverend sir.'

'Then, sire, is something other than the pole, axle, wheels, frame, banner-staff, yoke, reins, goad together the chariot?'

'No, reverend sir.'

'Sire, although I question you closely, I fail to find any chariot. Chariot is only a sound, sire. What is the chariot? . . .'

'Reverend Nagasena . . . it is because of the pole, axle, wheels, frame, banner-staff, yoke, reins, and goad that "chariot" exists as a designation, appellation, denotation, as a conventional usage, as a name.'

'Good: sire, you understand the chariot. It is just like this for me, sire: because of the hair of the head and because of the hair of the body . . . and because of the brain of the head, form, feelings, discriminations, compositional factors, and consciousness that "Nagasena" exists as designation, appellation, denotation, as a conventional usage, as a name. But ultimately there is no person to be found here. . . .'

'Wonderful, reverend Nagasena! Marvelous, reverend Nagasena! The replies to the questions that were asked are truly brilliant. If the Buddha were still here, he would applaud. Well done, well done, Nagasena!'

Source: *Milinda-panho,* 2.25–28.

MAHAYANA SCRIPTURES

THE *HEART OF PERFECT WISDOM SUTRA*

The passage below is the entire text of the Heart of Perfect Wisdom Sutra, *one of the shortest texts of the Perfection of Wisdom corpus. It is said by Mahayanists to contain the essence of the teachings of this voluminous literature.*

Thus have I heard: At one time the Exalted One was dwelling on the Vulture Peak in Rajagriha together with a great assembly of monks and a great assembly of bodhisattvas. At that time, the Exalted One was immersed in a meditative absorption (*samadhi*) on the enumerations of phenomena called "perception of the profound." Also at that time, the bodhisattva, the great being, the superior Avalokiteshvara was consider-ing the meaning of the profound perfection of wisdom, and he saw that the five aggregates (*skandha*) are empty of inherent existence. Then, due to the inspiration of the Buddha, the venerable Shariputra spoke thus to the bodhisattva, the great being, the superior Avalokiteshvara: 'How should a son of good lineage train if he wants to practice the profound perfection of wisdom?'

The bodhisattva, the great being, the superior Avalokiteshvara spoke thus to the venerable Shariputra: 'Shariputra, sons of good lineage or daughters of good lineage who want to practice the profound perfection of wisdom should perceive [reality] in this way: They should correctly perceive the five aggregates also as empty of inherent existence. Form is emptiness; emptiness is form. Emptiness is not other than form; form is not other than emptiness. In the same way, feelings, discriminations, com-positional factors, and consciousness are empty. Shariputra, in that way, all phenomena are empty, without characteristics, unproduced, unceasing, undefiled, not undefiled, not decreasing, not increasing. Therefore, Shariputra, in emptiness there is no form, no feelings, no discriminations, no compositional factors, no consciousness, no eye, no ear, no nose, no tongue, no body, no mind, no form, no sound, no odor, no taste, no object of touch, no phenomenon. There is no eye constituent, no mental con-stituent, up to and including no mental consciousness constituent. There is no ignorance, no extinction of ignorance, up to and including no aging and death and no extinction of aging and death. In the same way, there is no suffering, no source [of suffering], no cessation [of suffering], no path, no exalted wisdom, no attainment, and also no non-attainment.

'Therefore, Shariputra, because bodhisattvas have no attainment, they depend on and abide in the perfection of wisdom. Because their minds are unobstructed, they are without fear. Having completely passed beyond all error, they go to the fulfillment of nirvana. All the buddhas who live in the three times [past, present, and future] have been completely awakened into unsurpassable, complete, perfect awakening through relying on the perfection of wisdom.

'Therefore, the *mantra* of the perfection of wisdom is the *mantra* of great knowledge, the unsurpassable *mantra*, the *mantra* that is equal to the unequaled, the *mantra* that thoroughly pacifies all suffering. Because it is not false, it should be known to be true. The *mantra* of the perfection wisdom is as follows:

Om gate gate paragate parasamgate bodhir svaha [*Om* gone, gone, gone beyond, gone completely beyond; praise to awakening.]

'Shariputra, bodhisattvas, great beings, should train in the profound perfection of wisdom in that way.'

Then the Exalted One arose from that meditative absorption and said to the bodhisattva, the great being, the superior Avalokiteshvara: 'Well done! Well done, well done, son of good lineage, it is just so. Son of good lineage, it is like that; the profound perfection of wisdom should be practiced just as you have indicated. Even the Tathagatas admire this.' When the Exalted One had spoken thus, the venerable Shariputra, the bodhisattva, the great being, the superior Avalokiteshvara, and all those around them, and those of the world, the gods, humans, demigods, and *gandharvas* were filled with admiration and praised the words of the Exalted One.

Source: *Prajnaparamita-hridaya-sutra.*

EXCERPTS FROM THE *DIAMOND SUTRA*

Perfection of Wisdom texts contain many warnings against holding too rigidly to doctrines, even Buddhist doctrines. In the following passage, Buddha warns his disciple Subhuti against conceiving sentient beings as truly existing, and then applies the reasoning of emptiness to other Buddhist categories.

[Buddha:] 'Subhuti, due to being established in the bodhisattva vehicle, one should give rise to the thought, "As many sentient beings there are that are included among the realms of sentient beings . . . whatever realms of sentient beings can be conceived, all these should be brought by me to nirvana, to a final nirvana that is a realm of nirvana without remainder; but, although countless sentient beings have reached final nirvana, no sentient being whatsoever has reached final nirvana." Why is this? Subhuti, if a discrimination of a sentient being arises in a bodhisattva [literally, "awakening-being"], he should not be called an awakening-being. Why is this? Subhuti, one who gives rise to the discrimination of such a self, the discrimination of a sentient being, the discrimination of a soul, or the discrimination of a person should not be called a bodhisattva. . . .

'Subhuti, all of them produce and acquire an immeasurable and incalculable store of merit. Why is this? Subhuti, it is because these bodhisattvas, great beings, do not give rise to the discrimination of a self,

the discrimination of a sentient being, the discrimination of a soul, or the discrimination of a person. Also, Subhuti, these bodhisattvas, great beings, do not give rise to discriminations of phenomena, nor do they give rise to discriminations of non-phenomena, nor do they give rise to discrimination or to non-discrimination. Why is this? Subhuti, if these bodhisattvas, great beings, gave rise to discriminations of phenomena, this would be grasping a self, grasping a sentient being, grasping a soul, grasping a person. If they gave rise to discriminations of non-phenomena, this also would be grasping a self, grasping a sentient being, grasping a soul, grasping a person. Why is this? Subhuti, in no way should a bodhisattva, a great being, grasp either phenomena nor non-phenomena. Therefore, this has been said by the Tathagata with hidden intent: "For those who understand the teaching of *dharma* that is like a raft, *dharma* should be abandoned, and still more non-*dharma*."'

Source: *Vajracchedika-prajnaparamita-sutra* selections.

WHY BODHISATTVAS
ARE SUPERIOR TO HEARERS

Some early Mahayana texts have a distinctly sectarian tone, particularly when they compare the ideals of the arhat and the bodhisattva. In the following passage from the 8,000 Line Perfection of Wisdom Sutra, Buddha describes to Subhuti the differences between the attitudes of Hinayanists and Mahayanists.

[Buddha:] 'Subhuti, bodhisattvas, great beings, should not train in the way that persons of the hearer vehicle and solitary realizer vehicle train. Subhuti, in what way do persons of the hearer vehicle and the solitary realizer vehicle train? Subhuti, they think thus, "[I] should discipline only myself; [I] should pacify only myself; [I] should attain nirvana by myself." In order to discipline only themselves and pacify themselves and attain nirvana, they begin to apply themselves to establishing all the virtuous roots. Also, Subhuti, bodhisattvas, great beings, should not train in this way. On the contrary, Subhuti, bodhisattvas, great beings, should train thus, "In order to benefit all the world, I will dwell in suchness; and, establishing all sentient beings in suchness, I will lead the immeasurable realms of sentient beings to nirvana." Bodhisattvas, great beings, should begin applying themselves in that way to establishing all virtuous roots, but should not be conceited because of this. . . .

'Those who say, "In this very life, having thoroughly freed the mind from contamination, without attachment, [I] will pass beyond sorrow" are "at the level of hearers and solitary realizers." With respect to this, bodhisattvas, great beings, should not give rise to such thoughts. Why is this? Subhuti, bodhisattvas, great beings, abide in the great vehicle and put on the great armor; they should not give rise to thoughts of even a little elaboration. Why is this? These supreme beings thoroughly lead the world and arc a great benefit to the world. Therefore, they should always and uninterruptedly train well in the six perfections.'

Source: *Ashtasahasrika-prajnaparamita-sutra ('Phags pa shes rab kyi pha rol tu phyin pa brgyad stong pa'i mdo),* ch. 11]

ON THE DIFFERENCES
BETWEEN MEN AND WOMEN

The dialogue below applies the doctrine of emptiness to the commonly accepted differences between men and women. When these are closely examined, they are found to be merely the results of misguided conceptuality, since there is no inherently existent difference between the sexes.

The dialogue occurs in the house of Vimalakirti, a lay bodhisattva who is pretending to be sick in order to initiate a discourse on the dharma. The Buddha's disciples follow Manjushri—an advanced bodhisattva who is said to embody wisdom—to Vimalakirti's house in order to hear the two discuss the perfection of wisdom.

The interchange is so profound that a young goddess who lives in Vimalakirti's house rains down flowers on the assembly. The Hinayana monks who are present try frantically to brush them off, because monks are forbidden in the Vinaya to wear flowers or adornments. The bodhisattvas in the audience, however, are unaffected by such rigid adherence to rules, and so the flowers fall from their robes.

This causes Shariputra—described in Pali texts as the most advanced of Buddha's Hinayana disciples in the development of wisdom—to marvel at the attainments of the goddess and the bodhisattvas. She chides him for viewing the fruits of meditative training as things to be acquired, and in response Shariputra asks her why she does not change from a woman into a man. The question appears to be based on traditional Indian perceptions of authority, according to which wisdom is associated with elder males. The goddess violates these principles, because she is young and female. But it is clear from the dialogue that she is very advanced in understanding the perfection of wisdom.

The goddess responds to Shariputra's challenge by turning him into a woman and herself into a man. This leads to one of the most poignant scenes in the sutra, in which Shariputra experiences discomfort in his new body, apparently because of the Vinaya injunctions preventing monks from physical contact with women. Shariputra, now in a woman's body, is unable to avoid such contact, and tells the goddess that he is a woman without being a woman. The goddess replies that all women are women without being women, because "woman" is merely a conventional designation with no ultimate referent.

A goddess who lived in the house of Vimalakirti, having heard the doctrinal teaching of the bodhisattvas, the great beings, was very pleased, delighted, and moved. She took on a material form and scattered heavenly flowers over the great bodhisattvas and great hearers. When she had thrown them, the flowers that landed on the bodies of the bodhisattvas fell to the ground, while those that fell on the bodies of the great hearers remained stuck to them and did not fall to the ground. Then the great hearers tried to use their supernatural powers to shake off the flowers, but the flowers did not fall off. Then the goddess asked the venerable Shariputra: 'Venerable Shariputra, why do you try to shake off the flowers?'

'Goddess, flowers are not fitting for monks; that is why we reject them.'

'Venerable Shariputra, do not speak thus. Why? These flowers are perfectly fitting. Why? The flowers are flowers and are free from conceptuality; it is only yourselves, the elders, who conceptualize them and create conceptuality toward them. Venerable Shariputra, among those who have renounced the world to take up monastic discipline, such conceptualizations and conceptuality are not fitting; it is those who do not conceive either conceptualizations nor conceptuality who are fit.

'Venerable Shariputra, take a good look at these bodhisattvas, great beings: the flowers do not stick to them because they have abandoned conceptuality. . . . Flowers stick to those who have not yet abandoned the defilements; they do not stick to those who have abandoned them. . . .'

'Well done! Well done, Goddess! What have you attained, what have you gained that enables you to have such eloquence?'

'It is because I have not attained anything nor gained anything that I have such eloquence. Those who think that they have attained or gained something are deluded with respect to the well-taught disciplinary doctrine. . . .'

'Goddess, why do you not change your womanhood?'

'During the twelve years [that I have lived in this house], I have looked for womanhood, but have never found it. Venerable Shariputra, if a skillful magician created an illusory woman through transformation, could you ask her why she does not change her womanhood?'

'Every illusory creation is unreal.'

'In the same way, venerable Shariputra, all phenomena are unreal and have an illusory nature; why would you think of asking them to change their womanhood?'

Then the goddess performed a supernatural feat that caused the elder Shariputra to appear in every way like the goddess and she herself to appear in every way like the elder Shariputra. Then the goddess who had changed into Shariputra asked Shariputra who had been changed into a goddess: 'Why do you not change your womanhood, venerable sir?'

[Shariputra:] 'I do not know either how I lost my male form nor how I acquired a female body.'

[Goddess:] 'Elder, if you were able to change your female form, then all women could change their womanhood. Elder, just as you appear to be a woman, so also all women appear in the form of women, but they appear in the form of women without being women. It was with this hidden thought that the Exalted One said: "Phenomena are neither male nor female."'

Then the goddess cut off her supernatural power and the venerable Shariputra regained his previous form. Then the goddess said to Shariputra: 'Venerable Shariputra, where is your female form now?'

[Shariputra:] 'My female form is neither made nor changed.'

[Goddess:] 'Well done! Well done, venerable sir! In the same way, all phenomena, just as they are, are neither made nor changed. Saying that they are neither made nor changed is the word of the Buddha. . . .'

[Shariputra:] 'Goddess, how long will it be before you reach awakening?'

[Goddess:] 'Elder, when you yourself return to being a worldly person, with all the qualities of a worldly person, then I myself will reach unsurpassed, perfect awakening.'

[Shariputra:] 'Goddess, it is impossible that I could return to being a worldly person, with all the qualities of a worldly person; it cannot occur.'

[Goddess:] 'Venerable Shariputra, in the same way, it is impossible that I will ever attain unsurpassed, perfect awakening; it cannot occur. Why? Because unsurpassed, perfect awakening is founded on a non-foundation. Thus, since there is no foundation, who could reach unsurpassed, perfect awakening?'

[Shariputra:] 'But the Tathagata has said: "Tathagatas as innumerable as the sands of the Ganges river attain, have attained, and will attain unsurpassed, perfect awakening."'

[Goddess:] 'Venerable Shariputra, the words, "buddhas past, future, and present" are conventional expressions made up of syllables and numbers. Buddhas are neither past, nor future, nor present, and their awakening transcends the three divisions of time. Tell me, elder, have you already attained the level of arhat?'

[Shariputra:] 'I have attained it because there is nothing to attain.'

[Goddess:] It is the same with awakening: it is attained because there is nothing to attain.

Source: *Vimalakirti-nirdesha-sutra* (*'Phags pa dri ma med par grags pas bstan pa'i mdo*), ch. 6.

THE *LOTUS SUTRA*: PARABLE OF THE BURNING HOUSE

The parable of the burning house is a famous allegory for the practice of "skillful means" (upaya-kaushalya), which is one of the important abilities of bodhisattvas and buddhas. It involves adapting the dharma to the interests and proclivities of individual listeners, telling them things that will attract them to the practice of Buddhism. The question posed in the dialogue concerns whether such tactics should be considered underhanded or dishonest. The answer, not surprisingly, is no: The means used are for the good of the beings, and benefit them greatly in the long run. Moreover, with beings who are thoroughly enmeshed in the concerns of the world it is necessary to draw their attention away from mundane pleasures toward the dharma, which can lead to lasting happiness.

[Buddha:] "Shariputra, let us suppose that in a village somewhere . . . there was a householder who was . . . very wealthy. Suppose that he owned a great mansion, lofty, spacious, built long ago, inhabited by hundreds of living beings. The house had one door and was covered with thatch, its terraces were collapsing, the bases of its pillars were rotting, and the plaster and coverings of the walls were falling apart. Now suppose that all of a sudden the whole house burst into flames and that the householder managed to get himself out, but that his little boys [were still inside]. . . ."

[He thought:] "I was able to get out of the burning house through the door safely, without being touched by the flames, but my children remain in the house, playing with their toys, enjoying themselves. They do not realize . . . that the house is on fire, and so are not afraid. Even though they are caught up in the fire and are being scorched by flames, though they are actually suffering, they are unaware of it, and so they do not think to come out. . . ."

"So he called to the boys: 'Come, my children, the house is burning with a mass of flames! Come out, so that you will not be burned in the inferno and come to disaster!'

"But the ignorant boys paid no attention to the man's words, even though he only wished for their well-being. . . . They did not care, and did not run from the house, did not understand, and did not comprehend even the meaning of the word 'inferno.' Instead, they continued to run and play here and there, occasionally looking at their father. Why? Because they were ignorant children.

"So then, Shariputra, the man thought: . . . 'I should use a skillful method to cause the children to come out of the house.' The man knew the mental dispositions of his children and clearly understood their interests. He knew of the kinds of toys they liked. . . . So he said to them: 'Children, all the toys that you like . . . such as little ox carts, goat carts, and deer carts, which are pleasing and captivating to you, have all been put outside by me, so that you can play with them. Come, run out of the house! I will give each of you what you want! Come quickly! Come and get these toys!

"Then the boys, hearing him mentioning the names of the toys they liked . . . quickly ran from the burning house, not waiting for each other, and calling, 'Who will be first? Who will be foremost?'

"Then the man, seeing that his children had come out of the house safely, knowing that they were out of danger . . . gave his children . . . ox carts only. They were made of seven precious metals, and had railings, were hung with strings of bells, were high and lofty, adorned with wonderful and precious jewels, illuminated by garlands of gems, decorated with wreaths of flowers. . . .

"Now what do you think, Shariputra, did that man lie to his children by first promising them three vehicles and then later giving them only great vehicles, the best vehicles?"

Shariputra said: "No indeed, Lord! Not at all! There is no reason to think that in this case the man was a liar, because he was using skillful means in order to cause his children to come out of the burning house, and because of this he gave them the gift of life. Moreover, Lord, in addition to keeping their lives, they also received those toys. But, Lord, even if the man had not given them a single cart, he would still not have been a liar. Why is this? Because, Lord, that man first thought, 'By using skillful means, I will liberate those children from a great mass of suffering. . . . '"

"Well said, Shariputra, well said! You have spoken well! In the same way, the Tathagata also . . . is the father of the world, who has attained the supreme perfection of understanding of great skillful means, who is greatly compassionate, who has a mind that is unwearied, who is concerned for the well-being of others. He appears in this triple world, which is like a burning house blazing with the whole mass of suffering and despair . . . in order to liberate from desire, aversion, and obscuration those beings who remain trapped in the mists of ignorance, in order to liberate them from the blindness of ignorance, birth, old age, death, sorrow, grief, suffering, sadness, and dissatisfaction, in order to awaken them to supreme, perfect awakening. . . . In this triple world, which is like a burning house, they enjoy themselves and run here and there. Even though they are afflicted by a great deal of suffering, they do not even think that they are suffering. . . .

"Therefore, Shariputra, the Tathagata, who is just like that strong-armed man who . . . employed skillful means to coax his children from the burning house . . . speaks of three vehicles: the hearers' vehicle, the solitary realizers' vehicle, and the bodhisattvas' vehicle. . . .

"So the Tathagata is not a liar when he uses skillful means, first holding out the prospect of three vehicles and then leading beings to final nirvana by means of a single great vehicle."

Source: *Saddharma-pundarika-sutra*, ch. 3; tr. John Strong, *The Experience of Buddhism*, pp. 135–137.

EVERYTHING IS CONTROLLED BY THE MIND

The passage below comes from the Cloud of Jewels Sutra. *It indicates that all phenomena are productions of mind and that everything is created by mind. Ordinary beings allow the mind to wander at will, thus enmeshing them in confused and harmful thoughts, but bodhisattvas are advised to train the mind in order to bring it under control.*

All phenomena originate in the mind, and when the mind is fully known all phenomena are fully known. For by the mind the world is led . . . and through the mind karma is piled up, whether good or bad. The mind swings like a firebrand, the mind rears up like a wave, the mind burns like a forest fire, like a great flood the mind carries all things away. Bodhisattvas, thoroughly examining the nature of things, remain in ever-present mindfulness of the activity of the mind, and so do not fall into the mind's power, but the mind comes under their control. And with the mind under their control, all phenomena are under their control.

Source: *Ratnamegha-sutra*, from the *Shiksha-samuchchaya*, ch. 6.

THE BASIS CONSCIOUSNESS

The passage below from the Sutra Explaining the Thought *is one of the earliest descriptions of the "basis consciousness"* (alaya-vijnana), *a doctrine that was central to the Indian Yogacara school and that was also influential in other Mahayana countries, particularly Tibet and China. The basis consciousness is the most fundamental level of mind, and it is said to be comprised of the "seeds" of past actions and mental states.*

The seeds become part of the continuum of the basis consciousness, which is moved along by their force. If one cultivates positive actions and thoughts, for example, one's mind will become habituated to positive actions and thoughts. The converse is true of those who engage in negative actions and thoughts.

Under appropriate conditions, the seeds give rise to corresponding thoughts and emotions, and these are the phenomena of ordinary experience. Mind and its objects are said to arise together, and so there is no substantial difference between subject and object. Because of this, phenomena are said to be "cognition-only" (vijnaptimatra), *meaning that all we ever perceive are mental impressions, and not things in themselves.*

[Buddha:] 'Initially in dependence upon two types of appropriation—the appropriation of the physical sense powers associated with a support and the appropriation of predispositions which proliferate conventional designations with respect to signs, names, and concepts—the mind which has all seeds ripens; it develops, increases, and expands in its operations. . . .

'Consciousness is also called the "appropriating consciousness" because it holds and appropriates the body in that way. It is called the "basis consciousness" because there is the same establishment and abiding within those bodies. . . . It is called "mind" because it collects and accumulates forms, sounds, smells, tastes, and tangible objects.

Source: *Samdhinirmochana-sutra*, ch. 5.

NAGARJUNA ON EMPTINESS

Nagarjuna, founder of the Madhyamaka school of Indian Mahayana, emphasized the centrality of the doctrine of emptiness in his philosophy. In the following verses he indicates that concepts are empty because language is simply an interconnected system of terms that do not capture actual things. They simply relate to other words.

One who fully recognizes this fact becomes freed from the snares of language and attains correct realization, an important part of the path to liberation.

1. Through the force of worldly conventions, buddhas
   Have spoken of duration, arising, disintegration, existence, non-existence,
   Inferior, middling, and superior,
   But they have not spoken [of these] in an ultimate sense.
2. Self, non-self, and self-non-self do not exist,
   And so conventional expressions do not [really] signify.
   Like nirvana, all expressible things are empty of inherent existence.
3. Since all things completely lack inherent existence—either in causes or conditions, [in their] totality, or separately—they are empty.
4. Because it exists, being does not arise;
   Because it does not exist, non-being does not arise.
5. Because they are discordant phenomena, being and non-being [together] do not arise.
   Thus they neither endure nor cease. . . .
7. Without one, many does not exist; without many, one is not possible.
   Thus, dependently arisen things are indeterminable. . . .
56. In dependence upon the internal and external sense spheres (*ayatana*)
   Consciousness arises.
   Thus, just like mirages and illusions, consciousness is empty.
57. In dependence upon an apprehendable object, consciousness arises.
   Thus, the observable does not exist [in itself].
   [The subject of consciousness] does not exist without the apprehendable and consciousness.
   Thus, the subject of consciousness does not exist [by itself]. . . .
65. Due to correctly perceiving that things are empty, one becomes non-deluded.
   Ignorance ceases, and thus the twelve limbs [of dependent arising] cease. . . .
67. Nothing exists inherently, nor is there non-being there.
   Arising from causes and conditions, being and non-being are empty.
68. All things are empty of inherent existence,
   And so the incomparable Tathagata teaches dependent arising with respect to things. . . .
72. One with faith who seeks the truth, who considers this principle with reason,
   Relying on the dharma that is free of supports, is liberated from existence and non-existence [and abides in] peace.
73. When one understands that "this is a result of that," the net of wrong views is eradicated.
   Due to abandoning attachment, obscuration, and hatred, undefiled, one attains nirvana.

Source: Nagarjuna, *Shunyata-saptati*, tr. Christian Lindtner, in *Master of Wisdom: Writings of the Buddhist Master Nagarjuna* (Berkeley: Dharma Publishing, 1986), pp. 95–119.

THE BODHISATTVA'S
VOWS OF UNIVERSAL LOVE

The following verses, written by Shantideva, are among the most eloquent expressions in Mahayana literature of the ideal mind-set of bodhisattvas, who should dedicate all of their energies to helping other beings in every possible way.

16. May those who malign me, or harm me, or accuse me falsely, and others all be recipients of awakening.
17. May I be a protector of the helpless, a guide for those on the path, a boat, a bridge, a way for those who wish to cross over.
18. May I be a lamp for those who need a lamp, a bed for those who seek a bed, and a slave for those who desire a slave.
19. May I become a wish-fulfilling jewel, an inexhaustible jar, a powerful mantra, a cure for all sickness, a wish-fulfilling tree, and a cow of plenty for all creatures.
20. As earth and the other elements are enjoyed in various ways by innumerable beings living throughout space,
    So may I be the sustenance for various kinds of beings in all the realms of space for as long as all are not satisfied.

Source: Santideva, *Bodhicaryavatara*, *"Bodhicitta-parigraha"* tr. Marion Matics, *Entering the Path of Enlightenment* (London: Macmillan, 1970), pp. 154–155.

TANTRIC SKILL IN MEANS

Tantric texts claim that the system of tantra skillfully uses aspects of reality that cause bondage for people who are enmeshed in mundane conceptuality—things like desire and other negative emotions. The following excerpt from the Hevajra Tantra *indicates that these may serve as aids to the path of liberation if the proper means are used.*

Those things by which evil men are bound, others turn into means and gain thereby release from the bonds of existence. By passion the world is bound, by passion too it is released, but by heretical Buddhists this practice of reversals is not known.

Source: *Hevajra-tantra* I.ix.2–3, tr. David Snellgrove, *Indo-Tibetan Buddhism* (Boston: Shambhala, 1987), vol. I, pp. 125–126.

THE STAGE OF COMPLETION

The tantric practice of deity yoga involves first creating a vivid image of a buddha in front of one, and then visualizing the buddha as merging with oneself. One views oneself as a buddha—with the body, speech, and mind of a buddha—and as performing the activities of an awakened being. The first procedure is called the "generation stage," and the second, which is described in the following passage from the Guhyasamaja Tantra, *is termed the "completion stage." In order to avoid becoming attached to the visualization, one should be aware that both the buddha and oneself are empty of inherent existence. Thus at the end of the session, one dissolves both oneself and the buddha into emptiness.*

> Everything from the crown of the head to the feet dissolves into the heart; you engage in the perfect yoga (meditation on emptiness). . . . All sentient beings and all other phenomena dissolve into clear light and then dissolve into you; then you yourself, as the deity, dissolve into your heart. . . . Just as mist on a mirror fades toward the center and disappears, so does everything—the net of illusory manifestation—dissolve into the clear light of emptiness. Just as fish are easily seen in clear water, so does everything—the net of illusory manifestation—emerge from the clear light of emptiness.

Source: *Guhyasamaja-tantra;* quoted in Khenpo Könchog Gyaltsen *The Garland of Mahamudra Practices* (Ithaca: Snow Lion, 1986), pp. 56–57.

WOMEN SHOULD BE HONORED

One of the notable features of the tantric movement is an emphasis on the spiritual capacities of women. Classical Indian literature indicates that extereme misogyny was prevalent in the society, which makes this aspect of tantra even more significant. An example of the emphasis on the equality of women is the fact that one of the basic vows required of all tantric practitioners is a pledge not to denigrate women, "who are the bearers of wisdom." The following passage from the Chandamaharoshana Tantra *expresses a similar sentiment in its praises of women.*

> When women are honored,
> They provide instant accomplishments (*siddhi*)
> To those who wish for the welfare of all beings.
> Thus one should honor women.
> Women are heaven, women are dharma,
> Women are also the supreme asceticism (*tapas*).
> Women are Buddha, women are the sangha;
> Women are the perfection of wisdom.

Source: *Candamaharosana-tantra,* 8.27–30.

SAMSARA AND NIRVANA ARE ONE

The following excerpts from the Hevajra Tantra *discuss the tantric idea that there is no fundamental difference between cyclic existence and nirvana. Buddhas perceive them as undifferentiable, but ordinary beings, because of their delusions, think in terms of dichotomies, and so imagine that the path and goal are separate.*

Then the essence is declared, pure and consisting in knowledge, where
there is not the slightest difference between cyclic existence and
nirvana.
Nothing is mentally produced in the highest bliss, and no one
produces it,
There is no bodily form, neither object nor subject,
Neither flesh nor blood, neither dung nor urine,
No sickness, no delusion, no purification,
No passion, no wrath, no delusion, no envy,
No malignity, no conceit of self, no visible object,
Nothing mentally produced and no producer,
No friend is there, no enemy,
Calm is the Innate and undifferentiated. . . .
The Enlightened One is neither existence nor non-existence; he has a form
with arms and faces and yet in highest bliss is formless.
So the whole world is the Innate, for the Innate is its essence.
Its essence too is nirvana when the mind is in a purified state.

Source: *Hevajra-tantra*, ch. I.x.32–34, II.ii.43–44, tr. David Snellgrove, *The Hevajra Tantra: A Critical Study* (London: Oxford University Press, 1959), vol. I, p. 92.

USING DESIRE TO ERADICATE DESIRE

Tantric adepts claim that the fact that tantra uses emotions like desire as means in the path is an example of the skillful practices of the system. The following passage from Viryavajra's Commentary on the Samputa Tantra *contends that there are four levels of the use of desire: visualizing a man and woman looking at each other; laughing with each other; holding hands; and sexual union. Each of these represents a progressively higher level of desire. One should engage in these practices, however, in order to utilize the energy of desire as a force that can be used to eradicate mental afflictions. The skillful use of desire is said in some texts to be like rubbing two sticks together to make a fire, which then consumes the sticks themselves. In this case, the process is compared to the way that insects are born in wood, and then later consume the wood.*

Within the sound of laughter non-conceptual bliss is generated; or it is generated from looking at the body, the touch of holding hands and the embrace of the two; or from the touch [of union] . . . just as an insect is generated from the wood and then eats the wood itself, so meditative stabilization is generated from bliss [in dependence on desire] and is cultivated as emptiness [whereupon desire is consumed].

Source: Viryavajra's *Commentary on the Samputa Tantra*; quoted in *Sngags rim chen mo*, II.7.

THE STATE OF PURE AWARENESS

The following passage from the Hevajra Tantra *describes the state of mind of one who has transcended all discursive and dichotomizing thought through direct, intuitive awareness of the boundless clarity of mind.*

> From self-experiencing comes this knowledge, which is free from ideas of self and other; like the sky it is pure and void, the essence supreme of non-existence and existence, a mingling of wisdom and method, a mingling of passion and absence of passion. It is the life of living things, it is the Unchanging One Supreme; it is all-pervading, abiding in all embodied things. It is the stuff the world is made of, and in it existence and non-existence have their origin. It is all other things that there are. . . . It is the essential nature of all existing things and illusory in its forms.

Source: *Hevajra-tantra* I.x.8–12, tr. David L. Snellgrove, *The Hevajra Tantra*, p. 81.

THE IMPORTANCE OF THE GURU

The special techniques of tantra are said to be very powerful, but they can also be dangerous. Thus tantric texts warn meditators to find qualified spiritual guides (guru) who can help them to avoid possible pitfalls. One of the central practices of tantra is "guru yoga," in which one visualizes one's guru as a fully awakened buddha. One who does this successfully is said to move quickly toward actualization of buddhahood. In the following passage the tantric master Tilopa teaches that finding a qualified guru is a prerequisite for successful tantric practice.

> The ignorant may know that sesame oil—the essence—exists in the sesame seed, but because they do not know how, they cannot extract the oil. So also does the innate fundamental wisdom abide in the heart of all migrators; but unless it is pointed out by the guru, it cannot be realized. By pounding the seeds and clearing away the husks, one can extract the essence—the sesame oil. Similarly, when it is shown by the guru, the meaning of suchness is so illuminated that one can enter into it.

Source: Tilopa, quoted in *The Garland of Mahamudra Practices*, p. 58.

TIBETAN BUDDHIST SCRIPTURES

ULTIMATE REALITY

The "great completion" (dzogchen) tradition of Tibetan Buddhism is practiced by all of the four main schools—Nyingma, Kagyu, Sakya, and Geluk—but most closely associated with the Nyingma. In this system all phenomena are said to be creations of mind that, like mind, are a union of luminosity and emptiness. In the following passage, meditators are instructed on the nature of ultimate reality, in which phenomena spontaneously appear to the mind although they have no real substance.

Since [things exist] only in the manner of mirages, dreams, and delusions, you should abandon [false appearances] and adopt [virtuous practices], work for the sake [of others], avoid [non-virtue] and practice [virtue]. Wash away the afflictions of desire, anger, and obscuration with the waters of their antidotes: [meditation on] repulsiveness, love, and dependent arising. Because ultimate reality is non-arisen and pure, it is free from elaborations (*spros pa, prapanca*) such as the duality of samsara and nirvana. . . . All phenomena merely appear naturally to your own mind on the mandala that is the sphere of the foundation, the buddha nature. They are falsities, not really things, empty, and only appear as forms, as the aggregates, realms, spheres, and so forth. . . . The unsurpassed, supreme, secret great completion directly actualizes the sphere of the spontaneously existent. This foundational sphere is unchanging, like space. [All good] qualities [reside] in it spontaneously, as the sun, moon, planets, and stars [reside] in the sky. There is no need to seek it, since it has existed since beginningless time. No work or effort [is necessary,] as this path is naturally manifest.

Source: Longchen Rapjampa, *Chos bzhi rin po che'i phreng ba (Four Themed Precious Garland)*.

BARDO, THE STATE BETWEEN LIVES

The following excerpts are drawn from a Tibetan classic on death and dying entitled Liberation through Hearing in the Intermediate State, *attributed to Padmasambhava. According to the tradition, it was hidden by Padmasambhava and rediscovered by the "treasure finder" Karma Lingpa in the fourteenth century. The book describes the "intermediate state" (bardo; translated here as "the between") that all beings are said to enter after death.*

During the process of dying, the physiological changes that occur are accompanied by mental changes in which the coarser levels of mind drop away, revealing progressively more subtle aspects of consciousness. At the moment of death, the most subtle level of mind dawns. This is called the "mind of clear light," and compared to it all other minds are adventitious.

At this point one enters the intermediate state and experiences strange and terrifying sights. These are all said to be aspects of one's own mind, and they include visions of mild and terrifying beings, deafening sounds, and other intense sense experiences. The intermediate state is a time of great opportunity, however, and if one is able to maintain awareness and focus on the clear light nature of mind and perceive all experiences as merely aspects of mind, one may become a buddha, or at least attain rebirth in the pure land of a buddha. In such places the conditions are optimal for beings who seek buddhahood. If one is unable to maintain mindfulness, one will be reborn in accordance with one's accumulated karma.

> Hey! Now when the life between dawns upon me,
> I will abandon laziness, as life has no more time,
> Unwavering, enter the path of learning, thinking, and meditating,
> And taking perceptions and mind as a path,
> I will realize the Three Bodies of enlightenment! . . .

> Conscious of dreaming, I will enjoy the changes as clear light.
> Not sleeping mindlessly like an animal,
> I will cherish the practice merging sleep and realization! . . .
> Now when the death-point between dawns upon me,
> I will give up the preoccupations of the all-desiring mind,
> Enter unwavering the experience of the clarity of the precepts,
> And transmigrate into the birthless space of inner awareness;
> About to lose this created body of flesh and blood,
> I will realize it to be impermanent illusion! . . .
> I will . . . enter into the recognition of all objects as my mind's own visions,
> And understand this as the pattern of perception in the between;
> Come to this moment, arrived at this most critical cessation,
> I will not fear my own visions of deities mild and fierce! . . .
> Now courage and positive perception are essential.

Source: *Bardo thos grol* from *Bar do thos grol: The Tibetan Book of the Dead: Liberation through Understanding in the Between,* tr. Robert A. F. Thurman (New York: Bantam, 1994), pp. 115–116.

MILAREPA ON MEDITATION

Milarepa, one of the most influential figures in Tibetan Buddhism, was born into a fairly well-to-do family, but his greedy aunt and uncle took everything away from him, his mother, and sister. Overcome by rage, his mother coerced Milarepa into learning black magic and sending a curse on the aunt and uncle, with the result that a number of people died, but not the primary objects of his revenge.

*Milarepa, terrified of the consequences of his evil deeds, searched for a spiritual guide (*lama*) who could help him escape the consequences of his actions. He eventually found Marpa, who gave Milarepa a series of difficult and dispiriting tasks, which cleansed his negative karma. After this Milarepa spent many years living in a cave and practicing solitary meditation, which culminated in his attainment of awakening. He is considered in Tibet to be the supreme example of the attainment of buddhahood in one lifetime through tantric practice.*

> Look up into the sky, and practice meditation free from the fringe and center.
> Look up at the sun and moon, and practice meditation free from bright and dim.
> Look over the mountains, and practice meditation free from departing and changing.
> Look down at the lake, and practice meditation free from waves.
> Look here at your mind, and practice meditation free from discursive thought.

Source: *Rje btsun mi la ras pa'i rnam thar, (Religious Biography of the Master Milarepa),* pp. 49bff.

NIGUMA ON MAHAMUDRA

Niguma is said by Tibetan tradition to have been the founder of the Shangpa lineage of the Kagyu tradition. In the following passage she describes the view of mahamudra (literally, "great seal"), which is said by the Kagyu school to be the supreme form of

Buddhist practice. In mahamudra, one dispenses with the visualizations and rituals of tantra and focuses on the natural state of mind, which is said to be a union of clear light and emptiness. All phenomena are viewed as the spontaneous play of mind, and by cultivating this awareness it is said that the meditator moves quickly toward the attainment of buddhahood.

> Do nothing at all with the mind;
> Abide in a non-artificial and natural state.
> Your own unwavering mind is the truth body (*dharma-kaya*).
> The important thing for meditation is an unwavering mind.
> You should realize the great [reality] that is free from extremes.
> The afflictions, desires, aversions, and conceptualizations
> That arise like bubbles on the ocean of cyclic existence
> Should be cut off with the sharp sword of non-production
> That is not different from the nature of things.
> When you cut off the trunk and roots,
> The branches will not grow.
> Just as in the clear ocean
> Waves pop up and sink into the water,
> So conceptualizations are not really different from reality.
> So don't look for faults, remain at ease.
> Whatever arises, whatever materializes,
> Don't hold on to it, but immediately let it go.
> Appearances, sounds, and phenomena are one's own mind;
> There are no other phenomena apart from mind.
> Mind is free from the elaborations of arising and cessation.
> The nature of mind, awareness,
> Enjoys the five qualities of the Desire Realm, but
> Does not wander from reality. . . .
> In the great realm of reality (*dharma-dhatu*)
> There is nothing to abandon or adopt,
> No meditative equipoise or post-meditation period.

Source: Niguma, *Rang grol phyag rgya chen po* (*Individual Liberation of the Great Seal*).

INSTRUCTIONS FROM MANJUSHRI

The following verses, according to the Sakya tradition of Tibetan Buddhism, were spoken to Günga Nyingpo (1092–1158). They are a summary of the entire Buddhist path, including the renunciation of the world, the development of compassion, and the importance of avoiding extreme views.

> If you cling to this life, then you are not a dharma practitioner.
> If you cling to existence, then you do not have renunciation.
> If you are attached to your own interests, then you do not have the mind of awakening.
> If you hold to [a position], then you do not have the correct view.

Source: Drakpa Gyeltsen, *Zhen pa bzhi bral* (*Parting from the Four Attachments*).

THE TRIPLE APPEARANCE

The Sakya school teaches that there are three main levels of awareness, which are sum-marized in the following stanzas from Virupa's Vajra Verses. *The first verse refers to the perceptions of ordinary beings, which are colored by ignorance and mental afflic-tion. The second verse describes the perceptions of people on the path, who have some experience with meditation and thus have overcome some of their mental afflictions. The final verse indicates that buddhas perceive the world unafflicted by ignorance, hatred, desire, etc., and so are at the level of the "pure appearance." The Sakya tradi-tion stresses that although they appear to be incompatible, the three appearances are fundamentally non-different.*

> For sentient beings with the afflictions is the impure appearance.
> For the meditator with transic absorption is the appearance of experience.
> For the ornamental wheel of the Sugata's [Buddha's] inexhaustible awakened body, voice and mind is the pure appearance.

Source: *Rdo rje tshigs rkang, (Vajra Verses)* ch. 1, quoted in Ngorchen Konchog Lhundrub, *The Beautiful Ornament of the Three Visions* (Ithaca: Snow Lion, 1991), p. xvi.

DEVELOPING THE MIND OF AWAKENING

Ordinary beings are consumed by self-centered desires and think primarily of their own narrow interests. Bodhisattvas spend countless eons working toward buddhahood for the benefit of all beings, cheerfully accepting all the tribulations that occur along the path. Given the vast gulf between the attitudes of bodhisattvas and ordinary beings, it is difficult for people enmeshed in mundane concerns to imagine making the transition to true altruism.

The following passage by Tsong Khapa (the founder of the Gelukpa school of Tibetan Buddhism) outlines a seven-step program for developing the "mind of awakening," which marks the beginning of the bodhisattva path. It begins by recognizing that because one has been reborn in an infinite variety of situations since beginningless time, one has been in every possible relationship with every other sentient being. Thus, every sentient being has been one's mother, and has been a nurturing and caring friend.

One should reflect on the kindness of one's own mother, and then think that every other being has been equally kind. One then resolves to repay this kindness, and gener-ates a feeling of love toward others, wishing that they have happiness and the causes of happiness. One then develops compassion for sentient beings, since they are experienc-ing suffering as a result of contaminated actions and afflictions.

In the next stage one attains the "unusual attitude," which involves vowing to work to free all beings from suffering and establish them in buddhahood. The final step is attainment of the mind of awakening, which is a resolve to do whatever is necessary to attain buddhahood in order to help all sentient beings.

From one's own viewpoint, since one has cycled beginninglessly, there are no sentient beings who have not been one's friends hundreds of times. Therefore, one should think, 'Whom should I value?' 'Whom should I hate?' . . .

Imagine your mother very clearly in front of you. Consider several times how she has been your mother numberless times, not only now, but from beginningless cyclic existence. When she was your mother, she protected you from all danger and brought about your benefit and happiness. In particular, in this life she held you for a long time in her womb. Once you were born, while you still had new hair, she held you to the warmth of her flesh and rocked you on the tips of her ten fingers.

She nursed you at her breast . . . and wiped away your filth with her hand. In various ways she nourished you tirelessly. When you were hungry and thirsty, she gave you drink, and when you were cold, clothes, and when poor, money. She gave you those things that were precious to her. Moreover, she did not find these easily. . . . When you suffered with a fever she would rather have died herself than have her child die; and if her child became sick, from the depths of her heart she would rather have suffered herself than have her child suffer. . . .

Source: *Lam rim chen mo*, (*Great Exposition of the Stages of the Path*), pp. 572.5, 575.1.

CHINESE AND JAPANESE BUDDHIST SCRIPTURES

WHY BUDDHISM IS SUPERIOR TO DAOISM AND CONFUCIANISM

The following passage, by Jizang (549–623), is an example of the sectarian debates between Buddhists and Daoists in China. Drawn from the Profound Meaning of the Three Treatises, *it compares the teachings of Buddhism to those of Laozi and Zhuangzi.*

Shi Sengzhao (374–414) says, 'Every time I read Laozi and Zhuangzi, it causes me to lament and say: 'It is beautiful, but as for the technique of abiding with the spirit, of quieting the mental ties [that bind us to life and death], they have not yet mastered [them]. . . .'

Kumarajiva long ago heard that the three mysteries, together with the nine teachings of Buddhism, were both definitive. Laozi, together with Shakyamuni [Buddha], were [held to be] comparable in actions. So [Kumarajiva] lamented thus, and lamenting said, 'Lao[zi] and Zhuang[zi] have entered the profound. Therefore, they certainly do lead astray the ears and eyes.' This is the wisdom of the ordinary person. These are reckless words [claiming that Buddhism and Daoism are comparable]. In saying this, it appears to be the ultimate, and still has not yet begun to approach it. . . .

Non-Buddhists are not yet able to consider the ultimate, and still wander among the myriad things. Buddhist teachings, without moving away from absolute truth, teach, still establishing the various phenomena. Non-Buddhists reside in the teachings of gain and loss. Buddhists vanquish the two extremes in the principle of negation. Non-Buddhists have not yet extinguished both the knower and known. Buddhists have extinguished both subject and object.

If we take these [two, Buddhists and non-Buddhists], and further examine them in detail, it is like comparing a small bird's wings to the wings of a *peng* bird, or comparing a well to the ocean. [These metaphors] are not yet sufficient to explain their difference. Kumarajiva doubted the final teachings [of the Daoists]. What more can I say?

Source: Jizang, *Sanlun Xuanyi* (*The Profound Meaning of the Three Treatises*) ch. 1.

THE *PLATFORM SUTRA* OF THE SIXTH PATRIARCH

The Chan (Japanese: Zen) school developed in China. Asserting that the teachings of the school were a "special transmission outside of the scriptures," Zen masters claimed that their tradition represents the authentic teaching of the Buddha, who is said to have passed on the essence of his awakened mind to his disciple Mahakashyapa. He in turn passed it on to his main disciple, and so it continued in India through an unbroken chain of transmission until Bodhidharma, the last Indian "patriarch," traveled to China.

Bodhidharma, a semilegendary figure, is said to have arrived at the Shaolin monastery in China, where he sat in silent meditation in front of a wall for several years. At the end of this period, he began teaching the tradition to Chinese disciples, one of whom became the first Chinese patriarch.

The following passage was spoken by Hui Neng, the sixth patriarch, to a group of disciples. It contains many of the important doctrines of the developed Chan tradition, including the doctrine of "sudden awakening," which holds that buddhas become awakened in a flash of insight, and not gradually, as traditional Indian Buddhism taught. According to Indian Buddhist meditation texts, meditators should enter into concentrated meditative states called samadhi, *and these states lead to the awakening of wisdom (*prajna*). Hui Neng, however, declared that such ideas impose a false dualism onto the path to buddhahood. He contended that both concentration and wisdom are present in every moment of thought and that they cannot legitimately be separated.*

*He also opposed the goal-oriented practices of traditional Mahayana, and said that one becomes awakened by eliminating discursive thought. When all conceptual thoughts drop away and one attains the state of "no-thought" (*wu nian*), the mind flows freely and unimpededly, in harmony with the rhythms of the world. This is the state of mind characteristic of buddhahood, and any notions of "path" and "goal," or "cultivation" and "attainment," are products of dualistic thinking that will impede one's progress toward awakening.*

The Master Hui Neng called, saying: 'Good friends, awakening (*bodhi*) and intuitive wisdom (*prajna*) are from the outset possessed by men of this world themselves. It is just because the mind is deluded that men cannot attain awakening to themselves. They must seek a good teacher to show them how to see into their own natures. Good friends, if you meet awakening, [Buddha]-wisdom will be achieved.

13. 'Good friends, my teaching of the dharma takes meditation (*ding*) and wisdom (*hui*) as its basis. Never under any circumstances say mistakenly that meditation and wisdom are different; they are a unity, not two things. Meditation itself is the substance of wisdom; wisdom itself is the function of meditation. At the very moment when there is wisdom, then meditation exists in wisdom; at the very moment when there is meditation, then wisdom exists in meditation. Good friends, this means that meditation and wisdom are alike. Students, be careful not to say that meditation gives rise to wisdom, or that wisdom gives rise to meditation, or that meditation and wisdom are different from each other. . . .

16. 'Good friends, in the Dharma there is no sudden or gradual, but among people some are keen and others dull. The deluded recommend the gradual method, the awakened practice the sudden teaching. To understand the original mind of yourself is to see into your own original nature. Once awakened, there is from the outset no distinction between these two methods; those who are not awakened will for long *kalpas* [eons] be caught in the cycle of transmigration.

17. 'Good friends, in this teaching of mine, from ancient times up to the present, all have set up no-thought as the main doctrine, non-form as the substance, and non-abiding as the basis. Non-form is to be separated from form even when associated with form. No-thought is not to think even when involved in thought. Non-abiding is the original nature of humanity.

   'Successive thoughts do not stop; prior thoughts, present thoughts, and future thoughts follow one after the other without cessation. If one instant of thought is cut off, the Dharma body separates from the physical body, and in the midst of successive thoughts there will be no place for attachment to anything. If one instant of thought clings, then successive thoughts cling; this is known as being fettered. If in all things successive thoughts do not cling, then you are unfettered. Therefore, non-abiding is made the basis.

Source: Hui Neng, *Platform Sutra* 12–16, tr. Philip Yampolsky, *The Platform Sutra of the Sixth Patriarch* (New York: Columbia University Press, 1967), pp. 135–138.

KUKAI: EXOTERIC AND ESOTERIC BUDDHISM

Kukai (774–835), posthumously known as Kobo Daishi, was one of the most influential thinkers of the Heian period (794–1185). He traveled to China in 804 to study Buddhism, and learned the doctrines and practices of Esoteric Buddhism (Chinese: Zhenyan; Japanese: Shingon) with the Chinese master Hui Guo. This school is a branch of Vajrayana ("Vajra Vehicle"), which is based on the tantras of Indian Buddhism.

Like its counterparts in South Asia, East Asian Esoteric Buddhism emphasizes the importance of visualizations, mantras, and rituals for bringing about a cognitive transformation of one's mind into the mind of a buddha.

In the following passage, Kukai compares the path of Esoteric Buddhism to that of Exoteric Buddhism. He contends that Esoteric Buddhism is far superior to the Exoteric teachings and practices and that it is more effective in bringing about mundane benefits as well as final awakening. Kukai believed that human beings have the capacity to become "awakened in this very body" (sokushin jobutsu) and that the rituals and symbols of Esoteric Buddhism appeal directly to their basic nature of buddha-potential and enable them quickly to attain the state of buddhahood. These practices bring the body, speech, and mind of the meditator into concordance with those of the truth body, and thus allow the primordial buddha Mahavairocana to communicate directly with advanced practitioners.

I have heard that there are two kinds of preaching of the Buddha. One is shallow and incomplete while the other is esoteric. The shallow teaching is comprised of the scriptures with long passages and verses, whereas the esoteric teaching is the *dharani* [esoteric prayers thought to have magical properties] found in the scriptures.

The shallow teaching is, as one text says, like the diagnoses of an illness and the prescription of a medicine. The esoteric method of reciting *dharani* is like prescribing appropriate medicine, ingesting it, and curing the ailment. If a person is ill, opening a medical text and reciting its contents will be of no avail in treating the illness. It is necessary to adapt the medicine to the disease and to ingest it in accordance with proper methods. Only then will the illness be eliminated and life preserved.

However, the present custom of chanting the *Sutra of Golden Light* at the Imperial Palace is simply the reading of sentences and the empty recital of doctrine. There is no drawing of buddha images in accordance with proper technique nor the practice of setting up an altar for offerings and for the ceremonies of empowerment. Although the reading of the *Sutra* may appear to be an opportunity to listen to the preaching of the nectar-like teachings of the Buddha, in actuality it lacks the precious taste of the finest essence of Buddhist truth.

I humbly request that from this year on, fourteen monks skilled in esoteric ritual and fourteen novices be selected who, while properly reading the *Sutra*, will for seven days arrange the sacred images, perform the requisite offerings, and recite *mantra* in a specially adorned room. If this is done, both the exoteric and esoteric teachings, which express the Buddha's true intent, will cause great happiness in the world and thereby fulfill the compassionate vows of the holy ones.

Source: Kukai, *Petition to Supplement the Annual Reading of Sutra in the Imperial Palace;* tr. David Gardiner.

DOGEN'S MEDITATION INSTRUCTIONS

Dogen (1200–1253), founder of the Soto *(Chinese: Zaodong) school of Zen, traveled to China in 1223 and studied with Rujing, a Chinese Chan master. One day during meditation practice, another monk fell asleep, and Rujing woke him up, admonishing him to practice meditation diligently in order to "drop off body and mind" (Japanese: shinjin datsuraku), an idea that became a cornerstone of Dogen's system of medita- tive practice. The following passage contains instructions on meditation practice (zazen), which in Dogen's system is based on the experience of "not thinking" (hishiryo).*

In the state of not thinking, a meditator moves beyond discursive and dichotomiz- ing thought (shiryo), transcends the tendency to stop ordinary thought by suppress- ing it (fushiryo), and thus enters into a spontaneous awareness of reality in which thoughts flow along of their own accord. In this state of spontaneous mindfulness, the meditator experiences his or her own "buddha nature," an inherent propensity toward awakening that is shared by all beings.

> Once you have settled your posture, you should regulate your breath- ing. Whenever a thought occurs, be aware of it; as soon as you are aware of it, it will vanish. If you remain for a long period forgetful of objects, you will naturally become unified. This is the essential art of *zazen*. Zazen is the dharma gate of great ease and joy. . . .

> Having thus regulated body and mind, take a breath and exhale fully. Sitting fixedly, think of not thinking. How do you think of not thinking? Nonthinking. This is the art of *zazen*. Zazen is not the practice of *dhyana* [meditation]. It is the dharma gate of great ease and joy. It is undefiled practice and verification.

Source: Dogen, *Shobogenzo* selections, from *Dogen's Manual of Zen Meditation*, tr. Carl Bielefeldt (Berkeley: University of California Press, 1988), p. 181.

THE MU KOAN

The Rinzai (Chinese: Linji) school of Zen is renowned for its use of koan, *riddles that cannot be answered by rational or discursive modes of thought. The following passage contains the koan that is generally given to beginning students, referred to as the "Mu koan." It reports that a monk asked the Zen master Joshu if a dog has the buddha nature, to which Joshu answered, "Mu!" Mu may be translated as "not," but in the koan Joshu's answer is not a denial, but rather an indication that the question makes no sense from the point of view of awakening.*

The dilemma behind the question is based on traditional Japanese Buddhist ideas about the path. It is widely accepted in Japanese Buddhism that all beings—including dogs—have the buddha nature, an inherent potential for buddhahood. Thus, from the point of view of tradition, Joshu's answer should be "Yes." But since Zen claims to transcend blind adherence to tradition, this would be an unacceptable answer. On the other hand, if Joshu were to state that dogs do not have the buddha nature, he could be accused of contravening Buddhist doctrine and setting himself above the buddhas.

Thus Joshu's answer is an invitation to move beyond tradition and conceptualiza- tion to a direct perception of truth. The Zen tradition refers to this koan as the "closed opening" or the "gateless barrier," because once a meditator perceives the meaning behind Joshu's statement, this marks the first dawning of realization that will eventu- ally culminate in full awakening, referred to in Zen as "satori." It is intended to cause a cognitive crisis as the meditator attempts to solve the riddle by means of conceptual thought, but finds all such attempts utterly frustrated. This leads to the development of the "great doubt" (daigi), which is said to burn inside of one like a red-hot ball of iron. When the koan is solved, however, the pain and frustration disappear, and are replaced by a serene, nonconceptual awareness.

A monk once asked Master Joshu, 'Has a dog the Buddha Nature or not?' Joshu said, 'Mu!'

Mumon's commentary: In studying Zen, one must pass the barriers set up by ancient Zen Masters. For the attainment of incomparable satori, one has to cast away his discriminating mind. Those who have not passed the barrier and have not cast away the discriminating mind are all phantoms haunting trees and plants.

Now Tell me, what is the barrier of the Zen Masters? Just this 'Mu'—it is the barrier of Zen. It is thus called 'the gateless barrier of Zen.' Those who have passed the barrier will not only see Joshu clearly, but will go hand in hand with all the Masters of the past, see them face to face. . . . Wouldn't it be wonderful? Don't you want to pass the barrier? Then concentrate yourself into this 'Mu,' with your 360 bones and 84,000 pores, making your whole body one great inquiry. Day and night work intently at it. Do not attempt nihilistic or dualistic interpretations. It is like having swallowed a red hot iron ball. You try to vomit it but cannot. . . .

You kill the Buddha if you meet him; you kill the ancient Masters if you meet them. On the brink of life and death you are utterly free, and in the six realms and the four modes of life you live, with great joy, a genuine life in complete freedom.

Source: From *Zen Comments on the Mumonkan,* tr. Zenkei Shibayama (New York: Mentor, 1974), pp. 19–20.

PURE LAND: SHINRAN ON AMIDA'S VOW

The Pure Land (Chinese: Jingdu; Japanese: Jodo) tradition focuses on a buddha named Amitabha ("Limitless Light") or Amitayus ("Limitless Life"), who as a merchant named Dharmakara is said to have made a series of vows concerning the sort of "buddha-land" he would create after his attainment of buddhahood. In the Sutra on the Array of the Joyous Land (Sukhavativyuha-sutra), *Dharmakara indicates that his land will be especially wonderful, a place in which the conditions for buddhahood are optimal. Beings fortunate enough to be born into this land will receive teachings from buddhas and bodhisattvas, and they will quickly progress toward awakening.*

Amitabha also teaches that beings may be reborn in his land if they have sincere faith in him. The Japanese Pure Land teacher Shinran (1173–1262) stated that anyone may be reborn in Amitabha's paradise, regardless of past actions. Previous teachers had contended that birth in Sukhavati required good moral character and constant repetition of the formula, "Praise to Amida Buddha" (Namu Amida Butsu), but Shinran declared that all that is necessary is one moment of sincere belief (shinjin, literally "believing mind"). Shinran makes a distinction between "self-power," which characterizes the practices of early Buddhism, and "other-power," in which one relies completely on the saving power of Amitabha. Shinran contends that the former practice was appropriate in the Buddha's day, but that the present age is one of degeneration, and human beings have become so depraved that their only hope is to rely on Amitabha. The Tannisho *was written by a direct disciple of Shinran, probably Yuien (d. 1290) in the decades after Shinran's death, and it remains a respected record of Shinran's teachings.*

When our hearts are moved to invoke the name of Amida, believing that we can achieve rebirth in His Pure Land through the workings of the wondrous power of His vow—at that very moment we are saved by Amitabha Buddha, and we become recipients of the benefits that He bestows without exception upon all living beings. Amida's primal vow [to save all living beings by enabling them to be reborn in his Pure Land] does not discriminate between young and old, or between doers of good or evil. All that is necessary is for us to put our faith in His vow. This is because Amida's vow was made with the intention to save all living beings, caught up as they are in their evil deeds and worldly desires. For this reason, putting our faith in Amida's primal vow does not require us to perform any other good deeds, because there can be no greater merit than that which is attained by calling on Amida's name. Neither should we fear doing evil: there is no act so evil as to be able to obstruct the workings of Amida's vow. . . .

Even a good person can be reborn in the Pure Land. How much easier it is for an evil person to achieve this! Contrary to this fact, lay people generally say: "Even an evil person can achieve rebirth in the Pure Land. It goes without saying that it is much easier for a good person." While at first glance there may seem to be some reason for this view, it goes against the purpose of Amida's vow, which is based on the saving power of reliance on the Other. Why is this? Those who practice good deeds, relying on their own power, are not of a mind to wholeheartedly avail themselves of the Other Power of Amida, and are therefore not acting in accord with His vow. If, however, they let go of their reliance on their own power, and place their trust in the Other Power of Amida, they will be able to achieve rebirth in the Pure Land.

Source: Shinran, *Tannisho* selections, from *Tannisho: A Primer,* tr. *Dennis Hirota* (Kyoto, Ryukoku University, 1982), pp. 22–24.

TRUTH DECAY: NICHIREN ON THE TITLE OF THE *LOTUS SUTRA*

Nichiren (1222–1282) was one of the most charismatic figures of Japanese Buddhism. Initially trained in the Tendai school, he became disenchanted with its doctrines and practices, considering them to be inappropriate to the current age, which he believed to be the "age of degenerate dharma" (Japanese: mappo*) that the Buddha had predicted* *would begin 1,500 years after his death. Many Japanese Buddhists of the Kamakura period (1185–1333) believed that the turmoils of the time indicated that the final age of dharma had arrived, and a number of teachers believed that in such a time new models and practices were required.*

Since in the final age people become progressively more degenerate, Nichiren contended that the practices of the past—including intensive meditation practice and adherence to monastic vows—were no longer possible for most people, and thus simpler and more effective practices, appropriate to mappo, were required. Nichiren focused on the Lotus Sutra (Saddharma-pundarika-sutra) *as the only viable teaching for mappo, and he counseled his followers to place all of their faith in it. Its teachings, however, were deemed too profound for most people to understand, and so Nichiren developed the practice of chanting the title of the sutra (*Namu Myohorengekyo *in Japanese) and trusting to the saving power of the sutra to bring worldly benefits and final salvation.*

Question: If someone did not know the real meaning of the *Lotus Sutra* and did not understand its import, but merely recited the words 'Namu Myohorengekyo' once a day or once a month or once a year or once in ten years or once in a lifetime, without being tempted by evil deeds, great or small, would that person not only avoid the four evil realms but also achieve that stage from which there is no return?

Answer: He would. . . .

The words 'Myohorengekyo' . . . include all the beings of the nine worlds and of the Buddha world. Since they include the ten worlds, they include all the conditions one may be born into in the ten worlds. If the words 'Myohorengekyo' include all dharmas, one word of the scripture is lord of all scriptures. It embodies all scriptures.

Source: Nichiren, *Hokke Damokushü* selections, from *Hokke Damokushü,* tr. Lauren Rodel, in *Nichiren: Selected Writings* (Honolulu: University of Hawaii Press, 1980), pp. 82, 85.

GLOSSARY

Anatman   "Selflessness," the doctrine that there is no permanent, partless, substantial essence or soul.

Arhat   The ideal of "Hinayana" Buddhism, who strives to attain a personal nirvana.

Avidya   "Ignorance," the primary factor that enmeshes living beings in the cycle of birth, death, and rebirth.

Bodhisattva   A compassionate being who resolves to bring other beings to liberation.

Buddha   "Awakened One," epithet of those who successfully break the hold of ignorance, liberate themselves from cyclic existence, and teach others the path to liberation.

Chan/Zen   A school that developed in East Asia, which emphasized meditation aimed at a non-conceptual, direct understanding of reality.

Completion Stage   *(nishpanna-krama)* Tantric practice in which one visualizes oneself as being transformed into a buddha.

Deity Yoga *(devata-yoga)* The tantric practice of visualizing oneself as a buddha.

Dependent Arising *(pratitya-samutpada)* Doctrine that phenomena arise and pass away in dependence upon causes and conditions.

Dharma Buddhist doctrine and practice.

Duhkha "Suffering," the first "noble truth" of Buddhism, which holds that cyclic existence is characterized by suffering.

Eightfold Noble Path Fourth of the "four noble truths," which involves cultivation of correct views, actions, and meditative practices in order to bring an end to suffering.

Five Aggregates The components of the psycho-physical personality, and the factors on the basis of which unawakened beings impute the false notion of a "self": (1) form; (2) feelings; (3) discriminations; (4) consciousness; (5) compositional factors.

Four Noble Truths Basic propositions attributed to the Buddha: (1) suffering; (2) the cause of suffering; (3) the cessation of suffering; (4) the eightfold noble path.

Generation Stage *(utpanna-krama)* Tantric practice of visualizing a vivid image of a buddha in front of oneself.

Hinayana "Lesser Vehicle," a term coined by Mahayanists to describe their opponents, whose path they characterized as selfish and inferior to their own.

Karma "Actions," which bring about concordant results.

Keyi "Matching Concepts," a translation style adopted for early Chinese versions of Buddhist texts, which involved using indigenous Chinese terms for Sanskrit words.

Madhyamaka "Middle Way School," one of the most influential systems of Indian Buddhism.

Mahayana "Greater Vehicle," the school of Buddhism that emphasizes the ideal of the bodhisattva.

Nirvana Liberation from cyclic existence.

Pure Land A school of Buddhism popular in East Asia whose adherents strive for rebirth in the realm of the Buddha Amitabha.

Samsara "Cyclic Existence," the beginningless cycle of birth, death, and rebirth in which ignorant beings are trapped.

Shakyamuni "Sage of the Shakyas," an epithet of the historical Buddha, whose name at birth was Siddhartha Gautama.

Shunyata "Emptiness," the lack of inherent existence that characterizes all persons and phenomena.

Skill in Means *(upaya-kaushalya)* The ability to adapt Buddhist teachings and practices to the level of understanding of one's audience.

Sutra Discourses attributed to the historical Buddha.

Tantra Discourses attributed to the historical Buddha, which appeared sometime around the seventh century and that advocate practices involving visualizing oneself as a buddha.

Yogacara "Yogic Practice School," a system of Indian Buddhism whose main early exponents were the brothers Asanga and Vasubandhu

Zen See **Chan**

FURTHER READINGS

BECHERT, HEINZ AND GOMBRICH, RICHARD. *The World of Buddhism.* New York: Thames and Hudson, 1984.

BIELFELDT, CARL, tr. *Dogen's Manuals of Zen Meditation.* Berkeley: University of California Press, 1988.

CH'EN, KENNETH. *Buddhism in China: A Historical Survey.* Princeton: Princeton University Press, 1984.

COLLINS, STEVEN. *Selfless Persons: Imagery and Thought in Theravāda Buddhism.* Cambridge: Cambridge University Press, 1982.

DUMOULIN, HEINRICH. *Zen Buddhism: A History,* 2 vols. New York: Macmillan, 1988.

GOMBRICH, RICHARD. *Theravāda Buddhism: A Social History from Ancient Benares to Modern Columbo.* London: Routledge & Kegan Paul, 1988.

GREGORY, PETER N., ed. *Sudden and Gradual: Approaches to Enlightenment in Chinese Thought.* Honolulu: University of Hawaii Press, 1987.

GRIFFITHS, PAUL J. *On Being Mindless: Buddhist Meditation and the Mind-Body Problem.* La Salle, IL: Open Court, 1986.

HUNTINGTON, C.W. *The Emptiness of Emptiness: An Introduction to Early Indian Mādhyamika.* Honolulu: University of Hawaii Press, 1989.

KIYOTA, MINORU, ed. *Mahāyāna Buddhist Meditation.* Honolulu: University of Hawaii Press, 1978.

LAMOTTE, ÉTIENNE. *History of Indian Buddhism.* Sara Webb-Boin, tr. Louvain: Peeters Press, 1988.

MATSUNAGA, DAIGAN AND ALICIA. *Foundation of Japanese Buddhism,* 2 vols. Los Angeles: Buddhist Books International, 1974.

MURCOTT, SUSAN. *The First Buddhist Women: Translations and Commentary on the Therigatha.* Berkeley: Parallax Press, 1991.

NAKAMURA, HAJIME. *Indian Buddhism: A Survey with Bibliographical Notes.* Delhi: Motilal Banarsidass, 1987.

PAUL, DIANA. *Women in Buddhism: Images of the Feminine in Mahāyāna Tradition.* Berkeley: Asian Humanities Press, 1979.

POWERS, JOHN. *Introduction to Tibetan Buddhism.* Ithaca: Snow Lion, 1995.

PREBISH, CHARLES S., ed. *Buddhism: A Modern Perspective.* University Park: The Pennsylvania State University Press, 1975.

RAHULA, WALPOLA. *What the Buddha Taught.* New York: Grove Press, 1959.

ROBINSON, RICHARD. *The Buddhist Religion.* Encino, CA: Dickenson Publishing, 1977.

RUEGG, DAVID S. *The Literature of the Madhyamaka School of Philosophy in India.* Wiesbaden: Otto Harrassowitz, 1981.

SNELLING, JOHN. *The Buddhist Handbook: A Complete Guide to Buddhist Schools, Teaching, Practice, and History.* Rochester, VT: Inner Traditions, 1991.

WILLIAMS, PAUL. *Mahāyāna Buddhism: The Doctrinal Foundations.* London and New York: Routledge, 1989.

WRIGHT, ARTHUR F. *Buddhism in Chinese History.* Stanford: Stanford University Press, 1959.

Sikhism

INTRODUCTION

Early one morning in 1499 Nanak (1469–1539), the founder of the Sikh tradition, went to a river to perform his daily religious ablutions. When he failed to return, search parties were sent out, but all they found were his clothes on the bank of the river. Assuming that the current had carried Nanak away, they returned to town and reported the news. Several days later, however, Nanak reappeared, and after refusing to speak for three days he told his friends and family that he had been taken to the presence of God and given a mission: to teach Hindus and Muslims that both groups in fact worship the same God. God, he said, was distressed by the sectarian violence perpetrated in His name in India and wanted Nanak to call his followers from rigid adherence to dogmas and the performance of empty rituals to the true essence of religion, which is known only by those who move beyond external observances like ceremonies, prayers, pilgrimages, and study to the rich inner life of true spirituality. This is characterized by selfless devotion (*bhakti*) to God.

Nanak summarized God's message with the statement, "There is neither Hindu nor Muslim, so whose path should I follow? I will follow God's path, and God is neither Hindu nor Muslim." These words were the cornerstone of his later speeches and writings, in which he stressed the unity of God and the idea that the differences in how religions characterize Him are merely due to human failure to grasp the divine essence. Nanak further contended that there is no reason for religious groups to fight each other, since any system is necessarily limited, and all theological ideas are inadequate.

After his meeting with God, Sikh texts refer to Nanak as "Guru," a teacher and devotee of God. Throughout his life he worked to reconcile Hindus and Muslims, to teach them that God is everywhere and continually calls His creatures to experience Him directly and intuitively. This cannot be accomplished by those who rely on external religious observances, and God is found only by practitioners of pure devotion who open themselves to the divine call and experience mystical union.

Nanak taught that devotion is the highest form of religious practice, but also the most difficult. The ego is a powerful force in human beings, and it causes us to recoil from the experience of union, in which all sense of individuality is swept away by a transcendent vision of the divine presence.

Nanak belonged to a widespread but unorganized group of mystics known as Sants, whose members stressed the unity of God and criticized both

Hindus and Muslims for being overly concerned with the external aspects of their traditions, while failing to recognize that all theistic religions worship the same ultimate source of all being. The greatest early exponent of this tradition was Kabir, a weaver from Varanasi. He was born into a Muslim family that converted from Hinduism, but his writings indicate that he saw himself as having transcended any sectarian affiliation.

In his poetry he accuses both Muslim and Hindu religious leaders of hypocrisy and of failing to grasp the true essence of religion. Hindu *pandits* (religious scholars) are portrayed as being mainly concerned with profit and position, with empty ceremonies and merely external observances. Muslim clerics, he contends, tend to be caught up in systems and words and so do not understand that God is one and that all religious traditions have their source in the same ultimate reality. This reality is beyond the reach of human thought; it cannot be grasped by words or doctrines, and is only truly understood by those who abandon external religious observances and devote themselves wholeheartedly to meditation and worship.

The poetry of Nanak stresses similar themes. He denounces idol worship and indicates that such practices as pilgrimages, ritual bathing, and ceremonies tend to keep the individual far from God. Nanak, like Kabir, views God as having two aspects: God is both immanent (*saguna*, literally, "having qualities") and transcendent (*nirguna*, "without qualities"). In essence God is completely transcendent, and any qualities imputed to God are merely human attempts to grasp the ultimate reality in terms that we are able to understand. God in essence is completely other, unknowable, and ineffable, but may still be experienced by those who empty themselves of ego and open themselves to the divine presence.

Nanak died in 1539 after founding and guiding a small group of followers he referred to as "Sikhs," or students. His students were both Hindus and Muslims, who saw Nanak as a great religious leader whose mystical experiences transcended their sectarian divisions. According to Sikh legends, he continually worked to help them to overcome their limitations of religious vision.

Nanak's final teaching was given on his deathbed. When it became clear that death was near, a dispute arose between Hindu and Muslim Sikhs. The former group wanted to cremate him in accordance with their traditions, while the latter argued for burying his body. Nanak settled the dispute by telling them that each group should place a garland of flowers on one side of his body, and that the group whose garland remained unwilted after three days would be able to dispose of his corpse in accordance with its traditions. The next morning the shroud was removed, but his body was gone. All that remained were two garlands of unwilted flowers. Thus even in death Nanak taught his followers the importance of overcoming sectarian differences.

Before Nanak died, he designated his disciple Guru Angad (1504–1552) as his successor. According to Sikh tradition, this event marks the inauguration of the Sikh path (*panth*). The office of Guru was in turn passed on to Amar Das (1479–1574), and then to Guru Ram Das (1534–1581). The fifth Guru, Arjan (1563–1606), worked to mold the Sikhs into a cohesive religious, social, and economic community. He initiated construction of the Golden Temple at Amritsar, which is today the holiest shrine of the Sikhs, and he directed the compilation of the *Adi Granth,* the holiest scripture of the tradition. This text contains writings by Nanak and the other early Gurus, as well as works by Kabir and other devotional poets. Today the *Adi Granth* is the center of the religious life of the community. Ornate copies of the text are placed on special pedestals in the center of each Sikh temple (*gurdvar,* literally, "door to the Guru"), and portions of it are chanted almost constantly while the temple is open.

Arjan's tenure marks a change of direction for the Sikh community. During the reigns of the first four Gurus the Panth had enjoyed generally amicable relations with the Muslim Mughal rulers who controlled northern India, but with the ascension of the emperor Jehangir the situation changed. Hearkening back to the militancy of the early Muslim conquerors, Jehangir actively persecuted other religious groups, including the Sikhs. He had Arjan captured, and tortured him with the intention of forcing the Guru to renounce his faith. Arjan refused to submit to the emperor's demands, and he eventually died in prison. Shortly before his death, he advised his son Hargobind (1595–1664) to "sit fully armed upon the throne," since Arjan recognized the threat the new Mughal ruler posed for his community.

Guru Hargobind followed the wishes of his father, Guru Arjan, and began wearing two swords at all times, one symbolizing his religious authority, and the other his temporal authority. His tenure marks the beginning of the transition of the Panth from a group of devotional mystics concerned with reconciling the differences between Hindus and Muslims into a tradition stressing the importance of combat readiness and willingness to fight—and die if necessary—in order to defend the faith.

The seventh Guru, Hari Rai (1630–1661) ruled during a time of increasing tensions between the Sikhs and the Mughal emperor. The eighth, Hari Krishan (1656–1664), died as a child, and was succeeded by Tegh Bahadur (1621–1675), who became another Sikh martyr as a result of his opposition to the emperor's imposition of a tax on all non-Muslims in his empire. Intending to make an example of the Guru, the emperor had him imprisoned and tortured. He was ordered to renounce his faith and his opposition to the tax. When he refused, Tegh Bahadur was executed.

His son Gobind Singh (1666–1708) became the tenth and last Guru. Realizing that the position made its holder a target, as the Guru lay dying from wounds inflicted by a Muslim assassin he declared that henceforth the *Adi Granth* would be the Guru. He told the community to view the text as the condensation of the inspired words of the Gurus, the mouthpieces of God, which should guide them in their religious lives.

Gobind Singh's other major contribution to the development of Sikhism was his institution of the Khalsa, the community of Sikh believers. He recognized that survival of the faith required that Sikhs become fully committed to preparing themselves to defend the community against attacks by its enemies, and in a special ceremony he called on the faithful to step forward if they were truly prepared to die for their religion. Five stepped forward, and they became the first members of the new community. The Guru then instructed his followers to adopt five distinctive marks symbolic of their new commitment, which are referred to as the "Five Ks" because their names in the Punjabi language all begin with the letter K. These are (1) *kesh,* hair, which refers to the Sikh practice of not cutting the hair; (2) *kangha,* a comb used to keep the hair neat; (3) *kirpan,* a short sword, symbolizing the warrior ethos of the Khalsa; (4) *kara,* a steel wristband; and (5) *kachch,* short pants. Many male members of the community also began wearing turbans as a way of managing their hair, and most males also changed their family name to Singh, meaning lion, as a symbol of their devotion to the Guru. Women changed their names to Kaur, meaning princess, and all Sikhs were declared by the Guru to be members of the warrior caste (*kshatriya*), symbolizing both their emphasis on combat readiness and the equality of all believers.

Nanak had established the Panth as a community dedicated to reconciling Hindus and Muslims, but Gobind Singh realized that peaceful relations with the Mughal emperor were no longer possible. In order to maintain its survival, the community would have to defend itself against attacks, and it would have to develop into a cohesive and well-trained military force in order to protect itself from its neighbors. It is ironic that Sikhism began as a movement dedicated to reconciling different faiths but was pushed by historical circumstances to become a tradition that stressed the differences of its members from other religious groups and that was determined to defend itself from hostile opponents.

Sikh Doctrines and Practices

Sikh theology contends that God is one without a second, the transcendent ultimate that cannot be grasped by human intelligence or described by language. God is commonly referred to by such negative terms as Timeless (*akal*) and Unproduced (*ajuni*), but is also described positively as Truth or Being (*sat*). God is both utterly transcendent and accessible to His creatures through grace. God chooses some beings to draw near to Him through devotion, and He speaks to all beings through the words of the Gurus.

Sikhs commonly refer to God as *Akal Purakh,* "Timeless Being." He creates and sustains the universe, and is known only by those who approach Him with devotion. God reveals Himself through the Divine Name (*nam*), which expresses aspects of the divine Reality as understood by the limited intellects of His creatures. All of creation reflects the glory and activity of God, and so in this sense everything is an expression of the Name. People are able to approach God through meditation on the Name, through which they may transcend ordinary understanding and approach the Divine Presence. The Name is said in Sikh texts to be "the total expression of all that God is," and those who open themselves to the Name through selfless devotion may come to know God in a way that transcends ordinary knowing.

One of the most important of Sikh meditative practices is "remembering the Name" (*nam simaran*), in which the devotee contemplates various epithets of God, along with the adumbrations of the divine essence that are found throughout creation. In this practice, the meditator generally repeats a particular word or *mantra,* or chants the songs of the Gurus, in order to bring about intuitive understanding of God.

Sikhism teaches that there is only one God, although He is known in various guises by different religions. In essence, however, God transcends all creeds and systems. Sikhism rejects the idea that God takes physical incarnations (*avatara*). God is utterly transcendent and cannot be contained within the limited form of a created being. Like Hinduism, however, Sikhism contends that living creatures are reborn in a beginningless cycle (*samsara*) and that each being's situation is a result of past actions (*karma*). The ultimate goal of Sikhism is liberation (*moksha*) from cyclic existence, but this can be attained only through God's grace, and not by personal effort.

The primary factor preventing the attainment of liberation is self-reliance (*haumai*), which causes beings falsely to imagine that they are independent and autonomous, that their fates are within their own control, and that salvation may be attained through actions. In order to combat self-reliance, one must cultivate proper attitude (*hukam*), which involves recognizing one's utter dependence upon God. Humble and devoted repetition of the Name helps one to develop humility and to recognize the transcendent glory of God.

God is within everyone, and so rituals are unnecessary, according to Sikhism, nor is there any point in making pilgrimages, since God is everywhere. One may worship God anywhere and at any time, and Sikhism urges its followers to strive toward realization of the Divine Presence all around them. Sikhism contends that ignorance (*avidya*) is the primary factor preventing one from knowing God, and that ignorance is eliminated only by those who humbly submit themselves to the divine will and listen to God's message as revealed by the words of the Gurus and other inspired devotional mystics.

Since God is the ultimate source of everything, all is really God, although ignorant beings fail to realize this fact. God's presence is hidden from us by the power of illusion (*maya*), a process of projection that causes beings mistakenly to imagine that they have an existence apart from Him. In reality, however, everything is a part of Him, and nothing can exist apart from Him. When one wakes up to the reality behind this illusion (which can occur only through God's grace), one realizes the unity of God and gradually comes to perceive God in everything. Sikhism's formulation of the doctrine of *maya* differs from that of Advaita Vedanta in that in Sikh philosophy *maya* is not an objective reality projected by God, but a subjective error resulting from a wrong point of view, a belief in duality rather than unity. This causes the mirage of the world to be seen as an end in itself. It is eliminated by devotion and meditation on the divine Name. One who is wholeheartedly immersed in this practice may through the grace of God escape the cycle of birth and death and attain final liberation, which Sikhism contends is an eternally blissful state of union with the Ultimate.

Sikh Scriptures

The first attempt to create a collection of authoritative Sikh texts was made during the tenure of the third Guru, Amar Das (1552–1574), who supervised a compilation of works by his predecessors. The fifth Guru, Arjan, began the collection of texts that became the *Adi Granth,* the most revered scripture of the tradition. Sikhs consider it to be the Guru, since it contains the collected wisdom of the early Gurus and their Sant predecessors.

There are three known recensions of the *Adi Granth:* (1) one believed to be the original text written by Bhai Gurdas and owned by a Sikh family in Kartarpur; (2) the "Damdama Recension," which was compiled during the 17th century and which includes works by Guru Tegh Bahadur; and (3) the "Banno Recension," which is widely regarded by Sikhs as noncanonical. The Damdama Recension is the standard text for all copies of the *Adi Granth* published in modern times. Modern published texts of the *Adi Granth* follow this version, even to the extent of adopting its pagination. Thus, all copies of the *Adi Granth* have 1,430 pages, and every individual page mirrors the contents of the original Damdama text.

The *Adi Granth* is divided into three main portions: (1) Introductory Material (pp. 1–13); (2) Ragas (pp. 14–1353); and (3) Miscellaneous Works (pp. 1353–1430). The introductory section begins with the *Mul Mantra,* the basic statement of Sikh faith. The next portions are the works of the *Japji* of Guru Nanak, which is regarded as containing his quintessential teachings. The introductory material ends with works by Guru Angad, Nanak's immediate successor. The second portion of the introductory section is referred to as the *Sodar,* so named because the first word of the first hymn is *sodar.* This section contains four poems by Guru Nanak, three by Guru Ram Das, and two by Guru Arjan. The third section of the introduction is named *Sohila* or *Kirtan Sohila.* It contains three works by Guru Nanak, one by Guru Ram Das, and one by Guru Arjan.

The term *Raga* refers to various metres used in the works of the second section of the *Adi Granth.* This is the largest portion of the text, and is divided into 31 sections, each of which contains hymns of a particular type. Within each *Raga,* works are arranged according to length and content. Hymns in four stanzas are placed at the beginning, followed by hymns in eight stanzas. The last part of the *Ragas* contains poems by predecessors of Sikhism whose religious visions are considered to be consonant with that of Guru Nanak and his successors. Works by Kabir and the devotional poets Namdev and Ravidas are found in this section.

The section containing Miscellaneous Works has more writings by Kabir, and some compositions by the Sufi teacher Sheikh Farid. The final portion of the *Adi Granth* consists of 57 verses by Guru Tegh Bahadur, two works by Guru Arjan, and the *Rag-mala,* which summarizes the contents of the *Ragas.*

The language of the *Adi Granth* is referred to as "*Sant Bhasa,*" the language of the Sants. Linguistically similar to modern Punjabi, it was the language adopted by the devotional Sant poets of the 15th and 16th centuries in northern India. The words of the *Adi Granth* are recorded in the Gurmukhi script, which is also used for modern Punjabi.

Another important scriptural source for Sikhism is the *Dasam Granth*, the compilation of which is associated with the tenth Guru, Gobind Singh. Like the *Adi Granth*, it is referred to as "Guru," and is widely regarded as an authoritative text, but it is far less important for the tradition than the *Adi Granth*. It contains a range of literature, including extensive portions of stories from Hindu literature, many of which are written in different dialects.

The compositions of the mystic poets Bhai Gurdas and Bhai Nand Lal are also highly regarded by Sikhs and have the status of scriptures. The former writer lived during the tenure of the third through sixth Gurus, and the latter was a follower of Guru Gobind Singh. Along with the *Adi Granth* and the *Dasam Granth*, their writings are the only works approved for recitation in Sikh temples.

Mention should also be made of the *janam-sakhis*, which are hagiographical stories of Guru Nanak's life; they stress the themes of the unity of God, the pointlessness of sectarianism, and the worthlessness of external religious observances. They were probably composed during the 16th century, and although they have not been granted the status of scriptures, these stories are widely popular.

SIKH SCRIPTURES

NANAK, THE FIRST GURU

According to the Sikh tradition, Guru Nanak was born in the northern Punjab in an area that today is part of Pakistan. In this region Muslims and Hindus frequently came into conflict, which deeply troubled Nanak. As a member of the Sant tradition, he believed that both groups worship the same God, and so they should not fight. Even as a child Nanak was drawn to religious contemplation, and as he grew up his interest in the divine Reality became so intense that he cared little for mundane things.

One day he went to a nearby river to perform his ritual ablutions, but he disappeared. A search was conducted, but all that was found of Nanak were his clothes. After three days he reappeared, but he refused to discuss where he had been. After three days he told his friends and relatives that he had been taken to the presence of God and given a special mission. God had informed him that Hindus and Muslims both worship Him and that He wished that they join together in faith and not fight against each other. Guru Nanak was to be the prophet of the message of reconciliation, and he spent the remainder of his life working to bring the two groups together.

Baba Nanak was born in Talvandi, the son of Kalu, who was a Bedi Khatri by caste. In this Age of Darkness he proclaimed the divine Name and founded his community of followers, the Panth. Baba Nanak was born in the year S. 1526 on the third day of the month of Vaisakh [April 15, 1469 A.C.]. . . . Celestial music resounded in heaven. A mighty host of gods hailed his birth, and with them all manner of spirit and divinity. 'God has come to save the world!' they cried. . . .

As he grew older he began to play with other children, but his attitude differed from theirs in that he paid heed to the spiritual things of God. When he turned five he began to give utterance to deep and mysterious thoughts. Whatever he uttered was spoken with profound understanding, with the result that everyone's doubts and questions were resolved. The Hindus vowed that a god had taken birth in human form. The Muslims declared that a follower of divine truth had been born. . . .

After returning home in the evening Baba Nanak would devote his nights to singing hymns, and when it came to the last watch of the night he would go to the river and bathe. One morning, having gone to bathe, he entered the waters of the Vein stream but failed to emerge. His servant looked for him until mid-morning and then taking his clothes returned home to tell Jai Ram what had happened. . . . [A] thorough search was made, but to no avail.

Eventually, however, Baba Nanak did return. After three days and three nights had passed he emerged from the stream, and having done so he declared: 'There is neither Hindu nor Muslim. . . .'

Source: *Janam-Sakhi* selections, tr. W. H. McLeod, *Textual Sources for the Study of Sikhism* (Chicago: University of Chicago Press, 1984), pp. 18–21.

GURU NANAK'S DEATH

Although Hindus and Muslims became Nanak's followers, members of each group often retained strong ties to their original religion, despite Nanak's efforts to wean them of sectarianism. As he was preparing to die, members of each group proposed to dispose of his physical remains in accordance with their respective burial customs. Nanak's final lesson to his followers gently chided them for this behavior.

Guru Baba Nanak then went and sat under a withered acacia which immediately produced leaves and flowers, becoming verdant again. . . . Baba Nanak's wife began to weep and the various members of his family joined her in her grief. . . . The assembled congregation sang hymns of praise and Baba Nanak passed into an ecstatic trance. While thus transported, and in obedience to the divine will, he sang the hymn entitled *The Twelve Months.* It was early morning and the time had come for his final departure. . . . 'Even the Guru's dogs lack nothing, my sons,' he said. 'You shall be abundantly supplied with food and clothing, and if you repeat the Guru's name you will be liberated from the bondage of human life.'

Hindus and Muslims who had put their faith in the divine Name began to debate what should be done with the Guru's corpse. 'We shall bury him,' said the Muslims. 'No, let us cremate his body,' said the Hindus. 'Place flowers on both sides of my body,' said Baba Nanak, 'flowers from the Hindus on the right side and flowers from the Muslims on the left. If tomorrow the Hindus' flowers are still fresh let my body be burned, and if the Muslims' flowers are still fresh let it be buried.'

Baba Nanak then commanded the congregation to sing. . . . Baba Nanak then covered himself with a sheet and passed away. Those who had gathered around him prostrated themselves, and when the sheet was removed they found that there was nothing under it. The flowers on both sides remained fresh, and both Hindus and Muslims took their respective shares. All who were gathered there prostrated themselves again.

Source: *Puratan Janam-Sakhi*, pp. 111–115: from *Textual Sources for the Study of Sikhism*, p. 25.

THE *MUL MANTRA*: THE BASIC STATEMENT

Guru Arjan placed the Mul Mantra, *the basic Sikh statement of faith, at the beginning of the holiest book of the Sikhs, the* Adi Granth. *It expresses the primary attributes of the Sikh conception of God, His absolute unity and absolute transcendence.*

There is one God, Eternal Truth is His Name.

Maker of all things, fearing nothing and at enmity with nothing, timeless is His image.

Not begotten, being of His own Being: by the grace of the Guru, made known to humanity.

Source: *Adi Granth* 1.1.

JAP: THE MEDITATION

As He was in the beginning: The truth, so throughout the ages, He ever has been the truth, so even now He is truth immanent, so forever and ever He shall be truth eternal.

Source: *Adi Granth* 1.1–2: from *Selections from the Sacred Writings of the Sikhs*, tr. Dr. Trilochan Singh et al. (London, George Allen & Unwin, 1960), p. 28.

THE DIVINE NAME

The divine Name (nam) is an important motif in the Adi Granth. *The nature of God is intimated through the various epithets used to call and describe Him, and although none of these is able adequately to convey God's essence, each provides some insight into what God is.*

If in this life I should live to eternity, nourished by nothing save air; if I should dwell in the darkest of dungeons, sense never resting in sleep; yet must your glory transcend all my striving; no words can encompass the Name.

He who is truly the Spirit Eternal, immanent, blissful, serene; only by grace can we learn of God's goodness, only by grace can we tell.

If I were slain and my body dismembered, pressed in a hand-mill and ground;
if I were burnt in a fire all-consuming, mingled with ashes and dust; yet must
your glory transcend all my striving; no words can encompass the Name.
If as a bird I could soar to the heavens, a hundred such realms in my reach; if I
could change so that none might perceive me and live without food, without
drink; yet must your glory transcend all my striving; no words can encompass
the Name.

Listening to the Name bestows truth, divine wisdom, contentment.
To bathe in the joy of the Name is to bathe in the holy places.
By hearing the Name and reading it one attains to honor;
By listening, the mind may reach the highest blissful poise of meditation on God.
Nanak says, the saints are always happy;
By listening to the Name sorrow and sin are destroyed.

Source: *Adi Granth*, "Siri Raga" selections, from *Textual Sources for the Study of Sikhism*, p. 40, and *Selections from the Sacred Writings of the Sikhs*, p. 34.

MEDITATION ON THE NAME

In this passage Nanak indicates that the writings of Hindus and Muslims fail to capture the true essence of God. All the scholars of these traditions are grasping futilely for what cannot be grasped.

Pilgrimages, penances, compassion and almsgiving bring a little merit, the
size of a sesame seed.
But one who hears and believes and loves the Name will bathe and be made
clean in a place of pilgrimage within.
All goodness is Yours, O Lord, I have none;
Though without performing good deeds none can aspire to adore You.
Blessed are You, the Creator and the Manifestation, You are the word, You are
the primal Truth and Beauty, and You are the heart's joy and desire.
When in time, in what age, in what day of the month or week, in what season
and in what month did you create the world?
The pundits do not know or they would have written it in the *Puranas;*
The Qazis do not know, or they would have recorded it in the *Qur'an;*
Nor do the yogis know the moment of the day;
Nor the day of the month or the week, nor the month nor the season.
Only God who made the world knows when He made it.
Then how will I approach You Lord?
In what words will I praise You?
In what words will I speak of You?
How will I know You?
Nanak, all humanity speaks of Him, and each would be wiser than the next one;
Great is the Lord, great is His Name,
What He ordains comes to pass,
Nanak, a person puffed up with his own wisdom
Will get no honor from God in the life to come.

Source: *Adi Granth*, "Siri Raga" 1: from *Selections from the Sacred Writings of the Sikhs*, pp. 39–40.

NUDITY DOES NOT MAKE ONE A SAINT

In this poem Kabir stresses the need for true devotion to God, referred to here as Ram (an incarnation of Vishnu). Kabir indicates that asceticism is useless, since one only reaches liberation through ecstatic love of God, in which all sense of self is eliminated and one is consumed by pure love.

> Whether you are naked or clothed, what does it matter
> If you have not recognized the inward Ram (*atmaram*)?
> If one could achieve yoga by wandering naked,
> Then would not deer in the forest achieve liberation?
> If by shaving one's head one could have spiritual mastery (*siddhi*)
> Then would sheep also not go to heaven?
> My brother, if by holding back your seed you could be saved,
> Then surely eunuchs would attain the highest place in heaven.
> Kabir says: Listen brother, without the name of Ram
> Who has ever achieved liberation?

Source: *Kabir Granthavali*, pad 174.

BOOKS AND LEARNING ARE OF NO USE

A central theme of Kabir's poems is a rejection of the value of study and prayer as performed by the religious leaders of his day, who are characterized as holding to the letter of the scriptures without grasping the true meaning.

> Pundit, why are you so foolish?
> You don't speak of Ram, you fool!
> Carrying your Vedas and Puranas, moving like a donkey loaded with
> sandalwood,
> Unless you learn about the name of Ram,
> You will come to grief.
> You slaughter living beings and call it dharma;
> What then, brother, would non-dharma be?
> You refer to each other as "Great Saint"; whom, then, should I call "Butcher"?
> Your mind is blind, your understanding dull.
> Brother, how can you preach to others?
> You sell your knowledge for money, and spend your human life in vain.

Source: *Kabir Granthavali*, pad 191.

EXTERNAL OBSERVANCES ARE OF NO USE

Like their Sant predecessors, Sikhs denounced the practice of external religious observances. Far from bringing people closer to God, Sikhs believe that such practices tend to obscure the divine presence, which is all around us, in all things, and directly accessible to human intuition.

He cannot be installed like an idol,
Nor can humans shape His likeness.
He made Himself and maintains Himself
On His heights sustained forever;
Honored are they in His shrine who meditate upon Him.
Sing, Nanak, the psalms of God as the treasury of sublime virtues.
If one sings of God and hears of Him, and lets love of God sprout within,
All sorrow will depart; in the soul, God will create abiding peace.
The word of the Guru is the inner music;
The word of the Guru is the highest scripture;
The word of the Guru is all-pervading.
The Guru is Shiva, the Guru is Vishnu and Brahma, the Guru is the mother
Goddess.
If I knew Him as He truly is
What words could utter my knowledge?
Enlightened by God, the Guru has unraveled one mystery
There is only one Truth, one bestower of life;
May I never forget Him.

Source: *Adi Granth*, "Japji" 5: from *Selections from the Sacred Writings of the Sikhs*, pp. 31–32.

ON *HUKAM*

Hukam *is central to Sikh meditative practice. It literally means propriety, putting things where they belong. It involves understanding one's relation to God and God's place in the universe. Cultivating hukam is necessary to overcoming self-reliance* (haumai), *the false notion that one is an autonomous individual independent of God's grace.*

Hukam is beyond describing, [but this much we can understand:] that all forms were created by *hukam,* life was created through *hukam,* greatness is imparted in accordance with *hukam.* Distinctions between what is exalted and what is lowly are the result of *hukam,* and in accordance with it suffering comes to some and joy to others. Through *hukam* one receives blessing and another is condemned to everlasting transmigration. All are within *hukam;* no one is beyond its authority. Nanak, if anyone comprehends *hukam,* his self-centeredness is purged.

Source: *Adi Granth,* "Japji" 2: from *Adi Granth: Guru Nanak and the Sikh Religion,* tr. W. H. McLeod (Oxford: Clarendon Press, 1968), p. 200.

ON *HAUMAI*

Haumai *is born of ignorance, which is the root cause of continued transmigration. It is a perceptual error in which one mistakenly believes that one is independent and autonomous, although the fact of the matter is that everything in the universe is created and sustained by God. Those who hold to mistaken views of separateness and individuality fail to recognize the omnipresence of God and their utter dependence upon his grace.*

Innumerable are the blind fools, sunk in folly;
Innumerable those living on thievery and dishonesty.
Innumerable the tyrants ruling by brute force;
Innumerable the violent cutthroats and murderers;
Innumerable those revolving in their own falsehood;
Innumerable the polluted living on filth;
Innumerable the slanderers bearing on their heads their loads of sin.
The sinner Nanak thus enumerates the evil-doers,
I who am unworthy even once to be made a sacrifice to You.
All that You will is good, Formless One, abiding in Your peace.

Source: *Adi Granth*, "Japji" 18.

THE TRUE GURU

Throughout Sikh literature the importance of the Guru is emphasized. In the early years of the tradition the Guru was human, and Sikhs believed that Nanak and his successors were mouthpieces through whom God revealed his message to humanity. Following the tenure of the 10th Guru, Gobind Singh, the Adi Granth *was designated as the Guru, since it contained the inspired messages of the human Gurus and their Sant predecessors. The Gurus are believed to provide essential guidance, since their words are the signposts provided by God to call His devotees to mystical realization of truth.*

If the True Guru is gracious, trust becomes complete.
If the True Guru is gracious, no one ever yearns.
If the True Guru is gracious, trouble is a thing unknown.
If the True Guru is gracious, God's pleasure is acclaimed.
If the True Guru is gracious, how could there be fear of death?
If the True Guru is gracious, lasting happiness is granted.
If the True Guru is gracious, one finds life's greatest treasures.
If the True Guru is gracious, one mingles with the Truth.

Source: *Var majh Pauri*, 25: *Sources of Indian Tradition*, ed. Ainslie Embree (New York: Columbia University Press, 1988), p. 505.

THE ECSTASY OF MYSTICAL UNION

Kabir's poetry contains a wealth of striking metaphors and images intended to convey nuances of the experience of mystical union that cannot be expressed through ordinary language. In this poem he describes the bliss of devotional union experienced by one who abandons ego and ritual and is granted the transcendent experience of union with God.

2. The radiance of the Supreme Brahman (*parabrahm*) cannot be imagined;
   Its beauty is ineffable, and seeing it is the only real evidence.
3. The fortunate hail fell to earth, and so lost its selfhood;
   When it melted, it became water and flowed into the lake.

4. I found the one I sought just where I was,
   And it has now become me, though I previously spoke of it as "Other."

5. Light shines in the Unapproachable, the Inaccessible.
   Kabir has brought his worship there, beyond the realm of "merit" and "sin.". . .

7. Love illuminated the cage [of physical existence], an eternal flame arose,
   My doubts disappeared, and happiness dawned when I encountered my Beloved. . . .

9. Water turned into ice, and then the ice melted;
   Everything that was has become It, and so what more can be said? . . .

12. Kabir has found the One, the Unapproachable, whose radiance is indescribable,
    The Luminous wife who is a *paras* [a stone that brings immortality]
    The god whom I now see. . . .

19. Sun and moon have become merged, and both dwell in one house.
    My mind has attained the goal of its search due to my past actions.

20. Transcending all limitations, I entered into the Boundless,
    Dwelling in Emptiness (*sunni*).
    I now reside in the palace that the sages cannot find.

Source: Kabir, *Sakhi* 9.

GUIDELINES FOR A HAPPY MARRIAGE

Guru Gobind Singh advises married couples to view themselves as one entity and to avoid deceit in their relationship. Wives are urged to remain faithful and to be subservient to their husbands, while husbands are warned of the negative consequences of mistreating their wives.

When husband and wife sit side by side why should we treat them as two?
Outwardly separate, their bodies distinct, yet inwardly joined as one.
Comply with whatever your Spouse may desire, never resisting, spurning deceit. . . .
Obey his commands in total surrender, this is the fragrance to bring. . . .
Abandon self-will, the Beloved draws near; no cunning will ever avail.
Be humble in manner and practice restraint, let sweetness of speech be your prayer.
If these are the garments adorning a bride the husband she seeks will be found.
Sweet is her speech, approved by the Loved One; grant that the joy may endure evermore.
Filled with the spirit of truth and contentment, the family's pride and joy.
The one who is constant in goodness and virtue is cherished and loved by the Spouse.
Behind closed doors and a forest of curtains he lies with another's wife.

When the angels of Death shall demand your account how then can the truth
be concealed?
This is the message the Guru has brought; let this be your vow while your
body has breath.
Bestow your affection on none save your wife; spurning temptation, avoid
other beds.
Watchful, untainted, even in dreams.

Source: *Sukhamani* 4.5: *Textual Sources for the Study of Sikhism*, pp. 117–118.

FORMATION OF THE *KHALSA*

*This passage tells the story of how the 10th Guru, Gobind Singh, inaugurated the
institution of the Sikh* Khalsa *(community). Besieged by Muslim rulers who wanted
to eliminate the Sikhs, the Guru realized that in order to survive his followers would
have to develop into a military force. In a move that permanently changed the character of the Sikh community, he gathered the faithful together and asked if any were
willing to die for their faith. Five men stepped forward, and the Guru led them one by
one to a tent, and then emerged with his sword dripping blood. Many of the people in
attendance believed that the Guru had gone mad, but Gobind Singh later showed them
that the five men were actually unharmed. He had killed five goats, and the blood they
had witnessed had been that of the animals. The following day the Guru completed the
process of transforming the community into a warrior group by declaring that henceforth the Sikhs would adopt external signs differentiating them from other communi-
ties. They would consider themselves to be members of the* Khalsa, *and membership
would henceforth be exclusive.*

On the day before . . . the Guru [Gobind Singh] arranged for a large
tent made of fine woolen fabric to be pitched on the area known as Kesgarh.
Earlier he had given instructions for a large dais to be erected at the edge of
the area. At that place he held a magnificent reception attended by five
thousand Sikhs, all with eyes for none save the Guru. While they were
gazing with rapture the Guru rose from his throne and in order to test them
addressed the mighty assembly as follows. 'I want the heads of five Sikhs to
offer as a sacrifice to God,' he proclaimed. 'Those Sikhs, beloved of the
Guru, who cheerfully give their heads will enjoy in the eternal hereafter all
the happiness that their hearts desire.'

Terror gripped the hearts of all who heard him. All fell silent, the
blood draining from their faces. The Guru drew his sacred sword and
called them again. 'Why are you silent?' he cried. 'Who amongst you sincerely believes his body to be of no account? Let him stand up.'

Hearing this Daya Singh, a pious Khatri from Lahore, stood with
hands respectfully joined. The Guru conducted him into the tent where
five goats were secretly tethered. He felled one of them, letting its blood
gush out. When he returned to the assembly the people were stunned by
the sight of his bloodstained sword. When he proceeded to demand the
head of another Sikh they stood petrified. 'He must have been bewitched

by the goddess,' they said. 'Why else should he demand the heads of Sikhs?' Some said one thing, some another. . . . [The Guru repeated the procedure with four other Sikhs.]

All were faithful disciples, pious men wholly given to worship and meditation who valued true wisdom and principle more than their own lives. When the Guru called for heads to be sacrificed these five Sikhs offered theirs. Faint-hearted Sikhs . . . tricked by the goat ruse into believing that men were really being killed, whispered anxiously to each other, desperately wanting to flee. This they were unable to do. Overpowered by the radiant presence of the Guru, each was firmly rooted to the spot.

Although many more Sikhs, faithful and brave, were by this time clamoring to give their heads the Guru demanded only five. . . . To those who responded, the Cherished Five, he gave new garments and fine weapons so that their appearance should resemble his own. Then he led them from the tent, back to his assembled Sikhs. All were thunderstruck, believing that the Guru had restored to life those whom he had previously slain. . . .

[The Guru said:] "Now it is clear for all to see that the Panth will win renown, that it will strike down the enemies of this land while it spreads abroad the message of the Sikh faith. All this will happen because God has made himself manifest in these five. . . . We give thanks to God that he has destroyed the religion of Muhammad and his successors, replacing it with the supremacy of the Guru's chosen five. . . ."

On the morning following this momentous event. . . . After pouring water from the Satluj river into a large iron vessel the Guru gave instructions for the Cherished Five to be clad in white garments together with a sword and other symbolic forms. He then had them stand before him and commanded them to repeat the divine name 'Vahiguru,' fixing their minds on God as they did so. This they were to continue doing while he stirred the sanctified water (*amrit*) in the iron vessel with a double-edged sword held vertically. . . .

The Guru then used the tip of his sword to take a small quantity of amrit from the iron vessel. This he did five times, letting each portion run from his sword on to his face. Then he applied amrit to each of the Cherished Five. . . . Finally he promulgated the code of conduct which they were to observe. . . . Thus did the Guru lay the foundations of the Khalsa, determine its form, and define the obligations of its members.

Sources: *Tavarikh Guru Khalsa* selections: from *Textual Sources for the Study Sikhism*, pp. 34–37.

JUSTIFICATION FOR USE OF FORCE

This poem, written by Guru Gobind Singh to the Mughal emperor Aurangzeb, accuses him of treachery and argues that Sikhs should fight to defend themselves against the unjust attacks of India's Muslim rulers. These verses stand in obvious contrast to the vision of religious harmony articulated by Nanak, who looked for ways to bring Hindus and Muslims together in a religious community that transcended their differences and emphasized the essential unity of religions.

> What could forty starving men do when they were suddenly attacked by ten thousand?
> The violators of solemn oaths came suddenly and began attacking.
> Then I was forced to do battle, using arrows and gunfire in self-defence.
> When all attempts at negotiation have failed, one is justified in unsheathing the sword.
> You tell me that I can rely on your oaths on the Qur'an,
> But if I had not done so earlier, this would not have come to pass. . . .
> One should know that it is evil to deviate from the truth. . . .
> You should not wield the sword carelessly in order to draw blood from anyone.
> God will shed your blood in the same way.
> You should not be indifferent, but should know that God cares nothing for human praise.
> He is the Lord of the earth and the sky, the Fearless,
> Creator of the universe and of all that is in it. . . .
> If you are strong, do not harm the poor,
> And do not renege on your promises with axes and clubs.
> When God is on one's side, what can an enemy do, even if he uses many tricks?
> Even if the enemy attacks thousands of times,
> He cannot harm one who has God on his side
> And who is protected by His benevolence.

Source: Guru Gobind Singh, *Japharnama.*

GOD, THE SWORD SUPREME

Gobind Singh realized that the continued existence of his religion required that Sikhs learn to defend themselves. In this poem he indicates that military preparedness is a sacred duty and that God requires his followers to become warriors in order to fight for the truth.

> Sword, that strikes in a flash, that scatters the armies of the wicked in the great battlefield; you symbol of the brave.
> Your arm is irresistible, your brightness shines forth the blaze of the splendor dazzling like the sun.
> Sword, you are the protector of saints, you are the scourge of the wicked; scatterer of sinners I take refuge in You.
> Hail to the Creator, Savior and Sustainer, hail to You: Sword supreme.

Source: Guru Gobind Singh, *Bachiter Natak,* 1: *Selections from the Sacred Writings of the Sikhs,* p. 270.

GLOSSARY

Adi Granth *"First Book,"* the holiest book of the Sikhs, which contains writings of Guru Nanak and his successors, along with poems of Sants.

Akal Purakh "Timeless Being," one of the Sikh names of God.

Avidya "Ignorance," the basic factor that enmeshes beings in the cycle of birth, death, and rebirth.

Bhakti Selfless devotion to God.

Five Ks Distinctive marks of Sikh believers, instituted by Guru Gobind Singh: (1) *kesh,* unshorn hair; (2) *kangha,* comb; (3) *kirpan,* short sword; (4) *kara,* steel wristband; (5) *kachch,* short pants.

Gobind Singh The 10th Guru, founder of the khalsa (1666–1708).

Guru "Teacher," a designation for Nanak and his successors, and later for the *Adi Granth.*

Haumai Self-reliance, the false notion that one is independent of God.

Hukam An attitude of humility, brought about by the realization of one's utter dependence on God.

Karma Actions that lead to concordant results.

Khalsa The Sikh community, founded by Guru Gobind Singh.

Maya "Illusion," a falsehood caused by ignorance, which causes beings to perceive multiplicity instead of the unitary truth of God.

Moksha "Release" from the cycle of birth, death, and rebirth, which is brought about by God's grace.

Mul Mantra "Root Prayer," the fundamental statement of Sikh doctrine.

Nam "Divine Name," which refers both to the various epithets of God and to His manifestations in the world.

Nam Simaran "Remembering the Name," the practice of contemplating God's attributes and actions.

Nanak The founder of the Sikh tradition (1469–1539).

Nirguna "Without Qualities," a designation of God's essential nature.

Samsara "Cyclic Existence," the beginningless cycle of birth, death, and rebirth in which ordinary beings are trapped.

Sant Indian mystics who advocated pure devotion to God and who denounced religious sectarianism.

Sikh "Disciple," a term coined by Guru Nanak to designate his followers.

FURTHER READINGS

ANAND, BALWANT SINGH. *Guru Nanak: His Life Was His Message.* New Delhi: Guru Nanak Foundation, 1983.

BARRIER, N. GERALD. *The Sikhs and Their Literature: A Guide to Tracts, Books, and Periodicals, 1849–1919.* Delhi: Manohar, 1985.

COLE, W. OWEN and PIARA SINGH SAMBHI. *The Sikhs: Their Religious Beliefs and Practices*. London: Routledge & Kegan Paul, 1978.

GANDHI, SURJIT SINGH. *History of the Sikh Gurus: A Comprehensive Study*. Delhi: Gur Das Kapur, 1978.

JUERGENSMEYER, M. and BARRIER, N. G. (eds.). *Sikh Studies: Comparative Perspectives on a Changing Tradition*. Berkeley: Berkeley Religious Studies Series, 1979.

KOHLI, SURINDAR SINGH. *A Critical Study of the Adi Granth*. New Delhi: Punjabi Writers' Cooperative Society, 1961.

LOEHLIN, C. H. *The Sikhs and Their Scriptures*. Lucknow: Lucknow Publishing House, 1958.

MANSUKHANI, GOBIND SINGH. *Aspects of Sikhism*. New Delhi: Punjabi Writers' Cooperative Industrial Society, 1982.

McLEOD, W. H. *The Sikhs: History, Religion and Society*. New York: Columbia University Press, 1989.

SETHI, AMARJIT SINGH. *Universal Sikhism*. New Delhi: Hemkunt Press, 1972.

SHACKLE, C. *An Introduction to the Sacred Language of the Sikhs*. London: School of Oriental and African Studies, 1983.

SINGH, HAKAM. *Sikh Studies: A Classified Bibliography of Printed Books in English*. Patiala: Punjab Publishing House, 1982.

Confucianism

INTRODUCTION

Of all the traditions discussed in this book, Confucianism probably has the least in common with what most contemporary Westerners associate with "religion." Confucius (ca. 551–479 B.C.E.), the founder of Confucianism, did not assert the existence of a creator God, although he did mention an impersonal force called "Heaven" (*tian*) that watches over human affairs and confers a mandate on rulers that legitimates their power. Confucianism has no churches and no ecclesiastical hierarchy, and Confucius never clearly articulated any vision of the afterlife or a path to salvation. The focus of Confucius was squarely on human beings and their social relations with others. Confucius's philosophy articulated his vision of the Way (*dao*) of the "superior person" (*junzi*), who embodies the qualities of a truly good human being. When asked about "religious" topics such as the nature of Heaven, the existence and propitiation of spirits, and so forth, Confucius generally cautioned his audiences to focus on the present life and on their personal conduct, and not to waste time on idle speculation.

Confucius is the latinate form of Kong Fuzi, or "Master Kong." According to Chinese tradition, he lived during the fifth century B.C.E. He was born in the small state of Lu, in modern-day Shandong Province. Some accounts claim that he was a descendant of the royal house of the Shang Dynasty (1751–1122 B.C.E., the earliest authenticated dynasty of China), but his family had become impoverished by Confucius's time. His father is said to have been a soldier, and his mother was not the first wife. According to later tradition, when Confucius was born dragons appeared in his house and a unicorn was sighted in his village.

His father died when Confucius was young, and his mother died while he was still a child. According to Sima Qian, when Confucius was a boy he had little interest in the games of other children, and instead preferred to arrange sacrificial implements and pretend to be performing rituals. Apparently Confucius did not have a formal education, but through independent study managed to become renowned for his learning.

In his twenties he began to attract students. He married young and held a minor government position that required him to keep records of stores of grains and animals used for official sacrifices. According to some accounts, his interest in rituals led him to visit Laozi to seek advice on the performance of sacrifices, but Confucius was admonished for being excessively concerned with external observances and thus neglecting the Dao.

Confucius was married around the age of 19 to a woman from Bin Guan in the state of Song. They had a son and a daughter. Fearing the onset of social disruption in Lu, he traveled to the state of Qi, hoping to gain a position of influence. He was well received but failed to achieve his primary objective, and so returned to Lu at the age of 51. There he was appointed minister of justice, and according to Confucian accounts he instituted a period of good government. Records of his tenure claim that articles left on the road were returned to their owners, and people could travel freely without fear of crime. He became an advisor to the duke of Lu, but reportedly resigned in disgust after the duke received a present of 80 dancing girls from the rival duke of Qi, after which he no longer attended to his duties in the morning.

Confucius lived during a time of social and political turmoil, and this had a powerful effect on his thinking. The Zhou dynasty (1111–249 B.C.E.), which had unified China and fostered the development of Chinese culture, was losing control, and China was in the process of breaking up into fiefdoms that were vying with each other for territory and power. Confucius lamented this social disintegration and hoped to guide his country back to the norms and practices of the early days of the Zhou dynasty as reported in The *Book of Poetry* and the *Book of History,* both of which extolled the superior qualities of sage-emperors of the Shang and Zhou dynasties. Confucius hoped to find a position of political power that would allow him to help the rulers of his time to rediscover the traditions of the past, which he believed would help China to correct its problems and reestablish good government.

Unable to find a suitable position in Lu, at the age of 53 Confucius began a trek through China in search of a ruler who would allow him to put his ideas into practice. During the course of 13 years he journeyed to nine states. Some received him warmly and asked his advice, but in one state he was surrounded and threatened, and he was made a target of assassination in another, and detained by government authorities in a third state.

He promised that any state that allowed him significant control of domestic matters and foreign affairs would soon enjoy prosperity and enhanced prestige, and that it would have a contented populace that fully supported the policies of the rulers, but his ideas of government by wise and humane rulers were considered dangerous at a time when most rulers controlled their domains by force. After realizing that no one would give him an opportunity to implement his ideas, he returned to Lu at the age of 68 and devoted himself to teaching, convinced that his life's mission had been a failure.

His fame as a teacher grew, however, and traditional sources report that young men came from far and wide to study with Confucius and that he never turned away a student who was unable to pay him. As a result, young men of humble origins had access to education, which was an important factor in finding employment in government.

Confucius taught his students to cultivate themselves and urged them to aspire to become "noble men." The noble man, according to Confucius, possesses an unwavering moral compass, and thus knows what is correct in all situations. He has the virtue of "human-heartedness" (*ren*), the coalescence of the moral qualities that characterize those who are truly good. A noble man is honest, is courageous, stands in awe of Heaven and constantly seeks to perfect himself, is learned but does not boast of his learning, does not set his mind "for" or "against" anything, holds to no particular political philosophy, but rather seeks to follow what is right in every situation. He has no needs of his own, and so is able to work selflessly for others. His unassuming manifestation of good qualities inspires others to become better. Society, according to Confucius, is perfected by such people, who set a moral standard that subtly motivates others to correct themselves in order to emulate them.

Although Confucius was unable to acquire the political power he desired during his lifetime, his students passed on his teachings, becoming teachers themselves. Some of them became influential educators and helped to install his notion of the superior person as a standard for conduct among the educated elite of China. In addition, Confucius introduced to China the idea that the primary criteria for holding public office should be intelligence, learning, and highly developed moral character rather than hereditary status. He believed that universal standards of ethical behavior are outlined in the classics, and so he urged his students to study these texts in order to develop their moral awareness.

The Confucian Revival

In the centuries following Confucius's death, many of his disciples became educators, and as a result Confucian philosophy became a part of the standard curriculum of educated Chinese. Despite its widespread influence, however, the vitality of the tradition languished from the 4th through 10th centuries. Most of the best minds of China were either Daoists or Buddhists, and although Confucianism was widely studied there were few notable interpreters of the tradition.

This situation changed dramatically in the 11th century, when several prominent Confucian philosophers began to revive the tradition. Many of them were influenced by Buddhism and Daoism, and several had been Buddhists in their early years, but they ultimately rejected Buddhism because they considered its doctrine of "emptiness" (*shunyata*) to be nihilistic. They also saw the Buddhist emphasis on monasticism as unnatural, but found that the Confucian tradition valued the family and the norms of traditional Chinese society. A growing number of Confucian thinkers characterized Buddhism as a religion of "barbarians," unsuited to refined Chinese sensibilities, and they found in Confucianism a tradition that accorded with the norms and values of cultured Chinese. Among the early figures of this revival—which is referred to in China as "Study of Nature and Propriety" (*xing li xue*) and by Western scholars as "Neo-Confucianism"—were such prominent philosophers as Zhou Dunyi (1017–1073), Shao Yong (1011–1077), Zhang Zai (1020–1077), and the two brothers Cheng Hao (1032–1085) and Cheng Yi (1033–1107).

The Neo-Confucian revival is divided by contemporary scholars into two streams, one rationalistic and one idealistic. The major figure of the rationalist tradition was Zhu Xi (1130–1200), while Wang Yangming (1427–1529) was the main exponent of the idealists. Confucians of the first group focused on the foundational principles (*li*) of the natural world, human behavior, and society, while the idealists were primarily concerned with how to develop a moral consciousness through training the mind (*xin*).

Confucian Scriptures

According to Confucian tradition, Confucius edited the texts that came to be regarded as the Confucian classics: the *Book of Poetry* (*Shijing*), the *Book of Changes* (*Yijing*), the *Book of History* (*Shujing*), the *Book of Rites* (*Liji*), and the *Spring and Autumn Annals* (*Qunqiu*). These are regarded as the primary canonical texts of the tradition, along with the "Four Books": the *Analects* (*Lunyu*), the *Centeredness* (*Zhongyong*), the *Great Learning* (*Daxue*), and the *Mencius* (*Mangzi*).

The *Book of Poetry* is the earliest anthology of Chinese poetry. It contains 305 poems dating from early times until the later part of the Zhou dynasty. Confucian tradition holds that Confucius selected these from an earlier collection of three thousand poems, choosing those written in the finest style and exhibiting a high level of moral consciousness. The poems in the collection are mostly written in a style using rhymed quatrains with four characters per line, which became the standard for Chinese poetic writing after the time of Confucius.

The *Book of Changes* discusses how natural systems change, and it has long been regarded as a manual for divination. It contains 64 hexagrams, along with explanations of the significance of each one and "ten wings" of commentary that indicate how they should be interpreted. According to Confucian tradition, the ten wings were composed by Confucius, but this attribution has been rejected by most contemporary scholars (although it is admitted that he may have had a hand in composing one of the wings).

The hexagrams are composed of two trigrams each, and the trigrams are composed of broken and unbroken lines. The lines signify interactions of *yin* and *yang*, the two opposing polarities whose movements govern the developments of natural systems. *Yin* is said to be passive, wet, yielding, and feminine, and is represented by broken lines, while *yang* is aggressive, dry, forceful, and masculine, and is represented by unbroken lines. The pattern of the lines of a hexagram is believed to provide indications of the directions of natural elements and forces.

The *Book of History* is a collection of historical records and speeches purportedly from the early dynasties of China. It is the earliest Chinese historical work, containing documents from 17 centuries, dating back to the time of the legendary sage kings (third millennium B.C.E.). According to tradition, it was compiled and edited by Confucius, who chose selections for their historical and moral import. Each selection reports an event in Chinese history and contains a colophon that indicates the moral judgments of the author.

The *Book of Rites* describes the implements used in state rituals, the rules of the royal court, and it contains ethical exhortations for women and children, discussions of education, descriptions of proper performance of funerals and sacrifices to ancestors, and how a scholar should behave.

The *Spring and Autumn Annals* are historical records from the state of Lu from the period between 722 to 481 B.C.E. It describes the behavior of rulers, and is composed in a way that indicates the moral judgment of the compiler, believed by tradition to be Confucius.

Confucian tradition also holds that Confucius edited the *Book of Music* (*Yuejing*), which is now lost. It was replaced in the 12th century by a ritual text entitled *Rites of Zhou* (*Zhouli*). During the Han period, these six texts came to be referred to as the "six disciplines" (*liu shu*), and later as the "six classics" (*liujing*). Modern scholarship questions whether or not Confucius actually had a hand in editing these texts, since no evidence exists for this, except for relatively late traditions. It is clear from accounts of his life that he was thoroughly familiar with these texts and that he taught them to his students, but contemporary scholars see little reason to accept the tradition that he edited them.

The *Analects* contains 492 chapters collected into 20 books, and it contains pithy instructions on the core concepts of Confucius's philosophy. The primary focus is the training and character of the noble man, who is morally upright, learned, and restrained in his appetites.

The *Centeredness* was originally chapter 42 of the *Book of Rites*. According to Confucian tradition it was authored by Zeng Can (ca. 505–436 B.C.E.), but Zhu Xi contended that the opening paragraph was written by Confucius and that the rest of the work was an explanation composed by Zeng Can. It outlines three goals for the noble man: "making luminous virtue shine" (*ming ming de*), "having sympathy for the people" (*qin min*), and "abiding in attainment of perfect goodness" (*zhiyu zhishan*). These are said to be the first steps toward ordering society and establishing good government.

The *Great Learning* was originally chapter 31 of the *Book of Rites*, but came to be regarded as a separate text by the Confucian tradition. Zisi, a grandson of Confucius, is traditionally held to be its author, but this attribution is rejected by most contemporary scholars. It discusses the Dao of Heaven, which is said to be a principle that transcends the world but is manifest in its workings.

The *Mencius* contains teachings of the Confucian scholar Mangzi. These were written down by his students. The writings of Mencius represented an influential commentary on the thought of Confucius concerning the conduct of the sage and the nature of good government. The text consists of seven chapters, divided into two parts each.

Qin Shihuangdi, the founder of the Qin dynasty (221–206 B.C.E.), ordered Confucian texts burned, and as a result some works were lost, but most of the important texts survived, hidden by scholars until the political climate changed. The emperor also ordered the execution of a number of Confucian scholars, since he viewed the Confucian ideals of benevolent government as being at odds with his own authoritarian style.

When the Qin was overthrown by the Han dynasty, Confucianism again became the state ideology, largely due to the efforts of the Confucian scholar Dong Zhongshu, who was an advisor to emperor Wudi (r. 140–87 B.C.E.). In 125 he created a university whose educational program was based on the study of the Five Classics (the *Book of Music* had been lost during the persecution of Confucianism) and the Four Books.

In the 12th century, Zhu Xi published an edition of the Four Books that became the primary text for Confucian studies, eclipsing the Five Classics. In his system, students were advised to read the *Great Learning* first in order to learn the basic patterns of Confucianism, and then to move on to the *Analects*, which developed the ideas contained in the *Great Learning*. After that they should study the *Mencius* for its ability to inspire thought, and finally they should study *Centeredness*, which he described as profound and subtle. Due to his influence, these texts formed the basis for topics of the imperial examination system until it was abolished in 1905.

Although Confucius himself seldom mentioned such topics as spiritual beings, the nature of Heaven, life after death, or spirituality in general, his teachings became the basis for the most influential tradition of philosophy in China, one that eventually developed religious characteristics. Later Confucians propounded elaborate cosmological theories, doctrines concerning death and afterlife, and cultic practices. The tradition spread into other parts of Asia, and has been an important influence in Korea, Japan, and Vietnam. Although officially proscribed by the current leadership of the People's Republic of China, the ideas and values of Confucianism continue to exert a powerful influence on the Chinese people today.

CONFUCIAN SCRIPTURES

SIMA QIAN'S ACCOUNT OF CONFUCIUS'S LIFE

Sima Qian's account of Confucius's life, compiled in the 2nd century B.C.E., is very influential in China, though considered to be rather unreliable by modern scholars. Written on the basis of legends that had arisen around the figure of Confucius, it purports to describe his early life and to provide a biography of his adult years. The admiration of the writer is evident throughout the account, and especially in the concluding remarks.

> Confucius was born in Zou, a village in the region of Zhangbing in the state of Lu. . . . As a child, Confucius liked to play with sacrificial implements, arranging them as if for a ceremony. . . . Confucius was poor and humble. Growing up and working as keeper of the granaries for the Ji clan he measured the grains fairly; when he was keeper of the livestock the animals flourished, and so he was made minister of works. Subsequently he left Lu, was dismissed from Ji, driven out of Song and Wei and ran into trouble between Zhen and Zai. Finally he returned to Lu.

Well over six feet, Confucius was called the Tall Man, and everybody marveled at his height. He returned to the state of Lu as it had treated him well. . . .

All the men of Lu from the ministers down overstepped their rightful bounds and did not act correctly. This is why Confucius did not take an official position, and instead edited the *Book of Songs, Book of History, Book of Rites,* and the *Book of Music* in his retirement, and more and more pupils came even from distant places to study with him. . . .

When Confucius had spent three years in Zai, Wu attacked Zhen, and Zhu sent its army. . . . Hearing that Confucius was living between Zhen and Zai, the people of Zhu sent an invitation to him. Before he was able to accept it, however, the ministers of Zhen and Zai discussed the situation and said, 'Confucius is a worthy man who has correctly pointed out the failings of every state. He has spent a great deal of time between Zhen and Zai, and he disapproves of all our actions and policies. Now the powerful state of Zhu has invited him. If he serves Zhu, it will be bad for us.' They sent men to surround Confucius in the countryside, keeping him from leaving. His supplies ran out, his followers were too weak to move, but Confucius went on teaching and singing, accompanying himself on the lute.

Zi Lu came up to him and said with indignation, 'Must a noble man endure privation?'

Confucius answered, 'A noble man can withstand privation, but a small man who faces privation tends to go wrong.'

Zi Kong looked unhappy, and Confucius said to him, 'Do you consider me to be a learned and educated man?'

Zi Kong replied, 'Of course; aren't you?'

Confucius said, 'Not at all; I have merely grasped the thread that links the rest. . . .'

Confucius taught his students the old songs, records, rituals, and music. In all he had 3,000 pupils, and seventy-two of them were proficient in all of the six arts. Many other people, such as Yan Zhuozou, were taught by him. In his teachings, Confucius stressed four things: culture, good conduct, loyalty, and honesty. He avoided four things: rash judgments, arbitrary opinions, hardheadedness, and vanity. He advocated caution during sacrifices, war, and illness, and he only helped those who were sincere. If he provided one corner of a square and a student could not infer the other three corners, he would not repeat himself. . . .

He said to Zi Kong, 'The world has strayed from the true Dao, and no one is able to follow me. . . . He died seven days later at the age of seventy-three, on the *ji zhou* day of the fourth month of the sixteenth year of the reign of Duke Ye of Lu (479 B.C.E.). . . .

[Sima Qian comments:] Although I cannot reach him, my heart goes out to him. When I read the words of Confucius, I try to see the man himself, and when in Lu I visited his temple and saw his carriage, clothes, and sacrificial implements. . . . The world has seen countless princes and powerful people who found fame and praise during their lives but were forgotten after death, while Confucius, though a commoner, has been revered by scholars for more than ten generations. From the emperor, princes, and nobles on down, all regard him as the highest authority. He is appropriately called the Supreme Sage.

Source: Sima Qian, *Shiji* (*Records of the Historian*).

THE *BOOK OF HISTORY*

The Book of History *purports to record events from early Chinese history. It was an important source for Confucius in his understanding of the exalted qualities of the sage emperors Yao and Shun, who are described as exemplars of righteousness, wisdom, and benevolent government.*

Examining into antiquity, we find that the Emperor Yao was called Fang Xun. He was reverent, intelligent, accomplished, sincere, and mild. He was sincerely respectful and capable of modesty. His light covered the four extremities of the empire and extended to Heaven above and the earth below. He was able to make bright his great virtue, and bring affection to the nine branches of the family. When the nine branches of the family had become harmonious, he distinguished and honored the hundred clans. When the hundred clans had become illustrious, he harmonized the myriad states. The numerous people were amply nourished and prosperous and became harmonious.

Source: *Shujing* selections: *Sources of Chinese Tradition*, vol. I, ed. William Theodore deBary, Wing-tsit Chan, and Burton Watson (New York: Columbia University Press, 1964), pp. 8–9.

CONFUCIUS: SELECTIONS FROM THE ANALECTS

The following selections are excerpted from the Analects (Lunyu), *which record instructions given by Confucius to his students and events in his life. The title of the text literally means "conversations," and it received this name because it mainly contains conversations between Confucius and his students. They emphasize an interrelated set of themes, including the character and training of the "noble man," the idea that rulers should govern by moral persuasion and should treat their subjects as a loving father treats his children, the importance of following tradition, the role of rituals and sacrifices in establishing a harmonious state, and the importance of providing for the basic needs of the populace.*

Confucius believed that the righteousness of leaders is the key to social stability and told rulers that it is important scrupulously to practice the social rituals that help a society to function harmoniously. The noble man, he taught, has a strong sense of propriety (li), a general term for the day-to-day norms of social interaction as well as for state ceremonies.

In addition, the noble man speaks the truth as he understands it, and so is concerned with the "rectification of names" (zheng ming), which involves calling things what they are and using terms in a nondeceptive manner. Rulers who equivocate and who use euphemisms that attempt to cloak the truth of things lose the confidence of the people as surely as those who are morally degenerate and who blunder in their decisions.

According to his student Zeng Zi, there is "one thread" running through all of Confucius's teachings: an emphasis on the centrality of morality and cultivation of an ethical foundation, which leads the noble man to treat others like himself (shu). Human beings are said to have a basically moral nature (zhong), which needs to be developed by education and contact with superior persons. Such people cultivate their own moral consciousness and seek to establish others in virtue.

Confucius taught that a person with the virtue of human-heartedness (ren) knows how to treat others and acts appropriately in all situations. A central virtue of such a person is filial piety (xiao), which is evidenced by respect for elders and persons in authority, as well as by proper performance of rituals for the ancestors. Such behavior accords with the dictates of Heaven.

Confucius believed that Heaven watches over human affairs and confers a mandate to rule (tianming). This concept was first developed by the founders of the Zhou dynasty to justify their conquest of the Shang rulers. According to this theory, the emperor is the "son of Heaven" (tianzi), appointed to oversee human affairs, but rulers who become lazy, corrupt, or despotic cause Heaven to withdraw the mandate, and so lose their legitimacy. Heaven first sends warnings in the form of natural disasters, internal turmoil, or personal crises, and those who reform themselves may again earn Heaven's favor. Those who persist in their immoral actions, however, are eventually deposed by Heaven, which appoints other rulers of better moral character.

I. 1. The Master said, 'Is it not a pleasure, having learned something, to try it out at due intervals? Is it not a joy to have friends come from afar? Is it not gentlemanly not to take offense when others fail to appreciate your abilities?'

4. Zeng Zi said, 'Every day I examine myself on three counts. In what I have undertaken on another's behalf, have I failed to do my best? In my dealings with my friends have I failed to be trustworthy in what I say? Have I passed on to others anything that I have not tried out myself?'

6. The Master said, 'A young man should be a good son at home and an obedient young man abroad, sparing of speech but trustworthy in what he says, and should love the multitude at large but cultivate the friendship of his fellow men. If he has any energy to spare from such action, let him devote it to making himself cultivated.'

9. Zeng Zi said, 'Conduct the funeral of your parents with meticulous care and let not sacrifices to your remote ancestors be forgotten, and the virtue of the common people will incline towards fullness.'

10. Zi Qin asked Zi Kong, 'When the Master arrives in a state, he invariably gets to know about its government. Does he seek this information. Or is it given him?'

Zi Kong said, 'The Master gets it through being cordial, good, respectful, frugal and deferential. The way the Master seeks it is, perhaps, different from the way other men seek it.'

11. The Master said, 'Observe what a man has in mind to do when his father is living, and then observe what he does when his father is dead. If, for three years, he makes no changes to his father's ways, he can be said to be a good son.'

14. The Master said, "The noble man (*junzi*) seeks neither a full belly nor a comfortable home. He is quick in action but cautious in speech. He goes to men possessed of the Way (*dao*) to be put right. Such a man can be described as eager to learn.'

II. 2. The Master said, 'The *Odes* are three hundred in number. They can be summed up in one phrase, "Swerving not from the right path."'

3. The Master said, 'Guide them by edicts, keep them in line with punishments, and the common people will stay out of trouble but will have no sense of shame. Guide them by virtue, keep them in line with the rites, and they will, besides having a sense of shame, reform themselves.'

4. The Master said, 'At fifteen I set my heart on learning; at thirty I took my stand; at forty I came to be free from doubts; at fifty I understood the Decree of Heaven; at sixty my ear was attuned; at seventy I followed my heart's desire without overstepping the line.'

6. Mang Wubo asked about being filial. The Master said, 'Give your father and mother no other cause for anxiety than illness.'

13. Zi Kong asked about the noble man. The Master said, 'He puts his words into action before allowing his words to follow his action.'

20. Ji Kangzi asked, 'How can one inculcate in the common people the virtue of reverence, of doing their best and of enthusiasm?'

The Master said, 'Rule over them with dignity and they will be reverent; treat them with kindness and they will do their best; raise the good and instruct those who are backward and they will be imbued with enthusiasm.'

III. 5. The Master said, 'Barbarian tribes with their rulers are inferior to Chinese states without them.'

IV. 4. The Master said, 'If a man sets his heart on benevolence, he will be free from evil.'

10. The Master said, 'In his dealings with the world the noble man is not invariably for or against anything. He is on the side of what is moral.'

14. The Master said, 'Do not worry because you have no official position. Worry about your qualifications. Do not worry because no one appreciates your abilities. Seek to be worthy of appreciation.'

15. The Master said, 'The noble man understands what is moral. The small man understands what is profitable.'

17. The Master said, 'When you meet someone better than yourself, turn your thoughts to becoming his equal. When you meet someone not as good as you are, look within and examine your own self.'

25. The Master said, 'Virtue never stands alone. It is bound to have neighbors.'

V. 16. The Master said of Zi Chan that he had the way of the noble man on four counts: he was respectful in the manner he conducted himself; he was reverent in the service of his lord; in caring for the common people, he was generous and, in employing their services, he was just.

VII. 1. The Master said, 'I transmit but do not innovate; I am truthful in what I say and devoted to antiquity.'

2. The Master said, 'Quietly to store up knowledge in my mind, to learn without flagging, to teach without growing weary, these present me with no difficulties.'

4. During his leisure moments, the Master remained correct although relaxed.

6. The Master said, 'I set my heart on the Way, base myself on virtue, lean upon benevolence for support and take my recreation in the arts.'

7. The Master said, 'I have never denied instruction to anyone who, of his own accord, has given me so much as a bundle of dried meat as a present.'

21. The topics the Master did not speak of were prodigies, force, disorder, and gods.

22. The Master said, 'Even when walking in the company of two other men, I am bound to be able to learn from them. The good points of the one I copy; the bad points of the other I correct in myself.'

37. The Master said, 'The noble man is easy of mind, while the small man is always full of anxiety.'

38. The Master was cordial yet not stern, inspiring yet not fierce, and respectful yet at ease.

VIII. 2. The Master said, 'Unless a man has the spirit of the rites, in being respectful he will wear himself out, in being careful he will become timid, in having courage he will become unruly, and in being forthright he will become intolerant.

'When the noble man feels profound affection for his parents, the common people will be stirred to benevolence. When he does not forget friends of long standing, the common people will not shirk their obligations to other people.'

7. Zeng Zi said, 'A noble man must be strong and resolute, for his burden is heavy, and the road is long. He takes benevolence as his burden. Is that not heavy? Only with death does the road come to an end. Is that not long?'

13. The Master said, 'Have the firm faith to devote yourself to learning, and abide to the death in the good way. Enter not a state that is in peril; stay not in a state that is in danger. Show yourself when the Way prevails in the Empire, but hide yourself when it does not. It is a shameful matter to be poor and humble when the Way prevails in the state. Equally, it is a shameful matter to be rich and noble when the Way falls into disuse in the state.'

IX. 14. The Master wanted to settle amongst the Nine Barbarian Tribes of the east. Someone said, 'But could you put up with their uncouth ways?' The Master said, 'Once a noble man settles amongst them, what uncouthness will there be?'

18. The Master said, 'I have yet to meet the man who is as fond of virtue as he is of beauty in women.'

XI. 12. Ji Lu asked how the spirits of the dead and the gods should be served. The Master said, 'You are not able even to serve man. How can you serve the spirits?'

'May I ask about death?'

'You do not understand even life. How can you understand death?'

XII. 1. Yan Yuan asked about benevolence. The Master said, 'To return to the observance of the rites through overcoming the self constitutes benevolence. If for a single day a man could return to the observance of the rites through overcoming himself, then the whole Empire would consider benevolence to be his. However, the practice of benevolence depends on oneself alone, and not on others.'

4. Sima Niu asked about the noble man. The Master said, 'The noble man is free from worries and fears.'

'In that case, can a man be said to be a noble man simply because he is free from worries and fears?'

The Master said, 'If, on examining himself, a man finds nothing to reproach himself for, what worries and fears can he have?'

7. Zi Kong asked about government. The Master said, 'Give them enough food, give them enough arms, and the common people will have trust in you.'

Zi Kong said, 'If one had to give up one of these three, which should one give up first?'

'Give up arms.'

Zi Kong said, 'If one had to give up one of the remaining two, which should one give up first?'

'Give up food. Death has always been with us since the beginning of time, but when there is no trust, the common people will have nothing to stand on.'

11. Duke Jing of Qi asked Confucius about government. Confucius answered, 'Let the ruler be a ruler, the subject a subject, the father a father, the son a son.' The Duke said, 'Splendid! Truly, if the ruler is not a ruler, the subject not a subject, the father not a father, the son not a son, then even if there is grain, would I get to eat it?'

16. The Master said, 'The noble man helps others to realize what is good in them; he does not help them to realize what is bad in them. The small man does the opposite.'

22. Fan Chi asked about benevolence. The Master said, 'Love your fellow men.'

He asked about wisdom. The Master said, 'Know your fellow men.' Fan Chi failed to grasp his meaning. The Master said, 'Raise the straight and set them over the crooked. This can make the crooked straight.'

XIII. 1. Zi Lu asked about government. The Master said, 'Encourage the people to work hard by setting an example yourself.' Zi Lu asked for more. The Master said, 'Do not allow your efforts to slacken.'

3. Zi Lu said, 'If the Lord of Wei left the administration of his state to you, what would you put first?'

The Master said, 'If something is to be put first, it is, perhaps, the rectification of names.'

Zi Lu said, 'Is that so? What a roundabout way you take! Why bring rectification in at all?'

The Master said, 'Yu, how boorish you are. Where a noble man is ignorant, one would expect him not to offer any opinion. When names are not correct, what is said will not sound reasonable; when what is said does not sound reasonable, affairs will not culminate in success; when affairs do not culminate in success, rites and music will not flourish; when rites and music do not flourish, punishments will not fit the crimes; when punishments do not fit the crimes, the common people will not know where to put hand and foot. Thus when the noble man names something, the name is sure to be usable in speech, and when he says something this is sure to be practicable. The thing about the noble man is that he is anything but casual where speech is concerned.'

13. The Master said, 'If a man manages to make himself correct, what difficulty will there be for him to take part in government? If he cannot make himself correct, what business has he with making others correct?'

18. The Governor of She said to Confucius, 'In our village there is a man named "Straight Body." When his father stole a sheep, he gave evidence against him.' Confucius answered, 'In our village those who are straight are quite different. Fathers cover up for their sons, and sons cover up for their fathers. Straightness is to be found in such behavior.'

20. Zi Kong asked, 'What must a man be like before he can be said truly to be a noble man?' The Master said, 'A man who has a sense of shame in the way he conducts himself and, when sent abroad, does not disgrace the commission of his lord can be said to be a noble man.'

XV. 37. The Master said, 'The noble man is devoted to principle but not inflexible in small matters.'

XVI. 8. Confucius said, 'The noble man stands in awe of three things. He is in awe of the Decree of Heaven. He is in awe of great men. He is in awe of the words of the sages. The small man, being ignorant of the Decree of Heaven, does not stand in awe of it. He treats great men with insolence and the words of the sages with derision.'

Source: *Lunyu* selections: excerpted from *The Analects*, tr. D. C. Lau (New York: Dorset Press, 1979; Chinese terms have been converted to Pinyin spellings).

THE GREAT LEARNING

According to Confucian tradition, the Great Learning *was composed by Zeng Can, a student of Confucius. It is a short work that contains a condensed blueprint for personal cultivation and the ordering of the state. It has been the focus of a debate between the Neo-Confucian schools of Zhu Xi and Wang Yangming. Zhu Xi contended that the text is concerned with propriety, while Wang Yangming believed that it accords with his theory of the unity of humanity and Heaven.*

The way of the Great Learning consists of making luminous virtue shine; this entails having sympathy for the people and abiding in attainment of perfect goodness. After knowing [where to] abide, one is settled; once one is settled, one is able to be calm; once one is calm, one is able to be tranquil; once one is tranquil, one is able to have foresight; once one has foresight, one is able to begin consideration. Only after beginning consideration will the goal be attained. Things have roots and branches. Affairs have beginnings and ends. Knowing what is first and later, one will thus be near the Dao.

The ancients who wished to make their luminous virtue shine in the world first ordered their own states. Wishing to order their states, they first put their families in order. Wishing to put their families in order, they first cultivated their persons. Wishing to cultivate their persons, they first rectified their hearts. Wishing to rectify their hearts, they first made their intentions sincere. Wishing to make their intentions sincere, they first perfected their knowledge to the highest level.

Perfecting one's knowledge to the highest level consists in examination of things. Once things are examined, knowledge is perfected. When knowledge is perfected, intentions are sincere. When intentions are sincere, the heart is rectified. When the heart is rectified, one's person is cultivated. When one's person is cultivated, families are put in order. When families are put in order, states are ordered. When states are ordered, the whole world is tranquil.

Source: *Daxue* (*The Great Learning*).

CENTEREDNESS

The following text, the title of which is often translated as "The Doctrine of the Mean," consists of 3,567 characters and contains teachings attributed to Confucius. It describes the workings of Heaven and how they affect human life. According to the text, the Dao is a transcendent principle that pervades the entire universe, setting a standard and paradigm that sages seek to understand and emulate in their thoughts and behavior.

1. That which is Heaven's decree is called innate, following nature is called the Way (Dao), and cultivating the Way is called education. One cannot deviate from the Way for a moment; if one could, it would not be the Way. Because of this, the noble man is wary of what he does not see and apprehensive of what he does not hear. Nothing is better seen than what is hidden, and nothing is more apparent than what is obscure. Hence the noble man guards over his private realm. When happiness, anger, sorrow and pleasure have not yet arisen, this refers to centeredness; when these arise and are all balanced, this refers to harmony. The great foundation of the world is centeredness, and its great Way is harmony. When centered harmony is realized, heaven and earth will thereby be correctly aligned and all things will be fully developed.

2. Zhongni [Confucius] said: "The noble man, in the round of his life, is centered, but the inferior man's life is contrary to centeredness. The centered life of the noble man comes from his persisting in that centeredness; the life of the inferior man's being contrary to centeredness comes from his lack of scruples."

3. The Master said: "Centeredness is of itself consummate, but few people have been adept in it for a long time now."

4. The Master said: "I know why the Way is not followed: Those who are wise exceed it, and those who are foolish do not reach it. And I know why the Way is not clear: Those who are worthy exceed it, and those who do not emulate it do not reach it. There is no one who does not eat and drink, yet few are able really to perceive flavors."

6. The Master said: "Shun was indeed a man of great wisdom. Shun liked to query people, liked to examine their most trivial words, putting aside the evil, exalting the good. He grasped the two extremes and employed centeredness in regard to the people. This is why he was Shun [the sage-emperor]."

12. The noble man's Way is extensive yet hidden. The most foolish of men and women may share in some knowledge of it, but when it reaches its utmost even sages are ignorant of it. The most worthless of men and women may be able to practice it, but when it reaches its utmost even sages are not adept in it. In all the greatness of heaven and earth, there are still things which people complain about. Nothing in the world has adequate capacity to bear what is large in the Way of the noble man; nothing in the world can split what is small in it. The noble man's Way originates in ordinary men and women; yet at its utmost reach it reveals all heaven and earth.

Source: *Zhongyong* (*Centeredness*); tr. Kurt Vall.

THE LIFE OF MENCIUS

According to Sima Qian's account of Mencius's life, he was born in the small state of Zou and followed the example of Confucius in seeking public office in order to put his ideas into practice. Like his predecessor, however, he was unable to realize his ambitions, and made his greatest impact as a teacher.

Mencius (Mangzi) was born in Zou and was taught by a student of Master Si. After mastering the Dao, he traveled abroad and served King Xuan of Qi (r. 342–324 B.C.E.). King Xuan was unable to use him, so he went to Liang. King Hui of Liang did not find his counsel helpful. He was considered impractical and removed from the reality of affairs. . . . Wherever he went, he did not fit in. He retired, and together with students such as Wan Zhang he discussed the *Songs* and *Documents* and elucidated the ideas of Confucius, composing [his text entitled] *Mencius* in seven sections.

Source: Sima Qian, *Shiji*.

SELECTIONS FROM THE MENCIUS

The Mencius *contains teachings attributed to the Confucian scholar Mangzi, the most influential early disciple of Confucius. Mencius believed that the first rule of "humane government" (ren zheng) is to provide for the basic needs of the people, and he agreed with Confucius that rulers should rectify their own behavior and cultivate moral awareness.*

He taught his students that human nature (xing) is basically good, but that people become corrupted through exposure to negative influences. No matter how depraved a particular person might become, however, the basic nature remains good, and through proper education one's fundamental goodness may be reawakened.

In one passage he compares human nature to the shoots of plants growing on a hill called Ox Mountain, on which cattle graze. Plants constantly send up shoots, but the cattle eat them, and so the plants are not able to grow. If the cattle leave, however, the plants will be able to grow, just as human nature will find its innate goodness if the conditions inhibiting its growth are removed. In order for this to happen, people must train their minds (xin), which provide guidance in the process of moral development. The mind provides a faculty of discernment that, when attuned to human nature, develops into an unwavering sense of right and wrong.

Like Confucius, Mencius believed that Heaven confers a mandate on rulers and that it acts to remove corrupt rulers, but Mencius also contended that the people may become instruments of Heaven's will. When rulers become cruel and oppressive, they lose all legitimacy, and thus it becomes permissible for their subjects to remove them from office. Such doctrines were viewed by the rulers of his day as dangerous, and not surprisingly he was unable to find anyone to give him a position of real power. The following selections are drawn from his collected teachings, entitled the Mencius.

Mencius went to see King Hui of Liang. 'Sir,' said the King, 'You have come all this distance, thinking nothing of [traveling] a thousand *li*. You must surely have some way of profiting my state?'

'Your majesty,' answered Mencius, 'What is the point of mentioning the word "profit"? All that matters is that there should be benevolence and rightness. If your Majesty says, "How can I profit my family?" and the noble man and commoners say, "How can I profit my person?" then those above and those below will be trying to profit at the expense of one another and the state will be imperiled. . . . [I]f profit is put before rightness, there is no satisfaction short of total usurpation. No benevolent man ever abandons his parents, and no dutiful man ever puts his prince last. Perhaps you will now endorse what I have said, "All that matters is that there should be benevolence and rightness. What is the point of mentioning the word "profit"'?

King Hui of Liang said, 'I have done my best for my state. When crops failed in He Nei I moved the population to He Dong and the grain to He Nei, and reversed the action when crops failed in He Dong. I have not noticed any of my neighbors taking such pains over his government. Yet how is it the population of the neighboring states has not decreased and mine has not increased?'

'Your majesty is fond of war,' said Mencius. 'May I use an analogy from it? After weapons were crossed to the rolling of drums, some soldiers fled, abandoning their armor and trailing their weapons. One stopped after a hundred paces, another after fifty paces. What would you think if the latter, as one who ran only fifty paces, were to laugh at the former who ran a hundred?'

'He had no right to,' said the King. 'He did not quite run a hundred paces. That is all. But all the same, he ran.'

'If you can see that,' said Mencius, 'you will not expect your own state to be more populous than the neighboring states. If you do not interfere with the busy seasons in the fields, then there will be more grain than the people can eat; if you do not allow nets with too fine a mesh to be used in large ponds, then there will be more fish and turtles than they can eat; if hatchets and axes are permitted in the forests on the hills only in the proper seasons, then there will be more timber than they can use. When the people have more grain, more fish and turtles than they can eat, and more timber than they can use, then in the support of their parents when alive and in the mourning of them when dead, they will be able to have no regrets over anything left undone. For the people not to have any regrets over anything left undone, whether in the support of their parents when alive or in the mourning of them when dead is the first step along the Kingly way. . . .

Now when food meant for human beings is so plentiful as to be thrown to dogs and pigs, you fail to realize that it is time for collection, and when men drop dead from starvation by the wayside, you fail to realize that it is time for distribution. When people die, you simply say, "It is none of my doing. It is the fault of the harvest." In what way is that different from killing a man by running him through, while saying all the time, "It is none of my doing. It is the fault of the weapon?" Stop putting the blame on the harvest and the people of the whole Empire will come to you.'

Mencius said to King Xuan of Qi 'Suppose a subject of Your Majesty's, having entrusted his wife and children to the care of a friend, were to go on a trip to Chu, only to find, upon his return, that his friend had allowed his wife and children to suffer cold and hunger, then what should he do about it?'

'Break with his friend.'

'If the Marshal of the Guards was unable to keep his guards in order, then what should be done about it?'

'Remove him from office.'

'If the whole realm within the four borders was ill-governed, then what should be done about it?'

The King turned to his attendants and changed the subject.

King Xuan of Qi asked, 'Is it true that Tang banished Jie and King Wu marched against Zou?'

'It is so recorded,' answered Mencius.

'Is regicide permissible?'

'He who mutilates benevolence is a mutilator; he who cripples rightness is a crippler; and a man who is both a mutilator and a crippler is an "outcast." I have indeed heard of the punishment of the "outcast Zou," but I have not heard of any regicide.'

There was a border clash between Zou and Lu. Duke Mu of Zou asked, 'Thirty-three of my officials died, yet none of my people would sacrifice their lives for them. If I punish them, there are too many to be punished. If I do not punish them, then there they were, looking on with hostility at the death of their superiors without going to their aid. What do you think is the best thing for me to do?'

'In years of bad harvest and famine,' answered Mencius, 'close on a thousand of your people suffered, the old and the young being abandoned in the gutter, the able-bodied scattering in all directions, yet your granaries were full and there was failure on the part of your officials to inform you of what was happening. This shows how callous those in authority were and how cruelly they treated the people. Zeng Zi said, "Take heed! Take heed! What you mete out will be paid back to you." It is only now that the people have had an opportunity of paying back what they conceived. You should not bear them any grudge. Practice benevolent government and the people will be sure to love their superiors and die for them.'

'The will is commander over the *qi* (material force) while the *qi* is that which fills the body. Where the will arrives there the *qi* halts. Hence it is said, "Take hold of your will and do not abuse your *qi*" . . .'

'May I ask what your strong points are?'

'I have an insight into words. I am good at cultivating my "flood-like *qi*."'

'May I ask what this "flood-like *qi*" is?'

'It is difficult to explain. This is a *qi* which is, in the highest degree, vast and unyielding. Nourish it with integrity and place no obstacle in its path and it will fill the space between Heaven and Earth. It is a *qi* which unites rightness and the Way. Deprive it of these and it will collapse. It is born of accumulated rightness and cannot be appropriated by anyone through a sporadic show of rightness. Whenever one acts in a way that falls below the standard set in one's heart, it will collapse. . . . You must work at it and never let it out of your mind. At the same time, while you must never let it out of your mind, you must not forcibly help it grow either. You must not be like the man from Song. There was a man from Song who pulled at his seedlings because he was worried about their fail-ure to grow. Having done so, he went on his way home, not realizing what he had done. "I am worn out today," said he to his family. "I have been helping the seedlings to grow." His son rushed out to take a look and there the seedlings were, all shriveled up. There are few in the world who can resist the urge to help their seedlings to grow. There are some who leave the seedlings unattended, thinking that nothing they can do will be of any use. They are the people who do not even bother to weed. There are others who help the seedlings to grow. They are the people who pull at them. Not only do they fail to help them but they do the seedlings positive harm.'

Mencius said, 'No man is devoid of a heart sensitive to the suffering of others. Such a sensitive heart was possessed by the former Kings and this manifested itself in compassionate government. With such a sensitive heart behind compassionate government, it was as easy to rule the Empire as rolling it in your palm.'

'My reason for saying that no man is devoid of a heart sensitive to the suffering of others is this. Suppose a man were, all of a sudden, to see a young child on the verge of falling into a well. He would certainly be moved to compassion, not because he wanted to get in the good graces of the parents, nor because he wished to win the praise of his fellow villagers or friends, nor yet because he disliked the cry of the child. From this it can be seen that whoever is devoid of the heart of compassion is not human, whoever is devoid of the heart of shame is not human, whoever is devoid of the heart of courtesy and modesty is not human, and whoever is devoid of the heart of right and wrong is not human. The heart of compassion is the germ of benevolence; the heart of shame, of dutifulness; the heart of courtesy and modesty, of observance of the rites; the heart of right and wrong, of wisdom. Man has these four germs just as he has four limbs. For a man possessing these four germs to deny his own potentialities is for him to cripple himself; for him to deny the potentialities of his prince is for him to cripple his prince. If a man is able to develop all these four germs that he possesses, it will be like a fire starting up or a spring coming through. When these are fully developed, he can bend the whole realm within the Four Seas. If he fails to develop them, he will not be able even to serve his parents.'

Gaozi said, 'Human nature is like whirling water. Give it an outlet in the east and it will flow east; give it an outlet in the west and it will flow west. Human nature does not show any preference for either good or bad just as water does not show any preference for either east or west.'

'It certainly is the case,' said Mencius, 'that water does not show any preference for either east or west, but does it show the same indifference to high and low? Human nature is good just as water seeks low ground. There is no man who is not good; there is no water that does not flow downwards.

'Now in the case of water, by splashing it one can make it shoot up higher than one's forehead, and by forcing it one can make it stay on a hill. How can that be the nature of water? It is the circumstances being what they are. That man can be made bad shows that his nature is no different from that of water in this respect.'

Source: Mangzi, *Mencius*, tr. D. C. Lau (Hong Kong: The Chinese University Press, 1979, vol. I), pp. 3ff. Chinese terms have been converted to Pinyin spellings.

XUNZI: THE NATURE OF HUMAN BEINGS IS EVIL

The most influential interpreter of Confucius prior to the Han dynasty was Xunzi (Xun Qing, d. 215 B.C.E.), a younger contemporary of Mencius who lived in the state of Zhao and who is best known today for his treatises on government and warfare. Unlike Mencius, Xunzi believed that human nature is basically evil and that rulers must employ strict controls in order to keep their subjects in line. He advocated strong centralized rule and the use of punishment to restrain the population, but he also believed that human beings can be taught to be good through discipline and education. He was reportedly a teacher of Han Fei, the exponent of the philosophy of Legalism that became the dominant ideology of the Qin dynasty.

Xunzi rejected Mencius's ideas about human nature, contending that humans have innate desires, which can never be fully satisfied. People naturally desire to possess things and envy others who have things that they do not, and these basic tendencies oppose the cultivation of virtue. Goodness is attained only through training that teaches people to restrain their urges and recognize higher goods. This training requires study of the classics and education in proper performance of rites. He also rejected Mencius's idea of Heaven as a moral force that oversees human affairs. For Xunzi, Heaven is simply nature, which is impersonal and has no ethical dimension, but operates in accordance with its own laws without regard to individual virtue or human desires.

Human nature is evil; any good in humans is acquired by conscious exertion. Now, the nature of man is such that he is born with a love of profit. Following this nature will cause its aggressiveness and greedy tendencies to grow and courtesy and deference to disappear. Humans are born with feelings of envy and hatred. . . .

This being the case, when each person follows his inborn nature and indulges his natural inclinations, aggressiveness and greed are certain to develop. . . . Thus it is necessary that man's nature undergo the transforming influence of a teacher and the model that he be guided by is ritual and moral principles. Only after this has been accomplished do courtesy and deference develop. Unite these qualities with precepts of good form and reason, and the result is an age of orderly government. If we consider the implications of these facts, it is plain that human nature is evil and that any good in humans is acquired by conscious exertion.

Source: *Xunzi*, III. 150–151: *Xunzi: A Translation and Study of the Complete Works*, vol. III, tr. John Knoblock (Stanford: Stanford University Press, 1994), pp. 150–151.

YANG XIONG: HUMAN NATURE IS A MIXTURE OF GOOD AND EVIL

The question of whether human nature is basically good or evil was an important one for the Confucian tradition after Confucius. Mencius declared that human nature is basically good, while Xunzi believed it to be basically evil. Confucius himself did not make a definitive statement on the matter, and only said that people are born alike but become different through training and practice. He did contend, however, that all men have the potential to become noble men, and so it seems clear that his view of human nature was probably closer to that of Mencius than to Xunzi's negative assessment.

In the following passage, Yang Xiong (53 B.C.E.–18 C.E.) stakes out a middle position, contending that human nature is a mixture of good and evil. He contends that people become either good or evil as a result of their training: the good cultivate good, while the evil cultivate evil. His treatise helped to focus the attention of Confucian thinkers on this issue, but was criticized by later Confucians for its contention that human nature is partially evil.

Human nature is a mixture of good and evil. If we cultivate goodness, we will be good people; if we cultivate evil, we will be evil people; substance (*qi*) is the horse on which we ride to good or evil. Because of this, the noble man strives hard in learning and exerts himself in practice. The consummate Way is for him to make his goods precious before selling them, to perfect his person before forming relations with other people, to complete his plans before acting.

Source: Fuyan 3.1a–b: tr. Kurt Vall.

HAN YU: ATTACK ON BUDDHISM AND DAOISM

Han Yu (768–824) was a public official who led a Confucian attack on Buddhism and Daoism and called on the emperor to suppress them. He described Buddhism as a religion of barbarians that is at odds with cultured Chinese sensibilities, and he denounced Daoism as a religion that panders to primitive superstition.

The following excerpt is from a letter he wrote to the emperor regarding the veneration of a relic of the Buddha. He advised the emperor to reconsider his decision to publicly view a fragment of bone believed to have been left over after the Buddha was cremated, on the grounds that this may seem to the common people to be lending imperial support to the Buddhist practice of relic veneration, which Han Yu considered barbaric.

Your servant begs leave to say that Buddhism is no more than a cult of the barbarian peoples which spread to China in the time of the Latter Han. It did not exist here in ancient times. . . . When Emperor Gaozu [founder of the Tang] received the throne from the House of Sui, he deliberated upon the suppression of Buddhism. But at that time the various officials, being of small worth and knowledge, were unable fully to comprehend the ways of the ancient kings and the exigencies of past and present, and so could not implement the wisdom of the emperor and rescue the age from corruption. . . .

Now Buddha was a man of the barbarians who did not speak the language of China and wore clothes of a different fashion. His sayings did not concern the ways of our ancient kings, nor did his manner of dress conform to their laws. He understood neither the duties that bind sovereign and subject, nor the affections of father and son. If he were still alive today and came to our court by order of his ruler, Your Majesty might condescend to receive him, but . . . he would then be escorted to the borders of the nation, dismissed, and not allowed to delude the masses. How then, when he has long been dead, could his rotten bones, the foul and unlucky remains of his body, be rightly admitted to the palace? Confucius said, 'Respect ghosts and spirits, but keep them at a distance, . . .' Now without reason Your Majesty has caused this loathsome thing to be brought in and would personally go to view it. . . . Your servant is deeply shamed and begs that this bone be given to the proper authorities to be cast into fire and water, that this evil may be rooted out, the world freed from its error, and later generations spared this delusion. . . . If the Buddha does indeed have supernatural power to send down curses and calamities, may they fall only upon the person of your servant, who calls upon High Heaven to witness that he does not regret his words.

Source: Han Yu, *Changli Xianshang Wenji,* 39.2b–42: *Sources of Chinese Tradition,* pp. 371–372.

ZHOU DUNYI: THE GREAT ULTIMATE

Zhou Dunyi (1017–1073) was one of the important early figures in the Neo-Confucian revival that took place during the Song dynasty (960–1279). His most significant text was The Diagram of the Great Ultimate Explained (Taiji tu shuo), *a short work that equates the "great ultimate" (taiji) with the "non-ultimate" (wuji), which he describes as a reality transcending space and time. Its movement generates yang, the active force in nature, and its rest gives rise to yin, the passive element of natural systems. Through the interaction of these two, the "five agents" or "five elements" (wuxing) are produced, and the combinations of these elements give rise to the phenomena of the world. Zhou conceives of the universe as a dynamic and holistic system in which natural forces and human conduct are interrelated.*

1. [It is] the non-ultimate, yet also the great ultimate.
2. The great ultimate moves and produces yang. Moving to the limit, it rests. Resting, it produces yin. Resting completely, it moves again. Movement and rest alternate: each is the other's root. It distinguishes yin and yang: the two modes are established by it.
3. Yang diversifies and yin harmonizes, producing water, fire, wood, metal, and earth. The five substances *(qi)* propagate accordingly, and the four seasons are brought about by it.
4. The five phases *(xing)* are the one yin and yang. Yin and yang are the one great ultimate. The great ultimate is based in the non-ultimate. As for the production of the five phases, each has its own nature.
5. The non-ultimate reality and the essence of the Two (yin and yang) and the Five Agents marvelously harmonize and integrate. The Way of *qian* [Heaven] becomes masculine, and the Way of *kun* [earth] becomes feminine. The two affect each other, the changes producing all things: producing and reproducing and changing endlessly.
6. Humans alone get the finest endowment, and are the most spiritually potent. It is thus that their physical form is produced, and their spirit obtains understanding. The five principles of their natures respond, good and evil are distinguished, and affairs thus proceed along their courses.
7. The sage settles these matters with centeredness and rectitude, humanity and righteousness (the Way of the sage is nothing but centeredness and rectitude, humanity and righteousness), makes tranquility dominant (he is without desire and thus tranquil). In this way he sets up a standard for human perfection. Thus the sage harmonizes his power with heaven and earth, his brilliance with the sun and the moon, his time with the four seasons, and his good and bad fortunes with the spirits.
8. The noble man cultivates these qualities and earns good fortune; the inferior man goes against them and suffers misfortune.

9. Thus it is said that yin and yang establish the Way of heaven, yielding and firmness establish the Way of earth, and humanity and righteousness establish the Way of humans. It is also said that by looking into the cycle of things the explanation of life and death will become known.

10. How great is the *Book of Changes!* This is where its utmost values lies!

Source: Zhou Dunyi, *Taiji tu shuo,* ch. 1: tr. Kurt Vall.

ZHU XI: NATURE AND HUMANITY

Zhu Xi's philosophy is sometimes referred to as "study of principle" (li xueh), *because he was concerned with developing understanding of the principles underlying human behavior and social interaction. He believed that society can be rectified through diligent study of the patterns of organization and development that underlie both human civilization and nature. In 1313 Zhu Xi's interpretations of Confucius were officially recognized as the orthodox system of Confucianism and became the basis for civil examinations administered by the government. As a result, they exerted tremendous influence in Chinese education until the abolition of the system by the Nationalist government in 1905.*

His philosophy was influenced by Zhou Dunyi's The Diagram of the Great Ultimate Explained. *Zhu Xi interpreted the "ultimate"* (ji) *as the furthest point that can be reached, and he defined the "great ultimate* (taiji) *as the sum total of the principles of all the phenomena of the universe and the highest principle of each individual thing. According to Zhu Xi, the entire universe is one principle, and he interpreted the notion of "investigation of phenomena" as described in the* Great Learning *as a procedure of examining things in order to become aware of how each phenomenon manifests principle.*

He also contended that principle and material force are separate factualities in phenomena, although they are inseparable. Principle is immaterial, unitary, eternal, changeless, and indestructible. He viewed it as constituting the essence of things and as being always good. Material force is the energy that sustains physical things and provides the impetus for their production and transformation. It is corporeal, manifold, changeable, differentiated, and impermanent. It can become either good or evil in accordance with the choices made by human beings.

Nature corresponds with the great ultimate, and mind corresponds with yin and yang. The great ultimate is just within yin and yang; it cannot be separated from it. Yet on fully considering the great ultimate, it is of itself the great ultimate, as yin and yang are of themselves yin and yang. Nature and mind are also this Way. It is what is meant by the [notion that] they are one and yet two, and yet one.

Though nature is insubstantial, it is a concrete principle; and though the mind is an actual thing, it is yet insubstantial; thus it can embrace all principle. This is something that comes to be grasped only when people examine their own being. Nature is thus the principles that the mind has, and the mind is where principles come together.

Nature is principle *(li)*, and the mind is what embraces everything and applies it to things.

Nature is before movement, and feelings are when it has already moved. Mind embraces the already moving and the not yet moving. So, the mind before it moves is nature, and when it has already moved it is feelings. Desire is what comes out of feelings. Mind is like water: nature resembles the water's stillness; feelings, the water's flow; desire, its great waves. But great waves have both what is good and what is not good. The good desires are the kind that resemble the idea, "I desire humaneness." The ones that are not good persistently race forth as if they were billowing waves. When such desires are preponderate, then heavenly principle is excluded. It is like water rising to burst the levee: there is nothing that is not damaged.

Mind designates what is in command, the ruler. It rules over both movement and stillness. It is incorrect to say that it is not doing anything during stillness, so that only when we get to movement is there a ruler. To call it "the ruler" is to say that it is an all-pervasive presence in both movement and stillness. The mind brings together nature and feelings. Yet it is incorrect to say that it is one thing that is all of a piece with them, not something separate on its own.

Source: Zhu XI, *Xing qing xin yi deng mingyi* selections: tr. Kurt Vall.

WANG YANGMING: QUESTIONS ON THE GREAT LEARNING

Wang Yangming (1472–1529) was an important opponent of Zhu Xi who lived during the Ming dynasty (1368–1644). He was a government official and scholar, as well as an eminent military strategist whose real name was Wang Shouren. He became known as Wang Yangming because he maintained a retreat in Yangming Valley in Chekiang Province. His Inquiry on the Great Learning *was his most important work and was widely debated by other Chinese thinkers. In this text he rejects Zhu Xi's explanation of the* Great Learning, *which places the investigation of things (kewu) before making thoughts sincere. Wang placed primary emphasis on the study of mind (xin xueh), which focuses on developing moral awareness through education and ethical instruction.*

Understanding, Wang contended, comes from within and not through external actions. He believed that knowledge of the good is innate and that principle (li) is a universal factor that is found in human beings as well as natural phenomena. He followed Mencius's idea that human beings are naturally good and that those who fully cultivate their nature are able to overcome selfish tendencies and embrace the truth of the Great Learning.

Wang also rejected Zhu Xi's notion that the investigation of things is an examination of external phenomena. Wang contended that goodness is an innate quality of the mind and believed that it involves "eliminating what is incorrect in the mind in order to preserve the correctness of its original nature." For Wang, the investigation of things entails an ethical imperative to put moral standards into practice and cultivate one's character.

A previous scholar considered the *Great Learning* to be the learning of great men. I venture to ask why the *Great Learning* should consist in manifesting lucid character? Master Yangming said: The great man takes heaven and earth and all the things as one entity; he sees that the world is but one family, and that the Middle Country is an individual in it. Now, those who make entities separate and self and other distinct are petty people. The great man's ability to take heaven and earth and all things as one entity is not a result of his attention to it; but because the humanity of his mind is fundamentally thus: he becomes one with heaven and earth and all things. This is surely not confined to the great man: even in an inferior man's mind this is so. It is he himself who nevertheless makes it inferior, and that's all. Thus if he sees a child falling into a well, he cannot fail to have a concerned and compassionate mind towards it. This comes from his humanity and the child forming one entity. A child is still one of his own kind. Yet even if he sees a bird or animal shivering fearfully and calling pitifully, his mind cannot abide it. This comes from his humanity and the birds and animals forming one entity. This then is the mind which is capable of forming one entity with other things, and even though someone's mind may be that of an inferior man, it cannot but possess this capacity. And this has its root in heaven-decreed nature, which is inherently clear and unobscured. That is why it is called "lucid character."

So when unobscured by selfish desires, even an inferior man with an inferior man's mind—because of his humaneness which is capable of forming one entity with other things—is yet a noble man. But when obscured by selfish desire, even a noble man, because he cuts himself off from other beings, is nevertheless an inferior man. So, engaging in the learning of the noble man just means getting rid of the obscuration of selfish desires, thereby spontaneously manifesting lucid character and resuming essential oneness with heaven and earth and all things. It is not that there is something separate, something that can be added onto his basic being.

The utmost good is the ultimate principle of manifesting character and loving people. Heavenly decreed nature is purely of the utmost good. It is clear and unobscured, thus evincing its perfection. It is the substance of lucid character: it is what is called innate understanding. As the highest good is manifested, right and wrong are known by it, and it is affected and responds commensurately with the situation. There is nothing that does not inherently possess Heaven's centeredness: this is the unchanging principle of people and things.

The Teacher said: The endeavor of great learning is manifesting lucid character; manifesting lucid character is just making thought sincere; the endeavor of making thought sincere is just plumbing things and gaining understanding. So making dominant the task of making thought sincere and then going on to practice the endeavor of examining things and gaining understanding means that that endeavor will have results from the beginning. This is to say that being good and getting rid of evil are nothing but the task of making thought sincere. With [Zhu Xi's] new edition [of the *Great Learning*] exhaustively examining the principle *(li)* of things and affairs comes first; but this approach makes the task vast and hazy, so that there will be no result at all. In the main, the endeavor of centeredness is just making the self sincere. When making the self sincere reaches its furthest point, then it is consummate sincerity. When making thought sincere is at the utmost, then it is consummate good. All these endeavors are the same.

Source: Wang Yangming, Daxue wen, ch. 1: tr. Kurt Vall.

GLOSSARY

Confucius   (ca. 551–479 B.C.E.; Chinese: Kong Fuzi): Founder of Confucianism and one of the great sages of China.

Dao   "Way," a pattern of action that applies to all human societies and to natural forces.

Junzi   "Noble Man," one who embodies the ideal qualities of a Confucian gentleman.

Li   "Propriety," one of the primary Confucian virtues, involving proper social conduct and rituals.

Lunyu   *(analects)* A collection of aphorisms attributed to Confucius.

Mencius   (ca. 4th century B.C.E; Chinese: Mangzi): One of the most influential Confucian thinkers.

Neo-Confucianism   A movement to revive Confucianism that began in the 11th century.

Rectification of Names   *(zhengming)* The principle of using words nondeceptively, of saying what one actually means.

Ren   "Human-heartedness," one of the primary Confucian virtues, evidenced by proper attitudes and actions toward others.

Tian   "Heaven," an impersonal force that watches over human affairs.

FURTHER READINGS

CHEN, LI FU. *The Confucian Way: A New and Systematic Study of the 'Four Books.'* London: KPI, 1986.

FINGARETTE, HERBERT. *Confucius: The Secular as Sacred.* San Francisco: Harper Torchbooks, 1972.

HALL, DAVID L. and AMES, ROGER T. *Thinking Through Confucius.* Albany: State University of New York Press, 1987.

MCNAUGHTON, WILLIAM, ed. *The Confucian Vision.* Ann Arbor: Ann Arbor Paperbacks, 1974.

SCHWARTZ, BENJAMIN. *The World of Thought in Ancient China.* Cambridge, MA: Belknap Press, 1985.

WEI-MING, TU. *Centrality and Commonality: An Essay on Confucian Religiousness.* Albany: State University of New York Press, 1989.

Daoism

INTRODUCTION

For modern Chinese, religion is primarily a matter of participation in community activities and rituals connected with important transitions rather than adherence to doctrines and codes of conduct. Chinese rituals mark and celebrate the important rites of passage of human existence: birth, marriage, and death, as well as events in the agricultural calendar, such as planting and harvest. These rituals developed in a culture that is overwhelmingly agrarian and rural, in which the majority of people were (and still are) engaged in agricultural work. Underlying many Chinese religious practices is a deeply felt sense of the importance of promoting community solidarity and an emphasis on the rootedness of the individual and the collective in the natural world.

Another important feature of Chinese religious traditions is their eclecticism. The indigenous Chinese religious systems borrowed elements from each other and from traditions like Buddhism that were imported to China, and the foreign systems in turn adopted Chinese motifs and ideas in order to accommodate themselves to Chinese sensibilities. Among contemporary Chinese, sharp distinctions are seldom drawn between the major religious traditions of China: Daoism, Confucianism, and Buddhism; rather, they are viewed as harmoniously intersecting with each other to form a comprehensive system that is able to adapt itself to a wide spectrum of religious needs. The three traditions are collectively referred to as "lineage of teachings" (*zongjiao*) or "the three teachings" (*sanjiao*), indicating that they are not perceived as separate systems of doctrine and practice but as mutually complementary emphases.

Confucianism is viewed as being primarily concerned with the interactions of people in a social context. It outlines the norms and values that ensure social harmony, along with the rituals and duties that enable people to act appropriately when in the company of others. Daoism focuses on the connections between human beings and their natural environment, how natural processes and forces affect human existence, and how to predict the movements of these forces and manipulate them for the benefit of individuals and society. The purview of Buddhism is mainly life after death, since Buddhism brought to China a highly developed eschatology and a pantheon of compassionate buddhas and bodhisattvas who are willing and able to give aid both in the present life and after death.

The origins of Daoism lie in popular religious practices and ideas of ancient China. According to popular Daoist belief, the earliest codification of the central concepts of the tradition was set forth by Laozi, who according to legend was a sage who lived in the sixth century B.C.E. and who worked as an archivist in the state of Lu. Credited with the authorship of the classic work entitled *The Way and Virtue (Daodejing)*, Laozi became concerned with the degeneration of his society and decided to leave China and travel beyond the Western Gate that marked the border between Chinese civilization and the regions inhabited by non-Chinese peoples. As Laozi was leaving, the gatekeeper Yin Xi asked him to write a short outline of his philosophy for the benefit of posterity. Initially reluctant to commit his ideas to writing because words inevitably distort the truth, Laozi eventually agreed and summarized the essentials of what later came to be Daoist philosophy.

It should be noted that the text makes no claim to originality. Rather, Laozi stresses that his thoughts accord with those of the sages of the past and merely recapitulate the wisdom found by all who understand the subtle and profound workings of the universe. His text has two primary concerns: the Way (*dao*) and Virtue or Power (*de*), which is connected with its manifest operations. The Dao is described as a universal force, subtle and omnipresent, that gives rise to all things and provides their sustenance. It is the vital energy that makes all life possible, and it pervades the entire universe, providing a pattern for the growth and development of living things.

Transcending and embracing all dichotomies, the Dao is comprised of two opposite but complementary polarities, *yin* and *yang* Originally these terms seem to have referred to the shady and sunny sides of mountains, respectively. *Yin* is described as yielding, wet, passive, dark, and feminine, while *yang* is said to be aggressive, dry, active, light, and masculine. These distinctions reflect distinctive tendencies within natural systems, but they are not diametrically opposed. Rather, each contains elements of the other, and their interaction provides the creative and dynamic force behind the changes that occur in the natural world.

The Dao is ineffable. It transcends all sense experience and all thought. It may, however, be understood by the sage who becomes open to it and thus "becomes one with the Great Thoroughfare." The primary obstacle to this attainment is the senses, in combination with the intellect, which trick people into thinking that ordinary perceptions and cognitions provide a true picture of reality. Those who seek to become sages are counseled to empty themselves, to cast off learning, reasoning, words, and intellection. In this way they become open to direct experience of Dao, through which they can find true harmony with their environment and enjoy a long and tranquil life.

The workings of Dao tend toward harmony and balance, and whenever any part of a natural system develops extreme qualities, this imbalance triggers a corresponding backlash. This is true of natural phenomena and human beings. Imbalances in nature are corrected by automatic reactions, and the more extreme the imbalance, the more powerful will be the reaction. Similar principles operate in individual human lives and the actions of collectives.

Any person or group that develops extreme qualities or that disturbs the natural harmony of the world will reap corresponding consequences, which will inevitably right the balance of nature. Thus the Daoist sage goes along with the operations of the Dao, not forcing things, and so is able to live long and peacefully. Those who do not understand this principle are doomed to waste their vital energies in fruitless aggression and activity, like a strong swimmer who pushes against a current but eventually becomes exhausted and is carried downstream.

Laozi compares human beings at birth to uncarved blocks of wood (*pu*), with rough edges and unsymmetrical, like natural phenomena that have not been tampered with. Confucians shared this idea, but while they proposed to carve the block in order to properly socialize it, Laozi sees this notion as profoundly misguided. Humans at birth are supple and yielding, full of life energy, but through the process of acculturation they are placed into artificial molds and unnatural situations, which dissipate their energies in useless activities. Those who allow themselves to become caught up in the rat race inevitably wear themselves down and become like withered, dead branches—hard, stiff, and unyielding—and so shorten their lifespans.

According to Laozi, the operations of Dao may be compared to the movement of water. When water encounters a hard obstacle like a rock, it simply flows around it, rather than battering against it. Water, which is soft and yielding, does not contend against obstacles placed in its way, but instead moves around them, finding the path of least resistance. As it does this, however, it also slowly and inexorably wears down the resistance of even the hardest rock, and over the course of time overcomes all obstacles and may even create deep chasms in solid rock. Similarly, the sage avoids direct confrontation and goes along with the natural flow of Dao, practicing the Daoist virtue of "non-action" (*wuwei*). A person who perfects this technique appears to do nothing, but in reality moves with the natural rhythms of the world, thus working in accordance with the Dao to promote harmony and prosperity.

Zhuangzi, the other major figure of the early Daoist mystical tradition, shares similar views of the workings of Dao and the way of the sage. Where Laozi's text uses terse aphorisms to make its points, however, Zhuangzi tells stories that describe the way of the sage. Many of these have bizarre characters and strange situations, and they are pervaded by a subtle humor that gently mocks the ordinary ways of the world and the concerns of human society.

Zhuangzi also differs from Laozi in that he has little interest in applying Daoist principles in the political arena. The second half of Laozi's text is concerned with how rulers should act and the principles of good governance, while Zhuangzi repeatedly emphasizes his utter disinterest in becoming involved in such matters. Rather, Zhuangzi counsels his readers to cultivate uselessness, since things that are truly useless cannot be used by others and thus are left alone. The sage, according to Zhuangzi, moves unobtrusively among the hustle and bustle of the world, living at the margins of society, and is generally not even recognized as a sage by his or her contemporaries.

The establishment of Daoism as a distinctive religious tradition dates back to 142 C.E., when Zhang Daoling received the first of a series of revelations from Taishang Laojun, Lord Lao the Most High. This deity is the personification of the Dao and is believed by Daoist tradition to be Laozi, who in reality was a human form taken by the Dao in order to teach the truth to human beings. Zhang Daoling began to spread the teachings he had received and established the first organized Daoist system, named True Unity of Celestial Masters. Because of his connection with the first revelation, he was recognized as the first of the Celestial Masters, the patriarchs of the school.

The tradition continues today. The 64th Celestial Master currently resides in Taiwan and is considered to be the direct descendant of Zhang Daoling. The Celestial Masters tradition traces its philosophical roots back to the works of Laozi and Zhuangzi, and it has also developed into a communal religion that emphasizes rituals for purification and exorcism, along with teachings on morality.

Contemporary scholars commonly distinguish two main streams of Daoist thought: the system of the philosophers of the fourth and third centuries B.C.E. is termed "philosophical Daoism," and the later tradition that was concerned with techniques leading to immortality is termed "religious Daoism." While this division does capture an important distinction of emphases within the tradition, it is also overly simplistic. Daoism has a long and complex history that has produced numerous strands of thought and practice, and recent research has shown that elements of the "religious" strand may be found in the works of the early "philosophical" Daoists, and texts of "religious" Daoism are strongly influenced by the thought of "philosophical" Daoists.

In Zhuangzi's stories there are several mentions of the "immortals" (*xian*), who are said to live on a remote mountain (or, according to other accounts, on a hidden island). They avoid eating cereals, guard their vital energies, and are able to fly through the air. While most people dissipate their vital energies through involvement in mundane affairs, worry, and eating unhealthy foods, the immortals practice physical regimens that safeguard the life force (*qi*), while also avoiding activities and environments that weaken it. The search for immortality was an important concern of the developed Daoist tradition, which created elaborate systems of practice designed to promote long life. Among these were physical exercises that emulated the movements of long-lived animals (who were considered to be naturally adept at guarding vital energies), sexual techniques (*fang zhong*) that were believed to increase one's store of energy, special diets that were believed to promote the cultivation of energy, and chemical elixirs designed to replenish lost energy. Many of these elixirs contained cinnabar (mercuric sulfide), a red-colored liquid metal that was widely believed to contain a high concentration of vital energy.

Daoist masters also developed systems of meditative practices designed to promote longevity, such as "meditation on the One" (*shouyi*), in which one guards the vital energies, concentrating on the universal life force emanated by the Dao. This practice culminates in an ecstatic vision of multicolored light. Other techniques described five primary energy centers in the body, each of which was inhabited by a particular god. Meditators were advised to increase the energy levels in these centers by safeguarding the energy drawn into the body through breathing, by avoiding grains, by ingesting specific medicinal plants, and by medical techniques such as acupuncture and control of the pulse.

Daoist Scriptures

Given the long and varied history of Daoism and the range of concerns of Daoist authors, it is not surprising that the Daoist canon (*daozang*) contains a great variety of texts. All traditions of Daoism trace their origins back to the works of Laozi, Zhuangzi, and other early masters such as Liezi. Later developments incorporate their ideas and symbols, although they often diverge from their systems in significant ways. Moreover, despite the importance of these early masters for the later tradition, the development of the religion of Daoism took place many centuries after their deaths. The dawn of an organized religion of Daoism was the second century C.E., and it can be traced back to the movements of the Great Peace (Taiping) and the Celestial Masters, which formed around charismatic leaders and spread throughout China, among both common people and the cultural and political elite.

During the fourth and fifth centuries, Daoism became a widely popular tradition which appealed to all classes of Chinese society, and it is during this time that it began to develop a distinctive collection of scriptures. The earliest listing of Daoist texts was attempted by Ban Gu (32–92), in his *History of the Han* (*Han shu*), but it was not until the latter part of the fifth century that the first comprehensive catalogue of Daoist scriptures was prepared by Lu Xiujing (406–477). Sponsored by Song Mingdi (r. 465–477), he compiled the *Index to the Scriptures of the Three Caverns* (*Sandong Jingshu Mulu*), which he presented to the emperor in 471. Now lost, this massive compilation was said to have listed over 1,200 fascicles (*juan*), including philosophical texts, alchemical works, and descriptions of talismans.

The next important listing of Daoist literature was prepared by order of Emperor Tang Xuanzong (r. 713–756), who believed himself to be a direct descendant of Laozi (who by this time was widely regarded as a celestial deity). The emperor ordered a search throughout his empire for all existing Daoist literature, which was eventually brought together in a collection called *Sublime Compendium of the Three Caverns* (*Sandong Qiong gang*), which is said to have comprised 3,700 texts. He had a number of copies made of the collection, which were then stored in Daoist temples. Shortly after this, however, the imperial libraries of the capitals of Chang'an and Loyang were destroyed during the An Lushan and Shi Siming rebellions, with the result that much of this huge collection was also lost.

Another compilation was ordered during the Song dynasty (960–1279). Song Zhenzong (r. 998–1022) ordered his advisor Wang Qinruo (962–1025) to compile a catalogue of existing Daoist literature, and later Zhang Junfang (ca. 1008–1029) headed a team of Daoist priests who compiled a collection of Daoist scriptures called *Precious Canon of the Celestial Palace of the Great Song*

(*Song Tiangong Daozang*), which had 4,565 titles. This is regarded by the tradition as the first definitive edition of the Daoist canon.

During subsequent dynasties other compilations of the Daoist canon were prepared. The latest version of the canon was printed in 1926, with the sponsorship of the Nationalist government. Consisting of 1,120 fascicles, it is the largest collection of Daoist literature ever completed. Fu Zengxiang (1872–1950), a former minister of education, convinced President Xu Shichang (1855–1939) to allocate government funds to preserve this literature. Based on the collection of the White Cloud Abbey (Baiyun Guan) of Beijing, it is believed to be descended from an edition of the canon prepared in 1445, and later emended in 1845.

Since the compilation of the canon by Lu Xiujing in 471, editions of the *Daozang* have traditionally followed his division of Daoist texts into the "Three Caverns": (1) Cavern of Perfection (*dongzhen*), which derives from the Supreme Clarity (*shangqing*) texts; (2) Cavern of Mystery (*dongxuan*), which derives from the Numinous Treasure (*lingbao*) literature; and (3) Cavern of Spirit (*dongshen*), which is based on the texts collectively called "Three Kings" (*sanhuang*). This division appears to be patterned on the division of Buddhist teachings into the Three Vehicles.

In addition to this central division, the Daoist canon also contains other texts, such as the "Four Supplements" (*sifu*), which follow the Three Caverns, named respectively *Great Mystery* (*taixuan*), *Great Peace* (*taiping*), *Great Purity* (*taiqing*), and *True Unity* (*zhengyi*). The first three of these have traditionally been regarded as supplements to the Three Caverns, although in fact their origins are believed by contemporary scholars to have been composed in reference to other texts. The *Great Mystery* supplement is based on the *Daodejing*; the *Great Peace*, *Great Purity*, and *True Unity* collections appear to be based on the *Scripture on the Great Peace* (*Taipingjing*); the *Great Purity* (*Taiqing*) texts are based on alchemy, and the True Unity or Celestial Masters tradition.

As Daoist literature developed, other texts found their way into the canon that did not fit neatly into the early divisions, and as a result the canon was further subdivided. In the modern canon, each of the Three Caverns is divided into 12 sections: (1) original revelations; (2) celestial talismans; (3) commentaries; (4) sacred diagrams; (5) histories and genealogies; (6) codes of conduct; (7) rules for ceremonies; (8) outlines of rituals; (9) techniques for alchemy, geomancy, and numerology; (10) hagiographical works; (11) hymns and prayers; and (12) memorial addresses. Despite the apparently detailed nature of this division, individual sections contain a range of literature, and individual texts within a given division may not correspond to the general category.

In addition to the *Daozang*, another important compilation of Daoist scriptures should be mentioned, the *Edition of Essentials from the Daoist Canon* (*Daozang Jiyao*), a smaller collection of texts compiled during the Qing dynasty (1644–1912). The 1906 edition of this corpus contains 287 titles, including works attributed to Sun Buer, some of whose writings are excerpted below. These two collections of scriptures contain hundreds of rituals for renewal (*jiao*), funeral liturgies (*zhai*), philosophical texts, cosmological treatises, rituals for festivals and healing, discussions of external and internal alchemy, medical literature, meditation texts, descriptions for identification and preparation of healing herbs and roots, mythological stories and hagiographies of great Daoist masters and immortals, and a variety of other types of literature.

Due to the diffuse nature of the Daoist canon, it is possible to provide only a small cross-section of this literature. The following selections attempt to give a representative sampling of some of the most important texts and genres of literature in the canon and focus on developments that have had a significant impact on the development of Daoism.

DAOIST SCRIPTURES

A BRIEF ACCOUNT OF LAOZI'S LIFE

A number of contemporary scholars believe that Laozi (whose name means "Old Master") may not have been a historical figure. In addition, there is significant textual evidence that the work attributed to him actually comprises materials from different authors and was compiled centuries after he lived. His historicity is doubted because there is little solid evidence that he ever lived and considerable confusion among the sources that mention him. According to the record composed by the historian Sima Qian (154–80 B.C.E.), Laozi was reportedly born in a small village in southern China in the later period of the Zhou dynasty. His surname was Li, and his personal name was Er. He worked as an archivist for most of his life but, after becoming concerned with what he perceived as a degeneration of his society, Laozi decided to leave through the Western Gate, which marked the boundary of China. According to Sima Qian, he was not heard from again. In later times, however, numerous sightings of Laozi were reported, and a wealth of legends concerning this mysterious figure circulated throughout China.

Laozi cultivated the Dao and the Virtue. His teaching focused on remaining apart [from society] and avoiding fame. After living under the Zhou for a long time, he saw that the Zhou was in decline, and he decided to leave. When he reached the pass [on the western frontier of China], Yin Xi, the Guardian of the Pass, said, 'Since you are about to completely withdraw, I ask you to write a text for me.' Laozi thus composed a book in two sections which described the meaning of the Dao and the Virtue in more than five thousand characters. He then left. No one knows what became of him.

Source: Sima Qian, *Shiji*, p. 63.2142.

LAOZI INSTRUCTS CONFUCIUS

According to traditional sources, Laozi was an older contemporary of Confucius, and the two supposedly met on several occasions. When Daoist texts report their meetings, Laozi is portrayed as utterly surpassing Confucius in his understanding of Dao and as admonishing him to give up his attachment to rituals, propriety, and learning and embrace simplicity. Not surprisingly, Confucian sources portray Confucius as the victor. In the following selection, drawn from Sima Qian's history, Confucius comes to Laozi for instruction on the proper performance of rituals, but is advised instead to give up his rigidity and affectations and embrace Dao.

Confucius traveled to Zhou with the intention of questioning Laozi about rites. Laozi said, 'The people you mention have decomposed, both the people and their bones. Only their words remain here. Also, when the noble person attains his season, he will harness his horses. If he does not attain it, he will be pushed along like a tumbleweed moving with the wind. . . . Get rid of your arrogant manners and many desires, get rid of your artificial mannerisms and your grand ambitions. These all are of no benefit to you. This is all I have to tell you.'

Confucius left and told his disciples, 'I know that birds can fly, I know that fish can swim, and I know that animals can run. One may make traps for things that run, one may put out lines for that which swims, and one may make arrows with attached twine for that which flies. But regarding the dragon, I may never know how it flies in the wind and clouds and ascends into the sky. Today I have met Laozi. Is he like the dragon?'

Source: Sima Qian, *Shiji*, p. 63.2139.

LAOZI CONVERTS THE BARBARIANS

When Buddhism first arrived in China, many Daoists welcomed it as a kindred system, but over time rivalries between the two traditions developed, although they continued to borrow from each other. In the following passage, a Daoist author claims that the Buddha was really Laozi, who traveled to India after passing through the Western Gate. He intended to teach them the essence of Daoism, but soon realized that they were only capable of understanding the "Lesser Way," an inferior version of his teaching suitable for barbarians. The passage reflects traditional Chinese attitudes toward non-Chinese peoples, who are seen as savages.

Using his divine powers, [Laozi] then summoned all the barbarian kings. Without question they appeared from far and near. There were numerous kings and nobles. . . . They all came with their wives and concubines, families and other dependents. They crowded around the Venerable Lord, coming ever closer in order to hear the law.

At this time the Venerable Lord addressed the assembled barbarian kings:

'Your hearts are full of evil! You engage in killing and harm other beings! Since you feed only on blood and meat, you cut short manifold lives!

'Today I will . . . prohibit meat-eating among you and leave you with a diet of wheat and gruel. This will take care of all that slaughter and killing! Those among you who cannot desist shall themselves become dead meat!

'You barbarians are greedy and cruel! You make no difference between kin and stranger. You are intent only to satisfy your greed and debauchery! Not a trace of mercy or sense of social duty is within you!

'Look at you! Your hair and beards are unkempt and too long! How can you comb and wash them? Even from a distance you are full of rank smell! How awfully dirty your bodies must be!

'Now that you are made to cultivate the Dao all these things will be great annoyances to your practice. I therefore order all of you to shave off your beards and hair. . . . By teaching you the Lesser Way, I will, by and by, lead you to more cultivated manners. In addition, I will give you a number of precepts and prohibitions, so that you gradually get to exercise mercy and compassion. Each month on the fifteenth day, you shall repent your sins.'

Source: *Huahujing*, p. 1266b: *The Taoist Experience: An Anthology,* tr. Livia Kohn (Albany: State University of New York Press, 1993), pp. 76–77.

LAOZI BECOMES AN IMMORTAL

The following excerpt is taken from the Scripture of the Western Ascension, *which portrays Laozi as an immortal after his departure from China. The text reports that he traveled to India, where he became known as the Buddha. He taught the essentials of Daoism to his Indian audiences, and shortly before leaving human society forever he returned to China to impart a final instruction to Yin Xi.*

Suddenly Laozi was nowhere to be seen. The office building was illuminated by a brilliance of five colors, simultaneously dark and yellow. Yin Xi went into the courtyard, bowed down and said: 'Please, dear spirit man, let me see you once again. Give me one more rule, and I can guard the primordial source of all.'

He looked up and saw Laozi suspended in midair several feet above the ground. He looked like a statue. The image appeared and disappeared; it was vague and indistinct and seemed to waver between young and old.

Laozi said: 'I will give you one more admonition; make sure you get it right: Get rid of all impurity and stop all thoughts; calm your mind and guard the One. When all impurities are gone, the myriad affairs are done. These are the essentials of my Dao.'

Then the vision vanished. Yin Xi did not know where it had gone. He cried bitterly and worshipped it in remembrance. Then he retired from office on grounds of illness. He gave up all thinking and guarded the One, and the myriad affairs were done.

Source: *Xishengjing* selections: Livia Kohn, *Early Chinese Mysticism: Philosophy and Soteriology in the Taoist Tradition* (Princeton: Princeton University Press, 1992), p. 131.

LAOZI: THE *DAODEJING*

Regarded by Daoist tradition as the oldest text of the canon, the Daodejing is attributed to Laozi. Containing about five thousand characters, it is also popularly known as "The Five Thousand Character Classic." Modern versions of the text are divided into two sections, the first of which describes the Dao, while the second is concerned with how rulers should follow the way of Dao in order to rule wisely and well. Some contemporary scholars believe that the text we have today is not in fact a unitary work, but instead contains materials from various periods. It is widely believed to have been compiled during the Warring States Period, around 250 B.C.E., and the earliest known version of the text dates back to the beginning of the Han dynasty (202–220). It has also been the subject of numerous commentaries, many of which may still be found today in the Daoist canon.

1. The Dao that can be described
    Is not the eternal Dao.
    The name that can be spoken
    Is not the eternal name.
    The nameless is the origin of Heaven and Earth;
    The named is the mother of all things.
    Remain always free from desire,
    And you will see its subtlety.
    Always hold onto desires,
    And you will only see its results.
    The two develop together
    But have different names.
    They are deep and mysterious.
    Deeper and more mysterious, the gate of all wonders.

2. When beauty is recognized, ugliness is born.
    When good is recognized, evil is born.
    Is and is not give rise to each other;
    Difficult requires easy;
    Long is measured by short;
    High is determined by low;
    Sound is harmonized by voice;
    Back follows front.
    Therefore, the sage applies himself to non-action (*wuwei*),
    Moves without speaking,
    Creates the ten thousand things without hindrance,
    Lives, but does not possess,
    Acts, but does not presume,
    Accomplishes, but takes no credit.
    Since no credit is taken, his accomplishments endure.

3. Do not exalt heroes,
    And people will not quarrel.
    Do not value rare objects,
    And people will not steal.
    Don't display things of desire,
    And their hearts will not be troubled.
    Therefore, the sage governs by emptying their hearts and filling their stomachs,
    Discouraging their ambitions and strengthening their bones;
    Leads people away from knowledge and desire;
    Keeps the learned from imposing on others;
    Practices non-action, and the natural order is not disturbed.

4. Dao is empty.
   Use it, and it will never overflow;
   It is bottomless, the origin of all things.
   It blunts sharp edges,
   Unties knots, softens light,
   Merges with the dust.
   I do not know from where it comes,
   Its appearance precedes the Ancestor.

6. The spirit of the valley never dies.
   It is called the mysterious female.
   The gate of the mysterious female
   Is called the root of heaven and earth.
   It is continuous and exists forever;
   Use it and you will never wear it out.

8. It is best to be like water;
   Which benefits the ten thousand things and does not compete.
   It collects in the places in which humans disdain to live,
   Near the Dao.
   Live in goodness;
   Keep your mind deep;
   Treat others with kindness;
   Keep your word;
   Do what is right;
   Work at the proper time;
   If you do not contend, you cannot be blamed.

10. Can you balance your life force
    And embrace the One without differentiation?
    Can you gently control your breath like an infant?
    Can you purify your profound insight so it will become stainless?
    Can you love people and govern the state without [clinging to] knowledge?
    Can you open and shut the Gate of Heaven
    Without clinging to the earth? . . .
    Produce and cultivate
    Produce but not possess,
    Act without depending,
    Excel but do not try to master [others]:
    This is called profound virtue (*de*).

14. We look at it and do not see it;
    It is called the Invisible.
    We listen to it and do not hear it;
    It is called the Inaudible.
    We touch it and do not feel it;
    It is called the subtle. . . .
    Infinite and boundless, it cannot be named;
    It subsists in nothingness.
    It is shape without shape, form (*xiang*) without form.
    It is the vague and elusive. . . .

17. With the best rulers
   The people know that they exist.
   The next best they see and praise.
   The next they fear.
   And the next they revile.
   If you do not have basic trust
   There will be no trust at all,
   Be circumspect in the use of words.
   When your work is done,
   The people will say, "We have done it ourselves."

18. With the decline of the great Dao,
   The [doctrines of] humanity and righteousness appeared.
   When learning and cleverness are recognized,
   Great hypocrisy arises.
   When family relations are forgotten,
   Filial piety and affection arise.
   When a country falls into chaos,
   Loyal citizens come forth.

22. The crippled becomes whole.
   The crooked becomes straight.
   The hollow becomes filled.
   The worn becomes renewed.
   The meager becomes increased.
   The full becomes deluded.
   Therefore, sages embrace the One
   And maintain the world.
   Do not display themselves
   And are therefore luminous.
   Do not assert themselves
   And are therefore exalted.
   Do not boast
   And therefore succeed.
   Are not complacent
   And thus endure.
   Do not contend
   And so no one in the world
   Can contend against them.

28. One who knows the male and maintains the female
   Becomes the valley of the world.
   Being the valley of the world,
   Virtue will endure.
   Return to the state of infancy.
   Know the white, maintain the black,
   Become the model for the world.
   Being the model for the world,
   One will never deviate from virtue.
   Return to the state of the uncarved block (*pu*).

37. The Dao does nothing
    Yet through it everything is done.
    If kings and princes could hold to it,
    The world would be transformed of its own accord.
    When transformed, beings wish to engage in action.
    Still them through wordless simplicity.
    Then there will be no desire.
    Absence of desire is tranquillity,
    And the world becomes peaceful of its own accord.

41. When superior people hear of Dao
    They endeavor to live in accordance with it.
    When the mediocre hear of Dao
    Sometimes they are aware of it, and sometimes they are not.
    When the lowest type hear of Dao
    They break into loud laughter.
    If it were not laughed at, it would not be Dao.

43. The softest thing in the world overcomes the hardest.
    Non-being penetrates that which has no space.
    This indicates the benefit of non-action.
    Few in the world can understand wordless teaching and the benefit of
    non-action.

48. In pursuing knowledge, one gains daily;
    Pursuing Dao, one loses daily.
    Through losing and losing again,
    One arrives at non-action.
    By doing nothing everything is done.
    View the whole world as nothing.
    When one makes the slightest effort,
    The world is beyond one's grasp.

49. The sage has no fixed opinions,
    The opinions of ordinary people become his own.
    I am good to people who are good;
    I am also good to those who are not good:
    That is the goodness of virtue.
    I believe honest people;
    I also believe the dishonest:
    This is the trust of virtue.
    Sages create harmony in the world.
    They mingle their hearts with the world.
    Ordinary people fix their eyes and ears on them,
    But sages become the children of the world.

63. Act without acting.
    Serve without serving.
    Taste without tasting.
    Whether it is great or small, many or few,
    Repay hatred with virtue.

Deal with the difficult through what is easy;
Deal with the big through the small.
The difficulties of the world
Should be dealt with through the easiest;
The great things of the world
Should be accomplished through the smallest.

65. The rulers of old did not enlighten the people,
But kept them ignorant.
Therefore, ruling through cleverness
Leads to rebellion.
Not ruling through cleverness
Leads to good fortune.

76. When people are born, they are soft and weak;
At death, they are stiff and strong.
The ten thousand plants and trees are born soft and supple,
And at death are brittle and dry.
Hardness and strength are the companions of death,
And softness and weakness are the companions of life.
Therefore, the strongest armies do not seek to conquer.
The mightiest trees are cut down.
The strong and great sink down;
The soft and weak rise.

78. Nothing in the world is softer and weaker than water
But nothing is superior to it in overcoming the hard and strong;
Weakness overcomes strength
And softness overcomes hardness.
Everyone knows this, and no one practices it.

81. True words are not fine-sounding;
Fine-sounding words are not true.
Good people do not argue;
Argumentative people are not good.
Wise people are not learned;
The learned are not wise.
The sage does not accumulate things;
Has enough by working for others;
Gives to others and has even more.
The Dao of Heaven benefits and does not harm.
The Dao of the sage accomplishes, but does not contend.

Source: *Daodejing*, selections.

WANG BI: COMMENTARY ON THE *DAODEJING*

Wang Bi (226–249), author of the most influential commentary on the Daodejing, *is renowned in China as one of the foremost representatives of the Dark Learning (xuanxue) school of Chinese philosophy. This school is based on the "Three Dark Texts": the* Yijing, *the* Daodejing, *and the* Zhuangzi. *The philosophers of the Dark*

Learning school proposed to return to the ancient classics, whose ideas they mingled with Confucian notions about the ideal society and Daoist metaphysics. One of Wang Bi's original contributions to Chinese thought was the notion of "original non-being" (benwu), according to which prior to the creation of the universe there was only undifferentiated non-being. From this arose the One, another way of conceiving the Dao. From the One arose the Two, and from this came the myriad things of the universe.

All being originates from nonbeing. Therefore, the time before there were physical shapes and names is the beginning of the myriad beings. When shapes and names are there, [the Dao] raises them, educates them, adjusts them, and causes their end. It serves as their mother. The text [the *Daodejing*] means that the Dao produces and completes beings on the basis of the formless and the nameless. They are produced and completed but do not know how or why.

Source: *Laozi* 1.1.1a: *Early Chinese Mysticism*, p. 61.

VISUALIZING THE DAO

The following passage is an example of how Laozi's ideas became mingled with long life practices in later Daoist literature. It indicates techniques for visualization that will enable the meditator to harmonize vital energies and acquire esoteric wisdom.

> These are the secret instructions of the Highest Lord.
> First burn incense and straighten your robes, greet the ten directions with three bows each. Concentrate your mind inside and visualize Master Yin and the Master on the River, as well as Laozi, the Great Teacher of the Law. Then recite the following in your mind:
> Mysterious, again mysterious, the origin of Dao,
> Above, virtue incorporates chaos and the prime. . . .
> In my room, the seven jewels come together,
> Doors and windows open of themselves.
> Utter in my purity, I strive for deeper truth,
> Riding on bright light, I ascend the purple sky.
> Sun and moon to my right and left,
> I go to the immortals, and eternal life.
> All seven ancestors arise, are reborn in heaven,
> The world, how true, the gate to virtue and to Dao.

Finish this mental recitation, then clap your teeth and swallow the saliva thirty-six times each. Visualize the green dragon to your left, the white tiger to your right, the red bird in front of you, and the dark warrior at your back. . . .

On three sides you are joined by an attendant, each having a retinue of a thousand carriages and ten thousand horsemen. Eight thousand jade maidens and jade lads of heaven and earth stand guard for you.

Then repeat the formula, this time aloud, and begin to recite the five thousand words of the Scripture [the *Daodejing*]. Conclude by three times clapping your teeth and swallowing the saliva.

Source: *Laozi Daodejing Xuzhui: The Taoist Experience*, pp. 173–174.

THE DAO OF IMMORTALITY

According to legend, Heshang Gong, the Master on the River, lived during the reign of the Han emperor Wen (179–156 B.C.E.), but the earliest dated stories of his life come from the third century C.E. He is said to have lived near the Yellow River, where he studied the Daodejing *in solitude. Eventually he came to the attention of the emperor, who asked him to teach the essentials of Laozi's text. In the passage below, he indicates how the ideas of the* Daodejing *became mingled with immortality practices such as breathing exercises and gymnastics. In the system of Heshang Gong, people receive vital energy* (qi) *from Heaven, but they ordinarily dissipate it unless they practice special techniques to keep it stored in the vital organs.*

The Dao of prolonged life lies with the Mysterious Female. Mysterious is heaven, within human beings it is the nose. Female is earth, within human beings it is the mouth.

Heaven feeds people with the five energies. They enter the body through the nose and are stored in the heart. These five energies are clear and subtle, they form essence and spirit, intelligence and clear perception, sound and voice, as well as the five kinds of inner nature.

Heaven's manifest counterpart is the spirit soul. The spirit soul is male. It enters and leaves the human body through the nose. It is aligned with the Dao of heaven. Thus the nose is the Mysterious.

Earth nourishes people with the five tastes. They enter the body through the mouth and are stored in the stomach. The five tastes are turbid and coarse, they form the physical body, bones and flesh, blood and arteries, as well as the six kinds of emotions.

Earth's manifest counterpart is the material soul. The material soul is female. It enters and leaves the human body through the mouth. It is aligned with the Dao of earth. Thus the mouth is the female.

The nose and the mouth are the gateways by which the primordial energy that pervades Heaven and Earth comes and goes. Inhalation and exhalation through the nose and the mouth continue without interruption, subtly and miraculously. It is as if it would go on forever, yet seems not to be there at all. In your application of breathing, remain relaxed and comfortable. Never make haste or labor the exercise.

Source: *Laozi Daodejing Xuzhui* 6.1.5ab: *Early Chinese Mysticism*, p. 68.

PURITY AND TRANQUILLITY

As the Daoist tradition developed, Laozi's successors developed techniques for incorporating his doctrines into religious practice. The following excerpt, which became popular during the Song dynasty (960–1260), was used as a guide to meditation practice by the Complete Perfection (Quanzhen) school of Daoism, and is still in use today in its religious services.

The Great Dao has no form;
It brings forth and raises heaven and earth.
The Great Dao has no feelings;
It regulates the course of the sun and the moon.
The Great Dao has no name;
It raises and nourishes the myriad beings.
I do not know its name—
So I call it Dao.
The Dao can be pure or turbid, moving or tranquil.
Heaven is pure, earth is turbid;
Heaven is moving, earth is tranquil.
The male is moving, the female is tranquil. . . .
Always be pure and tranquil;
Heaven and earth
Return to the primordial.
The human spirit is fond of purity,
But the mind disturbs it.
The human mind is full of tranquillity,
But desires meddle with it.
Get rid of desires for good,
And the mind will be calm.
Cleanse your mind,
And the spirit will be pure.

Source: *Qingjing jing: The Taoist Experience*, pp. 25–26.

ZHUANGZI'S LIFE AND WORK

Zhuangzi, one of the two main figures of "philosophical Daoism," is believed to have lived during the fourth century B.C.E. Little is known about his life except for the enigmatic descriptions found in his own works. Sima Qian reports that he lived in the southern country of Mang, in modern-day Henan, and that he died around 290 B.C.E. He is said to have held a minor government post but refused any offers of higher office, preferring to retain his autonomy and personal freedom. According to his own account, he sought to live apart from his society, refusing honors and political involvement, and cultivated the virtue of "uselessness," which enabled him to move unmolested in the world and to attain a state of harmony with the Dao.

Zhuangzi lived in Mang. His given name was Zhou. Zhou once worked as a functionary at Qiyuan in Mang. He was a contemporary of King Hui of Liang (r. 370–335 B.C.E.) and King Xuan of Qi (r. 342–324 B.C.E.). There was nothing his teachings did not consider, and their essence hearkened back to the words of Laozi. His texts, comprising more than 100,000 characters, all used allegories. . . . He mocked people like Confucius and elucidated the meanings of Laozi . . . and he was adept at creating texts with hidden allusions and analogies. He used them to attack the Confucians and followers of Mozi. Even the greatest scholars of his day could not defend themselves against him. His words flowed and swirled freely, at his whim, and powerful people could not use him, including kings, dukes, and others.

Source: Sima Qian, *Shiji*, 63.2144.

THE DAO IS IN EVERYTHING

In the following selection, Zhuangzi indicates that Dao is everywhere and in every-thing, and that those who truly know it understand that it pervades even the lowest and most despised parts of the world.

> Dong Guo asked Zhuangzi, "The thing called Dao: where does it exist?"
> Zhuangzi said, "There's no place it doesn't exist."
> "Come," said Dong Guo, "you must be more specific!"
> "It is in ants."
> "How can it be in something so low?"
> "It is in grass."
> "But that's even lower!"
> "It is in bricks and shards."
> "But that's even lower!"
> "It is in excrement."

Source: *Zhuangzi*, ch. 22.

THE VALUE OF KNOWING DAO

According to Zhuangzi, most people waste their energies striving and planning for the future, and so fail to live in the moment. Sages, however, learn to move with the flow of Dao, and so they lead long and peaceful lives.

> 'Dao is without beginning or end, but things have their life and death—you cannot rely upon their fulfillment. One moment empty, the next moment full—you cannot depend upon their form. The years cannot be held off; time cannot be stopped. Decay, growth, fullness, and empti-ness end and then begin again. It is thus that we must describe the plan of the Great Meaning and discuss the principles of the ten thousand things. The life of things is a gallop, a headlong dash—with every movement they alter, with every moment they shift. What should you do and what should you not do? Everything will change of itself, that is certain!'
> 'If that is so,' said the Lord of the River, 'then what is valuable about Dao?'
> Ruo of the North Sea said, 'One who understands Dao is certain to have command of basic principles. One who has command of basic principles is certain to know how to deal with circumstances. And one who knows

how to deal with circumstances will not allow things to cause harm. When a person has perfect virtue, fire cannot burn him, water cannot drown him, cold and heat cannot afflict him, birds and beasts cannot injure him. . . .'

Source: *Zhuangzi*, ch. 17: *Chuang-tzu: Basic Writings,* tr. Burton Watson (New York: Columbia University Press, 1964), pp. 103–104.

THE PITFALLS OF WORDS AND CONCEPTS

A central theme of Zhuangzi's philosophy is the limitations of language. Those who become caught up in expressions and concepts inevitably fail to recognize truth, which cannot be captured in words.

Now I am going to make a statement here. I don't know whether it fits into the category of other people's statements or not. But whether it fits into their category or whether it doesn't, it obviously fits into some category. So in that respect it is no different from their statements. However, let me try making my statement.

There is a beginning. There is a not yet beginning to be a beginning. There is a not yet beginning to be a not yet beginning to be a beginning. There is being. There is nonbeing. There is a not yet beginning to be nonbeing. There is a not yet beginning to be a not yet beginning to be nonbeing. Suddenly there is being and nonbeing. But between this being and nonbeing, I don't really know which is being and which is nonbeing. Now I have just said something. But I don't know whether what I have said has really said something or whether it hasn't said something.

There is nothing in the world bigger than the tip of an autumn hair, and Mount Tai is little. No one has lived longer than a dead child, and Pengzu died young. Heaven and earth were born at the same time I was, and the ten thousand things are one with me.

We have already become one, so how can I say anything? But I have just said that we are one, so how can I not be saying something? The one and what I said about it make two, and two and the original one make three. If we go on this way, then even the cleverest mathematician can't tell where we'll end, much less an ordinary person. If by moving from nonbeing to being we get to three, how far will we get if we move from being to being? Better not to move, but let things be! . . .

If Dao is made clear, it is not Dao. If discriminations are put into words, they do not suffice. If benevolence has a constant object, it cannot be universal. If modesty is fastidious, it cannot be trusted. If daring attacks, it cannot be complete. These five are all round, but they tend toward the square.

Source: *Zhuangzi*, ch. 2: *Chuang-tzu: Basic Writings.*

THE VALUE OF UNLEARNING

Zhuangzi teaches that most problems come from entanglement with words and concepts. As an antidote, he advises that we "unlearn" the lessons that others have taught us "for our own good." Ideas of morality, justice, truth, etc. merely confuse people and make them think of doing the opposite. To counteract this, an important meditative practice is "sitting and forgetting" (zuowang), in which one simply lets thoughts flow freely, in harmony with Dao, and thus artificial concepts disperse of their own accord. A person who perfects this is able to attain the state of "free and easy wandering" in which one acts spontaneously, in accordance with the impulses of the moment. The following passage contains a section from Zhuangzi and a commentary by Guo Xiang, who compiled the edition that is the only extant version of the Zhuangzi.

> "What does 'sitting in oblivion' mean?" Confucius asked. "I smash up my limbs and body," Yan Hui replied, "drive out perceptions and intellect, get rid of physical shape and abandon all knowledge. Thus I merge with the Great Thoroughfare."
>
> Guo Xiang comments,
>
> Practicing this forgetfulness, how can there be anything not forgotten? First forget the traces, such as benevolence and righteousness; then put that which caused the traces out of the mind. On the inside, unaware of one's body, on the outside never know there is a universe. Only then will one be fully open, become one with the process of change and pervade everything.

Source: Guo Xiang, *Zhuangzi Zhu*, p. 8.39a: *Early Chinese Mysticism*, pp. 74–75.

THE SAGE IS GODLIKE

A person who is in harmony with Dao is able to move freely in the world, unharmed by things that injure ordinary people. The following passage was cited by the later Daoist tradition as evidence that Zhuangzi was interested in immortality practices, since his description of the sage indicates that understanding of Dao makes a person godlike, able to fly and to transcend death.

> Wang Ni said, "The Perfect Man is godlike. Though the great swamps blaze, they cannot burn him; though the great rivers freeze, they cannot chill him; though swift lightning splits the hills and howling gales shake the sea, they cannot frighten him. A man like this rides the clouds and mist, straddles the sun and moon, and wanders beyond the four seas. Even life and death have no effect on such a man, much less the rules of profit and loss!"

Source: *Zhuangzi*, ch. 2: *Chuang Tzu: Basic Writings*, pp. 41–42.

DREAMS AND REALITY

In the following passage, Zhuangzi falls asleep and dreams that he is a butterfly, but when he awakes he is unsure whether he is Zhuangzi or a butterfly dreaming of being Zhuangzi. The passage exemplifies the way that Zhuangzi merges dreams and waking "reality" while indicating that the boundaries between the two are not as rigid as ordinary people assume.

Once Zhuang Zhou dreamt that he was a butterfly, a butterfly flitting and flying around, content with himself and doing as he pleased. He didn't know he was Zhuang Zhou. Suddenly he woke up and there he was, solid and clearly Zhuang Zhou. But he didn't know if he was really Zhuang Zhou who had dreamt he was a butterfly, or a butterfly now dreaming he was Zhuang Zhou. Between Zhuang Zhou and a butterfly there must be some difference! These are the transformations of things.

Source: *Zhuangzi*, ch. 2: *Chuang-tzu: Basic Writings.*

WORLDLY FAME IS LIKE A DEAD RAT

Throughout his life, Zhuangzi avoided all attempts to make himself useful to his society. When offered important positions, he turned them down, preferring instead to live in the moment, unharried by the concerns of busy and important people.

When Huizi was prime minister of Liang, Zhuangzi set off to visit him. Someone said to Huizi, 'Zhuangzi is coming because he wants to replace you as prime minister!'

With this Huizi was filled with alarm and searched all over the state for three days and three nights trying to find Zhuangzi. Zhuangzi then came to see him and said, 'In the south there is a bird called the Yuanchu. . . . The Yuanchu rises up from the South Sea and flies to the North Sea, and it will rest on nothing but the Wutong tree, eat nothing but the fruit of the Lien, and drink only from springs of sweet water. Once there was an owl who had gotten hold of a half-rotten old rat, and as the Yuanchu passed by, it raised its head, looked up at the Yuanchu, and said, "Shoo!" Now that you have this Liang state of yours, are you trying to shoo me?'

Source: *Zhuangzi*, ch. 17: *Chuang Tzu: Basic Writings*, pp. 109–110.

SIMPLICITY AND NATURALNESS

According to Zhuangzi, the sage completely transcends the limitations felt by ordinary beings, and cares nothing for their judgments.

The sage leans on the sun and moon, tucks the universe under his arm, merges himself with things, leaves the confusion and muddle as it is, and looks on slaves as exalted. Ordinary men strain and struggle; the sage is stupid and blockish. He takes part in ten thousand ages and achieves simplicity in oneness. For him, all the ten thousand things are what they are, and thus they enfold each other.

Source: *Zhuangzi*, ch. 2: *Chuang Tzu: Basic Writings*, p. 42.

THE TRUE MAN

The sage moves in the world without becoming attached to anything. Living in the moment, he simply takes things as they come, and so is at peace. Ordinary people, by contrast, are full of desires, cares, and worries, and so fail to realize their potential.

One who knows what Heaven does and knows what humanity does has reached the peak. Knowing what Heaven does, one lives with Heaven. Knowing what humanity does, one uses the knowledge of what one knows to help out the knowledge of what one doesn't know, and lives out the years that Heaven provides without being cut off midway—this is perfect knowledge. . . .

What do I mean by a True Man? The True Man of ancient times did not rebel against poverty, did not grow proud in plenty, and did not plan affairs. Being like this, he could commit an error and not regret it, could meet with success and not make a show. Being like this, he could climb the high places and not be frightened, could enter the water and not get wet, could enter the fire and not get burned. His knowledge could climb all the way up to the Way like this.

The True Man of ancient times slept without dreaming and woke without care; he ate without savoring and his breath came from deep inside. The True Man breathes with his heels; the mass of men breathe with their throats. Crushed and bound down, they gasp out their words as though they were retching. Deep in their passions and desires, they are shallow in the workings of Heaven.

The True Man of ancient times knew nothing of loving life, knew nothing of hating death. He emerged without delight; he went back in without a fuss. He came briskly, went briskly, and that was all. He didn't forget where he began, didn't try to find out where he would end. He received something and took pleasure in it; he forgot about it and handed it back again. This is what I call not using the mind to repel the Way, not using man to help out Heaven. This is what I call the True Man.

Since he is like this, his mind forgets; his face is calm; his forehead is broad. This person is chilly like autumn, balmy like spring, and his joy and anger prevail through the four seasons. He goes along with what is right for things and no one knows his limit. . . . Therefore, he who delights in bringing success to things is not a sage; he who has affections is not benevolent; he who looks for the right time is not a worthy man; he who cannot encompass both profit and loss is not a noble man; he who thinks of conduct and fame and misleads himself is not a man of breeding. . . . This was the True Man of old: with bearing that was lofty and did not crumble; he appeared to lack but accepted nothing; he was dignified in his correctness but not insistent; he was vast in emptiness but not ostentatious. Mild and cheerful, he seemed to be happy; reluctant, he could not help doing certain things. . . .

Therefore his liking was one and his not liking was one. His being one was one and his not being one was one. In being one, he was acting as a companion of Heaven. In not being one, he was acting as a companion of man. When man and Heaven do not defeat each other, then he may be said to have the True Man.

Source: *Zhuangzi*, ch. 6: *Chuang Tzu: Basic Writings*, pp. 73–76.

WHAT THE SAGE KNOWS

Zhuangzi's friend, the logician Huizi, is a favorite target of the subtle humor for which Zhuangzi is famous. Portrayed as a philosopher who is fond of hair-splitting distinctions, Huizi is chided by his friend for becoming overly attached to logic and words and thus failing to embrace the myriad mysteries of the natural world.

Zhuangzi and Huizi were walking on a bridge over the Hao River. Zhuangzi said, 'Minnows moving about freely—that is what fish enjoy!'

Huizi said, 'You're not a fish. How do you know [how] fish [think]?'

Zhuangzi said, 'You're not me, so how do you know I don't know what fish enjoy?'

Huizi said, 'I'm not you, so I certainly don't know what you know. On the other hand, you're certainly not a fish, and so you certainly can't know what fish enjoy.'

Zhuangzi said, 'Let's go back to your original point. You said, "How do you know what fish enjoy," and so you already knew I knew when you asked me. I know it by being here above the Hao.'

Source: *Zhuangzi*, ch. 17: *Chuang Tzu: Basic Writings*.

A PERSON WITHOUT FEELINGS

In this passage, Huizi attempts to turn the tables on Zhuangzi, suggesting that despite his friend's emphasis on naturalness, what he advocates is really contrary to nature. Human beings naturally have feelings of attachment toward certain things and aversion toward others, and it is absurd to suggest that anyone can truly view all things as equal.

Huizi said to Zhuangzi, 'Can a person really be without feelings?'
'Yes.'
'But a person who has no feelings—how can you call him a person?'

'The Dao provided a face; Heaven provided a human form—why can't you call him a human?'

'But once you've called him a person, how can he be without feelings?'

'That's not what I mean by feelings. When I talk about having no feelings, I mean that a person doesn't allow preferences and aversions to enter and do harm. Instead, he always lets things be the way they are and doesn't try to push life along.'

'If he doesn't try to push life along, then how does he keep himself alive?'

'The Dao gave him a human face; Heaven gave him a human form. He doesn't let preferences or aversions enter and do harm. You, now—you place your spirit outside. You exhaust your energy, leaning on a tree and moaning, slumping at your desk and dozing—Heaven picked out a human body for you and you use it to babble about verbal sophistry!'

Source: *Zhuangzi*, ch. 5: *Chuang Tzu: Basic Writings*, p. 72.

AN OLD USELESS TREE

In his writings, Zhuangzi frequently extols the value of becoming useless. Those who make themselves useful are used by others, and so they dissipate their vital energies and die young. The sage, however, appears to be stupid and blockish, and so others believe that he is useless, and thus they leave him alone.

Carpenter Shi went to Qi and, when he got to Crooked Shaft, he saw a serrate oak standing by the village shrine. It was broad enough to shelter several thousand oxen and measured a hundred spans around, towering above the hills. The lowest branches were eighty feet from the ground, and a dozen or so of them could have been made into boats. There were so many sightseers that the place looked like a fair, but the carpenter didn't even glance around and went on his way without stopping. His apprentice stood staring for a long time and then ran after Carpenter Shi and said, 'Since I first took up my axe and followed you, Master, I have never seen timber as beautiful as this. But you don't even bother to look, and go right on without stopping. Why is that?'

'Forget it—say no more!' said the carpenter. 'It's a worthless tree! Make boats out of it and they'd sink; make coffins and they'd rot in no time. Use it for doors and it would sweat sap like pine; use it for posts and the worms would eat them up. It's not a timber tree—there's nothing it can be used for. That's how it got to be that old!'

After Carpenter Shi had returned home, the oak tree appeared to him in a dream and said, 'What are you comparing me with? Are you comparing me with those useful trees? The cherry apple, the pear, the orange, the citron, the rest of those fructiferous trees and shrubs—as soon as their fruit is ripe, they are torn apart and subjected to abuse. Their big limbs are broken off, their little limbs are yanked around. Their utility makes life miserable for them, and so they don't get to finish out the years Heaven gave them, but are cut off in midjourney. They bring it on themselves— the pulling and tearing of the common mob. And it's the same way with all other things.

'As for me, I've been trying a long time to be of no use, and now that I'm about to die, I've finally got it. This is of great use to me. If I had been of some use, would I ever have grown this large? Moreover, you and I are both of us things. What's the point of this—things condemning things? You, a worthless man about to die—how do you know I'm a worthless tree?' When Carpenter Shi woke up, he reported his dream. His apprentice said, 'If it's so intent on being of no use, what's it doing there at the village shrine?'

'Shhh! Say no more! It's only resting there. If we carp and criticize, it will merely conclude that we don't understand it. Even if it weren't at the shrine, do you suppose it would be cut down? It protects itself in a different way from ordinary people. If you try to judge it by conventional standards, you'll be way off!'

Source: *Zhuangzi*, ch. 4: *Chuang Tzu: Basic Writings*, pp. 60–61.

DRAGGING HIS TAIL IN THE MUD

In ancient China, rulers often asked renowned sages to be their advisors in order to receive wise counsel. In the following story, Zhuangzi is approached with such a job offer.

Once, when Zhuangzi was fishing in the Pu River, the king of Chu sent two officials to go and announce to him: 'I would like to trouble you with the administration of my realm.'

Zhuangzi held on to the fishing pole and, without turning his head, said, 'I have heard that there is a sacred tortoise in Chu that has been dead for three thousand years. The king keeps it wrapped in cloth and boxed, and stores it in the ancestral temple. Now would this tortoise rather be dead and have its bones left behind and honored? Or would it rather be alive and dragging its tail in the mud?'

'It would rather be alive and dragging its tail in the mud,' said the two officials.

Zhuangzi said, 'Go away! I'll drag my tail in the mud!'

Source: *Zhuangzi*, ch. 17: *Chuang Tzu: Basic Writings*, p. 109.

ZHUANGZI'S WIFE DIED

Since death is an inevitable part of life, the sage embraces it along with other aspects of the natural world. For most people, death is fearful and oppressive, but for the sage death is part of the cosmic mystery constantly unfolding around us.

Zhuangzi's wife died. When Huizi went to convey his condolences, he found Zhuangzi sitting with his legs sprawled out, pounding on a tub and singing. 'You lived with her, she brought up your children and grew old,' said Huizi. 'It should be enough simply not to weep at her death. But pounding on a tub and singing—this is going too far, isn't it?'

Zhuangzi said, 'You're wrong. When she first died, do you think I didn't grieve like anyone else? But I looked back to her beginning and the time before she was born. Not only the time before she was born, but the time before she had a body. Not only the time before she had a body, but the time before she had a spirit. In the midst of the jumble of wonder and mystery a change took place and she had a spirit. Another change and she had a body. Another change and she was born. Now there's been another change and she's dead. It's just like the progression of the four seasons, spring, summer, fall, winter.

'Now she's going to lie down peacefully in a vast room. If I were to follow after her bawling and sobbing, it would show that I don't understand anything about fate. So I stopped.'

Source: *Zhuangzi*, ch. 18: *Chuang Tzu: Basic Writings*, p. 113.

THE LADY OF GREAT MYSTERY

Although the position of women was well below that of men in classical China, there are many stories of female sages in the Daoist canon. These women managed to transcend the boundaries imposed on them by their society. Applying esoteric lore in secret, they became recognized as teachers, and sometimes even as immortals. The following selection, from a collection of stories of immortals from the Han dynasty, reports on the life of the "Lady of Great Mystery," who is said to have successfully practiced the secret arts of immortality and to have ascended to heaven in broad daylight, a sign of exceptional accomplishment.

The Lady of Great Mystery had the family name Zhuan and was personally called He. When she was a little girl she lost first her father and after a little while also her mother.

Understanding that living beings often did not fulfill their destined lifespans, she felt sympathy and sadness. She used to say: 'Once people have lost their existence in this world, they cannot recover it. Whatever has died cannot come back to life. Life is so limited! It is over so fast! Without cultivating the Dao, how can one extend one's life?'

She duly left to find enlightened teachers, wishing to purify her mind and pursue the Dao. She obtained the arts of the Jade Master and practiced them diligently for several years.

As a result she was able to enter the water and not get wet. Even in the severest cold of winter she would walk over frozen rivers wearing only a single garment. All the time her expression would not change, and her body would remain comfortably warm for a succession of days.

The Lady of Great Mystery could also move government offices, temples, cities, and lodges. They would appear in other places quite without moving from their original location. Whatever she pointed at would vanish into thin air. Doors, windows, boxes, or caskets that were securely locked needed only a short flexing of her finger to break wide open. Mountains would tumble, trees would fall at the pointing of her hand. Another short gesture would resurrect them to their former state. . . .

The Lady of Great Mystery perfectly mastered all thirty-six arts of the immortals. She could resurrect the dead and bring them back to life. She saved innumerable people, but nobody knew what she used for her dresses or her food, nor did anybody ever learn her arts from her. Her complexion was always that of a young girl; her hair stayed always black as a raven. Later she ascended into heaven in broad daylight. She was never seen again.

Source: *Biographies of Spirit Immortals*, "The Lady of Great Mystery": *The Taoist Experience*, pp. 291–292.

SUN BUER: IMMORTALITY PRACTICES FOR WOMEN

Sun Buer, known in Daoist literature as "Clear and Calm Free Human," lived during the 12th century. Perhaps the best-known of Daoist women immortals, externally she lived an unremarkable life, raising three children and performing the duties expected of a Chinese wife. At the age of 51 she undertook the training of Daoist immortality practices, and it is reported that she quickly mastered difficult esoteric techniques. She composed a number of texts on immortality, most of which focus on distinctive techniques for women. A central concern is harnessing the vital energy and causing it to move up along the spine through subtle energy channels, and thus to the top of the head. It then cascades down the front of the body, bringing indescribable bliss and restoring vitality. The verses are written in a code using the terminology of the Daoist immortalists, and so an explanatory commentary by Zhen Yangming, a 20th-century Daoist master, is included.

> Tie up the tiger and return it to the true lair;
> Bridle the dragon and gradually increase the elixir.
> Nature should be clear as water,
> Mind should be as still as a mountain.
> Tuning the breath, gather it into the gold crucible;
> Stabilizing the spirit, guard the jade pass.
> If you can increase the grain of rice day by day,
> You will be rejuvenated.

Commentary by Zhen Yangming

The tiger is energy, while the dragon is spirit. The "true lair" is the general area between the breasts. To tie up the tiger and return it to the true lair is what was explained by the Master of Higher Light, One Who Has Reached

Emptiness, in these terms: "When women cultivate immortality, they must first accumulate energy in their breasts."

This is the distinction between primal and acquired energy. Refinement of acquired energy uses the method of tuning the breath and freezing the spirit; to gather primal energy, you wait until there is living energy stirring in your body to start. To bridle the dragon simply means to freeze the spirit so as to join it to energy. When spirit and energy unite, the earthly soul and the celestial soul link, and the elixir is crystallized. One of the Celestial Teachers of the Zhang clan, the Empty Peaceful One, said, "Once the original spirit emerges, then gather it back in; when the spirit returns, energy in the body spontaneously circulates. Do this every morning and every evening, and eternal youth will naturally form a spiritual embryo." This is the meaning of bridling the dragon and gradually increasing the elixir. . . .

"Nature should be clear as water, mind should be as still as a mountain." Real Human Zhang Sanfeng said, "Freezing the spirit, tune the breath; tuning the breath, freeze the spirit. This should be done all at once, as one operation. Freezing the spirit means gathering the clarified mind within. When the mind is clear and cool, peaceful and light, then you can practice gathering it into the lair of energy. This is called freezing the spirit. After you do this, you feel as though you are sitting on a high mountain, gazing at the myriad mountains and rivers, or as though you have lit a heavenly lamp that lights up all dark realms. This is what is called freezing the spirit in the void. And tuning the breath is not hard; once mind and spirit are quiet, following the breath spontaneously, I keep this spontaneity. . . ."

The Real Human Zhang said, "When you sit, you should embrace energy with spirit, and keep your mind on breath, in the elixir field, with clear serenity, concentrating undistracted. The energy stored within combines with energy coming from outside to crystallize in the elixir field, filling it and growing stronger day by day and month by month, reaching the four limbs, flowing through the hundred channels, striking open the double pass at the middle of the spine, floating up to the nirvana chamber in the center of the brain. Then it turns and goes down to the heart and enters the field of elixir below in the abdomen. Spirit and energy keep to one another, resting on one another with each breath, and the course of the Waterwheel (the cycle of energy circulation) is opened. When the work reaches this point, the effective construction of the foundation is already half done. . . ."

"If you can increase the grain of rice day by day, you will be rejuvenated." In response to questions about what this "grain of rice" is, I can bring up an alchemical classic by Zhang Boduan. This classic . . . says, "The Undifferentiated encloses Space, Space encloses the worlds of desire, form, and formlessness. When you look for the root source of it all, it is a particle big as a grain." It also says, "A grain, and grain again; at first scarcely perceptible, it eventually becomes clearly evident."

This is the meaning of the statement "If you can increase the grain of rice day by day. . . ." Put simply, it is a matter of gradual culling and refinement of spirit and energy, gradually solidifying and combining them. It does not mean that this little ball of spirit and energy combined has a definite shape like a grain of rice that you can find.

Source: *Cultivating the Elixir;* from *Immortal Sisters,* tr. Thomas Cleary (Boston: Shambhala, 1989), pp. 34–37.

SEXUAL TECHNIQUES FOR MEN

The Daoist canon contains a wealth of information on long-life practices developed over the centuries by Daoists intent on extending their lifespans. Among these are various sexual techniques that are said to allow people to increase their energy level. Sexual practices for men often include ways to increase yang energy, while females are taught how to increase yin energy. Many of these describe a sort of sexual vampirism in which the energy of the partner is transferred to the practitioner. In other texts, it appears that the sexual practices awaken and augment one's natural energy. The following passage is written for men, who are advised to take as many sexual partners as possible, and that they should ideally be in their early teens, since young women have a greater store of energy. They are also counseled to avoid partners who are familiar with these techniques, since female adepts may turn the tables on them and take their energy.

The Master of Pure Harmony says: 'Those who would cultivate their yang energy must not allow women to steal glimpses of this art. Not only is this of no benefit to one's yang energy, but it may even lead to injury or illness. . . .'

According to Pengsu the Long-Lived, if a man wishes to derive the greatest benefit [from sexual techniques], it is best to find a woman who has no knowledge of them. He also had better choose young maidens for mounting, because then his complexion will become like a maiden's. When it comes to women, one should be vexed only by their not being young. It is best to obtain those between fourteen or fifteen and eighteen or nineteen. In any event, they should never be older than thirty. Even those under thirty are of no benefit if they have given birth. My late master handed down these methods and himself used them to live for three thousand years. If combined with drugs, they will even lead to immortality.

In practicing the union of yin and yang to increase your energy and cultivate long life, do not limit yourself to just one woman. Much better to get three, nine, or eleven: the more the better! Absorb her secreted essence by mounting the "vast spring" and reverting the essence upward. Your skin will become glossy, your body light, your eyes bright, and your energy so strong that you will be able to overcome all your enemies. Old men will feel like twenty and young men will feel their strength increase a hundredfold.

When having intercourse with women, as soon as you feel yourself aroused, change partners. By changing partners, you can lengthen your life. If you return habitually to the same woman, her yin energy will become progressively weaker and this will be of little benefit to you.

Source: *Yufang Bizhui,* "Sexual Instructions of the Master of Pure Harmony," 636: *The Taoist Experience,* pp. 155–156.

SEXUAL TECHNIQUES FOR WOMEN

The procedure for women is similar to that for men: they are advised to have as many partners as possible, and that they should ideally be young, since the young have a greater store of energy. Women should avoid becoming aroused, since orgasm dissipates the energies cultivated by sexual activity. Those who succeed in restraining themselves will acquire the energy dissipated by their partners through seminal emission.

The Master of Pure Harmony says: 'It is not only that yang can be cultivated, but yin too.' The Queen Mother of the West, for example, attained the Dao by cultivating her yin energy. As soon as she had intercourse with a man he would immediately take sick, while her complexion would be ever more radiant without the use of rouge or powder. She always ate curds and plucked the five-stringed lute in order to harmonize her heart and concentrate her mind. She was quite without any other desire.

The Queen Mother had no husband but was fond of intercourse with young boys. If this is not fit to be taught to the world, how is it that such an elevated personage as the Queen Mother herself practiced it?

When having intercourse with a man, first calm your heart and still your mind. If the man is not yet fully aroused, wait for his energy to arrive and slightly restrain your emotion to attune yourself to him. Do not move or become agitated, lest your yin essence become exhausted first. If this happens, you will be left in a deficient state and susceptible to cold wind illnesses. . . .

If a woman is able to master this Dao and has frequent intercourse with men, she can avoid all grain for nine days without getting hungry. Even those who are sick and have sexual relations with ghosts attain this ability to fast. But they become emaciated after a while. So, how much more beneficial must it be to have intercourse with men?

Source: *Yufang Bizhui* 635: *The Taoist Experience*, p. 156.

THE GREAT MAN

The Great Man (daren) is an important motif in Daoist literature. Described as a perfected sage, the Great Man is said to wander to the farthest reaches of the cosmos, visiting strange and mysterious realms and acquiring esoteric knowledge, along with substances that promote immortality. The following excerpt is from Ruanji's (210–263) poem "Biography of Master Great Man," which describes the Great Man as a natural ruler with sovereignty over the whole universe.

Heaven and earth dissolve,
The six harmonies open out,
Stars and constellations tumble,
Sun and moon fall down.

I leap up and farther up,
What should I cherish?
My clothes are not seamed, but I am beautifully dressed;
My girdle has no pendants but is ornate naturally.
Up and down I wander, fluttering about:
Who could fathom my eternity?

Source: *Daren Xiansheng Zhuang*, ch.1: *Early Chinese Mysticism*, p. 102.

THE VALUE OF DRUNKENNESS

The following poem was written by Liu Ling (ca. 265 C.E.), one of the "Seven Sages of the Bamboo Grove," a group of poet-philosophers who came together to discuss ultimate reality and engage in "pure conversation" (shingtan). In this poem he appears to refer to his own way of life. He was renowned for his fondness for wine, and is said to have traveled throughout the Chinese countryside accompanied by a servant who carried a shovel and a jug of wine. The wine enabled him to maintain a constant state of inebriation (which he believed helped him to harmonize with the Dao). The purpose of the shovel was to allow the servant to bury him on the spot when he died.

There is Master Great Man—

He takes heaven and earth as a single morning
A thousand years as one short moment.
The sun and the moon are windows for him,
The Eight Wilds are his garden.

He travels without wheels or tracks,
Sojourns without house or hearth.
He makes heaven his curtain and earth his seat,
Indulges in what he pleases.

Stopping, he grasps his wine-cup and maintains his goblet;
Moving, he carries a casket and holds a jar in his hand.
His only obligation is toward wine,
And of this he knows abundance. . . .

Utterly free he is from yearnings and from worries,
Always happy and full in his contentment.
Without ever moving he gets drunk,
Then, with a start he sobers up.

Listens quietly, but does not hear the rolling of thunder . . .
Unaware of the cold biting the flesh he is,
Unmoved by the afflictions of covetousness.
Looking down he watches the myriad beings bustling about
Like tiny pieces of duckweed that float on the Han and Jiang. . . .

Source: *Jiu Desong 47: Early Chinese Mysticism*, pp. 105–106.

TRANSCENDING THE WORLD

In the texts of Laozi and Zhuangzi there are suggestions that sages transcend the world and that its cares no longer burden them. This theme was developed in other Daoist texts that extol the prowess of the "Great Man," who is portrayed as a mighty figure traveling in the remote corners of the world—and the highest reaches of heaven—without obstruction, complete master of all things.

> Heat and cold don't harm me; nothing stirs me up.
> Sadness and worry have no hold on me; pure energy at rest.
> I float on mist, leap into heaven, pass through all with no restraint.
> To and fro, subtle and wondrous, the way never slants.
> My delights and happinesses are not of this world, how could I ever fight with it?

Source: *Yuan You: Early Chinese Mysticism*, p. 103.

THE MUSIC OF DAO

This excerpt is taken from the Scripture of the Western Ascension (Xishengjing), *a fifth-century text that brings together the "three traditions" of Daoism, Confucianism, and Buddhism into a harmonious religious vision. Most of the text reports oral teachings given by Laozi to Yin Xi, the guardian of the Western Gate and recipient of the Daodejing. In this text Laozi reveals that he is really a divinity, the manifestation of Dao, and he further describes its workings so that Yin Xi might merge with it and thus attain immortality. The text is notable for its description of Laozi's ascension into Heaven as an immortal and for its use of the Buddhist concepts of karma, rebirth, and selflessness. It also incorporates Buddhist meditation techniques, integrating them into the Daoist quest for immortality.*

> The Dao is nature.
> Who practices can attain [it]. Who hears can speak [about it].
> Who knows does not speak; who speaks does not know.
> Language is formed when sounds are exchanged.
> Thus in conversation, words make sense.
> When one does not know the Dao, words create confusion.
> Therefore I don't hear, don't speak; I don't know why things are.
> It can be compared to the knowledge of musical sound.
> One becomes conscious of it by plucking a string.
> Though the mind may know the appropriate sounds, yet the mouth is unable to formulate them.
> Similarly the Dao is deep, subtle, wondrous; who knows it does not speak.
> On the other hand, one may be conscious of musical sounds and melodies.
> One then dampens the sounds to consider them within.
> Then when the mind makes the mouth speak, one speaks but does not know.
> Laozi said: The Dao is deep and very profound, an abyss of emptiness and non-being.
> Though you may hear its doctrine, in your mind you don't grasp its subtlety.

Why is this so? The written word does not exhaust speech, and by relying on scriptures and sticking to texts your learning remains on the same [intellectual] level.

Rather, you must measure it: recollect it within, meditate on it and consider it carefully. . . .

Laozi said: Heaven, earth, people, and all beings originally contain the primordial source of the Dao.

They emerge together from the Grand Immaculate, from the first beginning of emptiness and non-being; they come from the radiance of essence, flickering softly, from supreme mystery, subtle and wondrous.

It can be compared to a dam ten thousand miles in height. It has gushing, gurgling streams beneath. Looking down they seem all turbid and confused; looking closer there are countless sand grains on the bottom.

Obscure in the extreme, utterly undifferentiated, we don't know where they come from: as in a person recently deceased one cannot see the numinous spirit soul:

It has merged with the engulfing power of yin, and yang can no longer shine forth to make it distinct.

Look at the past and the future as you look at the present.

If you can't even understand that, how will you know about not existing or being alive? . . .

Talented and analytical, you have a certain wisdom, receiving the teaching by word of mouth. But while you claim to have penetrated the innermost part of the Dao, you cannot intuit its true inner essence.

Therefore if you have lost the foundation of life, how could you know the primordial source of the Dao?

Source: *Xishengjing* selections: *Taoist Mystical Philosophy: The Scripture of the Western Ascension,* tr. Livia Kohn (Albany: State University of New York Press, 1991), pp. 235, 240.

GLOSSARY

Cinnabar   Mercuric sulfide, believed by Daoist alchemists to be the key to an elixir of immortality.

Dao   "Way," the impersonal force that sustains all life and dictates patterns of growth and development.

Daodejing   *The Way and Virtue,* a classic work of Daoism attributed to Laozi.

De   The power or virtue of Dao, which enables it to influence the movements of natural systems.

Immortals   (*xian*) Daoist sages and alchemists who have discovered the secrets of physical immortality.

Laozi   The legendary founder of Daoism, said to have lived during the sixth century B.C.E.

Philosophical Daoism   A term coined by Western scholars to designate the strand of Daoism represented by Laozi and Zhuangzi, which is concerned with the nature and activities of Dao.

Pu   "The Uncarved Block," a metaphor for human beings in their natural state before society distorts their true nature through training and education.

Qi   Vital energy or life force that sustains living beings.

Religious Daoism   A term coined by Western scholars to designate the strand of Daoism that was concerned primarily with the quest for immortality.

Wuwei   "Not Acting," the attitude of the Daoist sage, which involves allowing events to happen naturally, in accordance with the movements of Dao.

Yang   The active and aggressive aspect of Dao.

Yin   The passive aspect of Dao.

Zhuangzi   One of the most influential figures of early philosophical Daoism.

Zuowang   "Sitting and forgetting," a method of Daoist meditation involving dropping off the accumulated training that interferes with understanding of Dao.

FURTHER READINGS

AMES, ROGER T. "Is Political Taoism Anarchism?" *Journal of Chinese Philosophy*, 10 (1983), pp. 27–47.

——*The Art of Rulership: A Study in Ancient Chinese Political Thought*. Honolulu: University of Hawaii Press, 1983.

ANDERSEN, POUL. *The Method of Holding the Three Ones: A Taoist Manual of Meditation of the Fourth Century A.D.* London: Curzon Press, 1979.

BLOFELD, JOHN. *Taoism: The Quest for Immortality*. London, Boston: Mandala Books, Unwin Paperbacks, 1979.

CHANG, CHUNG-YAN. "The Philosophy of Taoism According to Chuang Tzu." *Philosophy East and West*, 27 (October 1977), pp. 409–422.

GIRARDOT, N. *Myth and Meaning in Early Taoism: The Theme of Chaos (hun-tun)*. Berkeley: University of California Press, 1983.

GRAHAM, A. C. *Disputers of the Tao: Philosophical Argument in Ancient China*. LaSalle: Open Court, 1989.

KOHN, LIVIA (ed.) *Taoist Meditation and Longevity Techniques*. Ann Arbor: University of Michigan, Center for Chinese Studies Publications, 1989.

LAGERWEY, JOHN. *Taoist Ritual in Chinese Society and History*. New York: Macmillan, 1987.

MAIR, VICTOR H. (ed.) *Experimental Essays on Chuang-tzu*. Honolulu: University of Hawaii Press, 1983.

SASO, MICHAEL. *Taoism and the Rite of Cosmic Renewal*. Pullman: Washington State University Press, 1972.

—— "The Taoist Tradition." *China Quarterly*, 41 (1979), pp. 83–102.

SCHWARTZ, BENJAMIN. *The World of Thought in Ancient China*. Cambridge, MA: Belknap Press, 1985.

STRICKMANN, MICHEL (ed.) *Tantric and Taoist Studies in Honour of R.A. Stein, Mélanges Chinois et Bouddhiques*, 21 (1983).

THOMPSON, LAURENCE G. *Chinese Religion: An Introduction*. Belmont, CA: Wadsworth Publishing, 1989.

WALEY, ARTHUR (tr.). *The Way and Its Power: A Study of the Tao Te Ching and Its Place in Chinese Thought*. London: Allen & Unwin, 1934.

WELCH, HOLMES. *Taoism: The Parting of the Way*. Boston: Beacon Press, 1957.

WELCH, HOLMES and SEIDEL, ANNA (eds.) *Facets of Taoism: Essays in Chinese Religion*. New Haven: Yale University Press, 1979.

YUNG-LAN, FUNG. *A History of Chinese Philosophy*. Princeton: Princeton University Press, 1953.

Shinto

INTRODUCTION

In ancient Japan there was no term for indigenous religious practices, but when Buddhism was introduced to the country in the sixth century the term Shinto, or "way of the *kami*," was coined in order to differentiate Japanese traditions from the foreign faith (which was labeled *butsudo,* or "way of the Buddha"). The *kami* are the indigenous gods of Japan, and Shinto is a general term referring to religious practices relating to them. Shinto has no founder, no organization based on believers' adherence to particular doctrines, and no beliefs or practices that are required of all. In contemporary Japan, Shinto is most visibly practiced at the many shrines found throughout the country, in popular festivals and pilgrimages, and in the continuing manifestations of reverence for the forces inhabiting the natural world that are celebrated in prayers and offerings to the kami.

The Japanese have traditionally believed that their country is the residence of many powerful beings and that these beings directly influence the lives of humans, as well as natural phenomena. Kami are commonly associated with natural forces such as wind and storms, with awe-inspiring places such as mountains, waterfalls, and rivers, and with spirits of deceased humans.

Most kami have a delineated sphere of influence, and their worship generally centers on a particular shrine or area. Other kami have a national significance and are venerated throughout Japan. The most prominent kami is the sun goddess, Amatarasu Omikami (Great Heavenly Illuminating Goddess), who in ancient myths is said to be the progenitor of the Japanese race. Amatarasu is also closely associated with the ruling house of Japan, which claims descent from her. This claim is a part of the official legitimation for the rule of the emperor, who was traditionally believed to be semidivine. This was expressed in the title of "Living Kami" (*Akitsukami*), which was given to the emperor and implied that he was a direct descendant of Amatarasu.

Shinto is not a unified system of beliefs and practices, but rather a general term that encompasses many different traditions dating from the earliest periods of Japanese history. Some of the elements and practices of Shinto may be derived from the religious lives of Japanese who lived thousands of years ago in prehistoric times, while others are influenced by the imported traditions of Daoism, Buddhism, and Confucianism, along with various indigenous practices and beliefs.

For the average contemporary Japanese, Shinto is not concerned primarily with doctrines. Rather, practicing Shinto involves performing actions expected of Japanese people who recognize the existence and power of the kami and who engage in actions traditionally associated with them. In the broadest sense, Shinto includes all the actions—festivals, rituals, prayers, offerings, pilgrimages, etc.—that pertain to the kami.

Because kami are believed to reside throughout the Japanese archipelago, there are shrines to local and national kami scattered throughout the islands, and these are an important focus of Shinto practice. There are between 78,000 and 79,000 Shinto shrines in Japan today, and traditional households generally have an altar to the clan deity (*uchigami*), at which regular offerings are presented.

In the modern period, Shinto can be classified into three broad categories, which although distinguishable are interrelated: Shrine Shinto (*Jinja Shinto*), Sectarian Shinto (*Kyoha Shinto*), and Folk Shinto (*Minzoku Shinto*). The first type includes rituals and other activities performed at Shinto shrines. It centers on the prayers and offerings addressed to the kami, which are generally expected to lead to specific concrete results, such as material success, health, academic accomplishments, or protection. It is believed that prayers and offerings make the kami positively predisposed toward the people who present them and that the kami in return may grant their requests. The most important deity of Shrine Shinto is Amatarasu, whose main shrine is at Ise. The deities worshipped in Shinto shrines are collectively referred to as "the gods of heaven and earth" (*tenshin chigi*). Rituals and prayers are also offered for the well-being of deceased ancestors and to ensure the peace, stability, and prosperity of the country.

Contemporary Shinto thought commonly contends that ritual actions must be combined with a pure mind, since the kami will positively respond only to people whose thoughts are sincere. In order to gain the blessing and aid of the kami, one must have the "heart of truth" (*makoto no kokoro*) or "true heart" (*magokoro*), which is characterized by reverence for the natural world, concordance between one's thoughts and actions, and, most important, an attitude of truthfulness that is the result of cultivating purity of heart.

Sectarian Shinto includes a number of Shinto groups that have developed into cohesive religious movements. Primarily composed of 13 sects officially recognized by the government during the Meiji era (1868–1911), Sectarian Shinto groups generally have a historical founder and tend to emphasize group solidarity. In addition, their religious centers are often churches rather than shrines.

Folk Shinto is a general term applied to the practices and beliefs of the mass of Japanese people who visit shrines and engage in activities relating to the kami but who do not feel a strong affiliation with any particular sect. Such practices emphasize reverence for natural forces, purification, and the idea that by performing certain actions one may gain access to the power of the kami in order to influence particular aspects of one's life.

Although many Japanese believe that Shinto is an enduring tradition of indigenous religious practices, contemporary Shinto practice is in fact an amalgamation of numerous influences, including Buddhism, Confucianism,

Daoism, and Chinese philosophy. The focus of Shinto practice is the natural world, and Shinto emphasizes the connection of individuals with their environment. In modern times the development of Shinto has been strongly influenced by revivalist movements that seek to link it with Japan's past. One particularly important movement has been the school of Revival Shinto (*Fukko Shinto*), which was linked to the National Learning (*Kokugaku*) movement of the early Edo period (late seventeenth century). This movement was an attempt to purge Shinto of the influence of Buddhism and other foreign traditions and return to a "pure" and "original" form of Shinto. The most important exponent of Revival Shinto was Motoori Norinaga, whose study of Japanese classics such as the *Tale of Genji* convinced him that there is a discernible Japanese character, which is based on awareness of, and reverence for, the natural environment. Norinaga stressed the polytheistic character of Shinto and contended that mundane affairs are shaped by the will of the kami.

During the Meiji period the nationalistic tendencies of Revival Shinto were highlighted and Shinto became the official state cult. The government stressed the divine origin of Japan and pointed out that no foreign invasion of the nation had ever succeeded. This was attributed to the actions of the kami, who protected Japan and worked to ensure its well-being. The government also emphasized the traditional connection between the emperor and Amatarasu Omikami, which was believed to confer on the emperor a divine right to rule.

Because these nationalistic notions were a part of the militaristic policies of Japan prior to and during World War II, State Shinto was outlawed during the Allied occupation, and the emperor publicly repudiated his divine status. With the removal of government patronage, Shinto again became the popular religion of the Japanese people, a position that it holds today. Throughout the Japanese archipelago, people worship at the numerous Shinto shrines, participate in Shinto festivals, purchase amulets empowered by kami and believed to bring success, protection, or good health, and pay reverence to their clan deities and the spirits of their ancestors. Shinto remains a diffuse tradition that incorporates elements of other systems but that is distinctively Japanese.

Shinto Scriptures

Shinto is a practice-oriented tradition that focuses on rituals, prayers, and attitudes associated with worship and veneration of the kami, and it has no distinct canon and few traditional texts. The earliest literary use of the term Shinto is found in the *Nihonshoki* (*Chronicles of Japan,* written in 720), which purports to be a record of the early history of Japan and which is an important source of information on ancient Japanese religious ideas and practices. The *Nihonshoki* (also referred to as the *Nihongi*) and the *Kojiki* (*Records of Ancient Matters*) are among the oldest sources available for pre-Buddhist Japanese religious practices and myths, and these two works are the oldest known sacred literature of Shinto.

According to the accounts of these texts, before the arrival of humans on the Japanese islands, two kami named Izanami and Izanagi stood on the "floating bridge of heaven" and stirred the primordial waters with a jeweled spear. When the water began to coagulate they gathered up the sediment and let drops fall to form the islands of Japan.

Izanami died after giving birth to Kagutsuchi, the fire god, and Izanami followed her to the netherworld hoping to ask her to return to the land of the living. She replied that she had already eaten the food of the dead and so could not return without special permission. She then instructed him not to follow her when she made the request, but after waiting for a long time he became impatient and went after her. When he found her, however, her flesh was putrefying and decomposed, which revolted him, and so he fled the netherworld, returned to the land of the living, and bathed in order to purify himself. When he washed his eyes, the dripping water gave rise to Amatarasu, the sun goddess, and her brother, Tsukiyomi the moon god.

Both the *Kojiki* and *Nihonshoki* indicate that Amatarasu is the divine ancestor of the emperor, an idea that played an important role in the legitimation of the royal line. In addition, their descriptions of Japan as a special place created and guarded by the kami have been influential in shaping Japanese ideas about themselves and their country. The legends of these two works link the origin of the Japanese people with the kami and indicate that humans and kami are intimately interrelated. Humans need the power of kami in order to achieve their goals, and the kami for their part require reverence and offerings from humans.

Other important Shinto texts include the *Fudoki* (*Records of Wind and Earth*), written in the eighth century, which is a collection of myths and legends; the *Man'yoshu* (*Collection of Ten Thousand Poems*), compiled in the late eighth century, which contains poems expressing the beliefs and practices of the common people; and the *Sendai Kujihongi* (*Narrative of Ancient Matters*), compiled in the ninth century, which contains accounts of the practices of the Mononobe clan.

SHINTO SCRIPTURES

BIRTH OF THE KAMI OF SUN AND MOON

The following passage describes the birth of Amatarasu Omikami, the sun goddess, and her brother, Tsukiyomi the moon god. It also indicates that Izanami and Izanagi produced various other kami of various temperaments, some of which were good, while others were malevolent.

Izanagi no Mikoto and Izanami no Mikoto consulted together, saying: 'We have now produced the Great-Eight-Island Country [Japan], with the mountains, rivers, herbs, and trees. Why should we not produce someone who shall be lord of the universe?' They then together produced the Sun Goddess, who was called O-hiru-me no muchi.

The resplendent luster of this child shone throughout all the six quarters. Therefore the two Deities rejoiced, saying: 'We have had many children, but none of them have been equal to this wondrous infant. She ought not to be kept long in this land, but we ought of our own accord to send her at once to Heaven, and entrust to her the affairs of Heaven.' At this time Heaven and Earth were still not far separated, and therefore they sent her up to Heaven by the ladder of Heaven.

They next produced the Moon-god. His radiance was next to that of the Sun in splendor. This god was to be the consort of the Sun-goddess, and to share in her government. They therefore sent him also to Heaven.

Next they produced the leech-child, which even at the age of three years could not stand upright. They therefore placed it in the rock-camphor wood boat of Heaven, and abandoned it to the winds.

Their next child was Suso no o no Mikoto. This god had a fierce temper and was given to cruel acts. Moreover he made a practice of continually weeping and wailing. So he brought many of the people of the land to an untimely end. Again he caused green mountains to become withered. Therefore the two gods, his parents, addressed Susa no o no Mikoto, saying: 'You are exceedingly wicked, and it is not fitting that you should reign over the world. Certainly you must depart far away to the Nether-land.' So at length they expelled him.

Source: *Nihongi,* ch. 1: W. G. Aston, *Nihongi* (London: George Allen & Unwin, 1956) I, pp. 18–20; pp. 16–17.

THE BIRTH OF GREAT KAMI

According to the following account, the first beings to arise in the world were three kami. *They were followed by two more* kami, *and the five together became the progenitors of all the other* kami. *It then describes a confrontation between Amatarasu and her brother Susa no o, who is said to have a wicked and deceitful disposition. When he decided to ascend into Heaven, she stopped him and demanded to know what his intentions were. He assured her that he meant no harm, but she did not believe him. In order to ensure that he would remain true to his word, he proposed that both should swear and produce children, which apparently made Susa no o keep his promise.*

At the beginning of heaven and earth, there came into existence in the Plain of High Heaven the Heavenly Center Lord Kami, next, the Kami of High Generative Force, and then the Kami of Divine Generative Force.

Next, when the earth was young, not yet solid, there developed something like reed-shoots from which the Male Kami of Excellent Reed Shoots and then Heavenly Eternal Standing Kami emerged.

The above five kami are the heavenly kami of special standing. . . .

Then, there came into existence Earth Eternal Standing Kami, Kami of Abundant Clouds Field, male and female Kami of Clay, male and female Kami of Post, male and female kami of Great Door, Kami of Complete Surface and his spouse, Kami of Awesomeness, Izanagi (Kami-Who-Invites) and his spouse, Izanami (Kami-Who-Is-Invited). . . .

So thereupon His-Swift-Impetuous-Male-Augustness (Susa no o) said: 'If that be so, I will take leave of the Heaven-Shining-Great-August Deity (Amatarasu), and depart.' [With these words] he forthwith went up to Heaven, whereupon all the mountains and rivers shook, and every land and country quaked. So the Heaven-Shining-Deity, alarmed at the noise, said: 'The reason of the ascent hither of His Augustness my elder brother is surely no good intent. It is only that he wishes to wrest my land from me.' And she forthwith, unbinding her august hair, twisted it into august bunches; and both into the left and into the right august bunch, as likewise into her august head-dress and likewise on to her left and her right august arm, she twisted an augustly complete [string] of curved jewels eight feet [long] of five hundred jewels; and, slinging on her back a quiver holding a thousand [arrows], and adding a quiver holding five hundred [arrows], she likewise took and slung at her side a mighty and high [sounding] elbow-pad, and brandished and stuck her bow upright so that the top shook; and she stamped her feet into the hard ground up to her opposing thighs, kicking away [the earth] like rotten snow, and stood valiantly like a mighty man, and waiting, asked: 'Why do you ascend here?' Then Susa no o replied, saying: 'I have no evil intent. It is only that when the Great-August-Deity [our father] spoke, deigning to enquire the cause of my wailing and weeping, I said: "I wail because I wish to go to my deceased mother's land"; whereupon the Great-August-Deity said: 'You will not dwell in this land,' and deigned to expel me with a divine expulsion. It is therefore, solely with the thought of taking leave of you and departing, that I have ascended here. I have no strange intentions.'

Then the Heaven-Shining-Deity said: 'If that is so, how shall I know the sincerity of your intentions?' Thereupon Susa no o replied, saying: 'Let each of us swear, and produce children.' So as they then swore to each other from the opposite banks of the Tranquil River of Heaven, the august names of the Deities that were born from the mist [of their breath] when, having first begged Susa no o to hand her the ten-grasp saber which was girded on him and broken into three fragments, and with the jewels making a jingling sound and having brandished and washed them in the True-Pool-Well of Heaven, and having crunchingly crunched them, the Heaven-Shining Deity blew them away, were Her Augustness Torrent-Mist-Princess . . . next Her Augustness Lovely-Island-Princess . . . next Her Augustness Princess-of-the-Torrent.

Source: *Kojiki*, ch. 1: *Kojiki, Records of Ancient Matters*, ch. 1: *The Great Asian Religions: An Anthology* (New York: MacMillan, 1969), pp. 231–2.

THE CREATION OF JAPAN

When the earth was newly formed, the islands of Japan were still below the waters, and Izanami and Izanagi decided to create a special land. They thrust a spear into the waters, and the brine that dripped from it formed the islands of the Japanese archipelago. After this they united, and their union resulted in the birth of more kami.

Izanagi and Izanami stood on the floating bridge of Heaven, and held counsel together, saying: 'Is there not a country beneath?' Thereupon they thrust down the jewel-spear of Heaven, and groping about with it found the ocean. The brine which dripped from the point of the spear coagulated and became an island which received the name of Ono-goro-jima.

The two deities then descended and lived on this island. Accordingly they wished to become husband and wife together, and to produce countries. So they made Ono-goro-jima the pillar of the center of the land.

Now the male deity turning by the left, and the female deity by the right, they went round the pillar of the land separately. When they met together on the side, the female deity spoke first and said: 'How delightful! I have met with a lovely youth.' The male deity was displeased, and said: 'I am a man, and by right should have spoken first. How is it that on the contrary you, a woman, should have been the first to speak? This was unlucky. Let us go round again.' Upon this the two deities went back, and having met again, this time the male deity spoke first and said: 'How delightful! I have met a lovely maiden.'

Then he inquired of the female deity, saying: 'In your body is anything formed?' She answered, and said: 'In my body there is a place which is the source of femininity.' The male deity said: 'In my body again there is a place which is the source of masculinity. I wish to unite this source-place of my body to the source-place of your body.' Then the male and female first became united as husband and wife.

Now when the time of birth arrived, first of all the island of Ahaji was reckoned as the placenta, and their minds took no pleasure in it. Therefore it received the name Ahaji no Shima. Next was produced the island of O-yamato no Toyo-aki-tsu-sha (Rich-harvest Island of Yamato). Next they produced the island of Iyo no futa-na, and next the island of Tsukushi. Next the islands of Oki and Sado were born as twins. . . . Next was born the island of Koshi, then the island of O-shima, then the island of Kibi no Ko. Thus first arose the designation of the Great Eight-Island Country.

Source: *Nihongi*, ch. 1: *Nihongi*, pp. 10–17.

IZANAGI VISITS IZANAMI IN THE NETHERWORLD

This passage describes how Izanagi, longing for his deceased love, decided to visit her in the land of the dead and plead with her to return with him. When he saw her body putrefying and covered with maggots, however, he ran away in horror and purified himself by bathing. The drops of water from his eyes and nose produced three kami: *Amatarasu, Tsukiyomi (the moon god), and Susa no o.*

After giving birth to the land, they [Izanami and Izanagi] proceeded to bear kami [such as the kami of the wind, of the tree, of the mountain, and of the plains]. But Izanami died after giving birth to the kami of fire. . . .

Izanagi, hoping to meet again with his spouse, went after her to the land of Hades. When Izanami came out to greet him, Izanagi said, 'Oh my beloved, the land which you and I have been making has not yet been completed. Therefore, you must return with me.' To which Izanami replied, 'I greatly regret that you did not come here sooner, for I have already partaken of the hearth of the land of hades. But let me discuss with the kami of hades about my desire to return. You must, however, not look at me.' As she was gone so long, Izanagi, being impatient, entered the hall to look for her and found maggots squirming around the body of Izanami.

Izanagi, seeing this, was afraid and ran away, saying, 'Since I have been to an extremely horrible and unclean land, I must purify myself.' Thus, arriving at [a river], he purified and exorcised himself. When he washed his left eye, there came into existence the Sun Goddess, or Heavenly Illuminating Great Kami [Amatarasu], and when he washed his right eye, there emerged the Moon Kami [Tsukiyomi]. Finally, as he washed his nose there came into existence Valiant Male Kami [Susa no o].

Source: *Kojiki*, chs. 7, 9, 10, 11: *The Great Asian Religions*, pp. 232–233.

AMATARASU HIDES IN A CAVE

The passage below recounts a well-known Shinto myth in which Amatarasu decides to hide herself in a cave as a result of the misdeeds of Susa no o. When she enters the cave the world is plunged into darkness, and so the other kami *work together to draw her out again. When she leaves the cave, a sacred rope is placed across the entrance to ensure that she will never again conceal her radiance from the world.*

[At one time] the Sun Goddess [shocked by the misdeeds of her brother, Valiant Male Kami], opened the heavenly rock-cave door and concealed herself inside. Then the Plain of High Heaven became completely dark, and all manner of calamities arose.

Then the 800 myriads of kami gathered in a divine assembly, and summoned Kami of the Little Roof of Heaven and Kami of Grand Bead to perform a divination. They hung long strings of myriad curved beads on the upper branches of a sacred tree, and hung a large-dimensioned mirror on its middle branches. They also suspended in the lower branches white and blue cloth. These objects were held by Kami of Grand Bead as solemn offerings, while Kami of the Little Roof in Heaven intoned liturgical prayers (*norito*). Meanwhile, Kami of Heavenly Strength hid himself behind the entrance of the rock-cave, and Kami of Heavenly Headgear bound her sleeves with a cord of vine, and stamped on an overturned bucket which was placed before the rock-cave. Then she became kami-possessed, exposed her breasts and genitals. Thereupon, the 800 myriads of kami laughed so hard that the Plain of High Heaven shook with their laughter.

The Sun Goddess, intrigued by all this, opened the rock-cave door slightly, wondering why it was that the 800 myriads of kami were laughing. Then Kami of Heavenly Headgear said, 'There is a kami nobler than you, and that is why we are happy and dancing.' While she was speaking thus, Kami of the Little Roof and Kami of Grand Bead showed the mirror to the Sun Goddess. Thereupon, the Sun Goddess, thinking this ever more strange, gradually came out of the cave, and the hidden Kami of Grand Bead took her hand and pulled her out. Then as the Sun Goddess reappeared, the Plain of High Heaven was naturally illuminated.

Source: *Kojiki*, ch. 17: *The Great Asian Religions*, pp. 232–233.

THE SHRINE AT ISE

The Grand Shrine at Ise, dedicated to Amatarasu, is the most important Shinto shrine in Japan today. The following passage describes the events surrounding its inauguration and refers to the link between the emperor and Amatarasu.

25th year, Spring, and month, 8th day. The Emperor commanded the five officers, Takenu Kaha-wake, ancestor of the Abe no Omi; Hiko-kuni-fuku, ancestor of the Imperial Chieftains; O-kashima, ancestor of the Nakatome Deity Chieftains; and Tochine, ancestor of the Mononobe Deity chieftains . . . saying: 'The sagacity of Our predecessor on the throne, the Emperor Mimaki-iri-hiko-inie, was displayed in wisdom; he was reverential, intelligent, and capable. He was profoundly unassuming, and his disposition was to cherish self-abnegation. He adjusted the machinery of government, and did solemn worship to the Gods of Heaven and Earth. He practiced self-restraint and was watchful of his personal conduct. Every day he was heedful for that day. Thus the welfare of the people was sufficient, and the Empire was at peace. And now, under Our reign, will there be any remissness in the worship of the Gods of Heaven and Earth?'

3rd month, 10th day. The Great Goddess Amatarasu was taken from [the princess] Toyo-suki-iri-hime, and entrusted to [the princess] Yamato-hime no Mikoto. Now Yamato-hime sought for a place where she might enshrine the Great Goddess. So she proceeded to Sasahata in Uda. Then turning back from there, she entered the land of Omi, and went round eastwards to Mino, and so she arrived in the province of Ise.

Now the Great Goddess Amatarasu instructed Yamato-hime, saying: 'The province of Ise, of the divine wind, is the land in which the waves from the eternal world reside, the successive waves. It is a secluded and pleasant land. In this land I wish to reside.' In compliance, therefore, with the instruction of the Great Goddess, a shrine was erected to her in the province of Ise. Accordingly an Abstinence Palace was built at Kawakami in Isuzu. This was called the palace of Ise. It was there that the Great Goddess Amatarasu first descended from Heaven.

Source: *Nihongi*, ch. 5: *Nihongi*, p. 175.

WHY JAPAN IS SPECIAL

According to the legends of the Kojiki and Nihonshoki, Japan was created by the kami, *who continue to take an active interest in the Japanese islands and the people who inhabit them.*

> Japan is the divine country. The heavenly ancestor it was who first laid its foundations, and the Sun Goddess left her descendants to reign over it forever and ever. This is true only of our country, and nothing similar may be found in foreign lands. That is why it is called the divine country.

Source: *Kitabatake Chikafusa*: *Sources of Japanese Tradition*, ed. Ryusaku Tsunoda, Wm. Theodore deBary, and Donald Keene (New York: Columbia University Press, 1958), p. 274.

PROTECTING THE STABILITY OF THE COUNTRY

The following passage reflects an idea that is common in East Asia, that natural calamities reflect on the personality and moral character of the ruler and serve as a sign of the displeasure of Heaven. It reports that when the ancient emperor Sujin experienced difficulties he asked the kami *to explain the cause, and he was informed that he had failed properly to venerate the* kami *Omononushi. The problems he was experiencing were a manifestation of the* kami's *displeasure, and the emperor was told that they would end when the emperor provided the appropriate offerings.*

> During the reign of the tenth legendary emperor Sujin, there were many people who wandered away from their homes, and there were also some rebellions. The situation was such that the imperial virtue alone could not control the nation. Therefore, the emperor was penitent from morning till night, asking for divine punishment of the kami of heaven and earth upon himself. Prior to that time the two kami, the Sun Goddess and the Kami of Yamato, were worshipped together within the imperial palace. The emperor, however, was afraid of their potencies and did not feel at ease living with them. Therefore, he entrusted Princess Toyosukiri to worship the Sun Goddess at the village of Kasanui in Yamato, where a sacred shrine was established. Also he commissioned Princess Nunakiri to worship the Kami of Yamato.
>
> [Then] the emperor stated, 'I did not realize that numerous calamities would take place during our reign. It may be that the lack of good rule might have incurred the wrath of the kami of heaven and earth. It might be well to inquire the cause of the calamities by means of divination.' The emperor therefore assembled the eighty myriads of kami and inquired about this matter by means of divination. At that time the kami spoke through the kami-possession of Princess Yamatotohimomoso, 'Why is the emperor worried over the disorder of the nation? Doesn't he know that the order of the nation would be restored if he properly venerated me?' The emperor asked which kami was thus giving such an instruction, and

the answer was: 'I am the kami who resides within the province of Yamato, and my name is Omononushi-no-kami.' Following the divine instruction, the emperor worshipped the kami, but the expected result did not follow. Thus the emperor cleansed himself and fasted as well as purifying the palace, and addressed himself to the kami in prayer, asking, 'Is not our worship sufficient? Why is our worship not accepted? May we be further instructed in a dream as to the fulfillment of your divine favor toward us.'

That night a noble man who called himself Omononushi-no-kami appeared and spoke to the emperor in his dream, 'The emperor has no more cause to worry over the unsettled state of the nation. It is my divine wish to be worshipped by my child, Otataneko, and then the nation will be pacified immediately.' Upon learning the meaning of the dream, the emperor was greatly delighted and issued a proclamation throughout the country to look for Otataneko, who was subsequently found in the district of Chinu and was presented to the court. Whereupon the emperor asked Otataneko as to whose child he was, and the answer was: 'My father's name is the Great Kami Omononushi. My mother's name is Princess Ikutamayori.' The emperor then said, 'Now prosperity will come to us.' Thus, Otataneko was made the chief priest in charge of the worship of the Great Kami Omononushi. After that the emperor consulted divination as to the desirability of worshipping other kami, and found it desirable to do so. Accordingly he paid homage to the eighty myriads of kami. Thereupon the pestilence ceased and peace was restored in the nation, and good crops of the five kinds of grain made the peasantry prosperous.

Source: *Nihongi*, ch. 5, 6th and 7th years: *Nihongi*, pp. 239–240.

PRINCE SHOTOKU'S PROCLAMATION ON VENERATION OF KAMI

Prince Shotoku is a pivotal figure in Japanese history. He embraced Buddhism and propagated it throughout the country, but as the following passage indicates, he continued the ancient practices of venerating the indigenous kami.

[In 607 during the reign of Empress Suiko, r. 592–628] the following edict was issued [by the Prince Regent Shotoku, 573–621]: 'We are told that our imperial ancestors, in governing the nation, bent humbly under heaven and walked softly on earth. They venerated the kami of heaven and earth, and established shrines on the mountains and by the rivers, whereby they were in constant touch with the power of nature. Hence the winter (*yin*, negative cosmic force) and summer (*yang*, positive cosmic force) elements were kept in harmony, and their creative powers blended together. And now during our reign, it would be unthinkable to neglect the veneration of the kami of heaven and earth. May all the ministers from the bottom of their hearts pay homage to the kami of heaven and earth.'

Source: *Nihongi*, ch. 12: *Nihongi*, p. 241.

FESTIVAL OF THE GATES

This is a ritual prayer (norito) *recited to ask the* kami *to protect the imperial palace. It requests that they guard against evil spirits and safeguard the gates.*

We do most humbly invoke your hallowed names: Kushi-iha-mato, Toyo-iha-mato. For you dwell in all the inner and outer august gates of the four quarters, defending them like massive sacred rocks. For if from the four sides and the four quarters the hateful and unruly god Ame-no-maga-tsu-hi should appear, you are not enchanted by his wicked words, nor deceived into consenting to them. For if this evil should come from above you defend from above, and if it should come from below you defend from below, lying in wait to drive off and protect, and to exorcize with words. For you open the gates in the morning, and close the gates in the evening, and inquire and know the names of all who come in and of all who go out. For if there be any error or misdeed, you rectify it to the eye and to the ear as do the deities Kamu-naho-bi and Oho-naho-bi, and cause those in the service of the divine descendant to serve him in tranquility and peace. Thus do we most humbly praise your hallowed names, Toyo-iha-mato, Kushi-iha-mato. Thus humbly we speak.

Source: *Mikado Matsuri (Festival for the Imperial Palace Gates)*; tr. Meredith McKinney.

PRAYER TO AMATARASU DURING THE FESTIVAL OF THE SIXTH MONTH

This is a prayer spoken by the head priest of the Grand Shrine of Ise during a regular festival performed every six months. It asks Amatarasu to ensure that the emperor has a long life, to protect the country, and to promote the prosperity of the people.

By the solemn command of the Emperor,
[I pray] that you make his life a long life,
Prospering [his reign] as an abundant reign,
Eternal and unmoving as the sacred massed rocks,
That you favor also the princes who are born,
That you [protect] long and tranquilly the various officials,
As well as even the common people of the lands of the four quarters of the kingdom,
And that you cause to flourish in abundance
The five grains which they harvest.
With the prayer [I offer] the tribute threads habitually presented by the people of the Kamube
Established in the three counties and in the various lands and various places,

And the great wine and the great first fruits prepared in ritual purity,
Placing these in abundance like a long mountain range.
I, the great Nakatomi, abiding concealed behind the solemn *tama-gusi*,
On the seventeenth day of the sixth month of this year,
Do humbly speak your praises as the morning sun rises in effulgent glory.

Source: *Norito.*

PRAYER FOR MOVING THE SHRINE OF ISE

Every 20 years the grand shrine of Ise is rebuilt. There are two sites on which the shrines are constructed, and builders alternate between the two. When the time comes to construct a new shrine, the following prayer is spoken to the goddess in order to inform her that the time has come for her to move again.

By the solemn command of the Sovereign Grandchild,
I humbly speak in the solemn presence of the Great Sovereign Deity;
In accordance with the ancient custom,
The great shrine is built anew once in twenty years,
The various articles of clothing of fifty-four ages,
And the sacred treasures of twenty-one types are provided,
And exorcism, purification, and cleansing are performed.

Source: *Norito.*

MOUNT FUJI

Mount Fuji is widely viewed in Japan as a particularly sacred place and as the abode of powerful kami. *The following poem, contained in the* Manyoshi *collection, describes the grandeur of the mountain and the power of its* kami.

Between the provinces of Kai and Suruga
Stands the lofty peak of Fuji.
Heavenly clouds would not dare cross it;
Even birds dare not fly above it.
The fire of volcano is extinguished by snow,
And yet snow is consumed by fire.
It is hard to describe;
It is impossible to name it.
One only senses the presence of a mysterious kami. . . .
In the land of Yamato,
The land of the rising sun,
The lofty Mount Fuji is its treasure and its tutelary kami. . . .
One is never tired of gazing at its peak in the province of Suraga.

Source: *Manyoshi,* 3:319–321; *The Great Asian Religions,* p. 239.

LIFE IS TRANSITORY

A common theme in Shinto literature is the notion that things in the natural world are transitory. The following poem describes how the changes of the seasons are similar to the changes experienced by human beings.

> It has been told from the beginning of the world
> That life on earth is transitory. . . .
> Indeed we see even in the sky the moon waxes and wanes. . . .
> In the spring flowers decorate mountain-trees,
> But in the autumn with dew and frost
> Leaves turn colors and fall on the ground. . . .
> So it is with human life:
> Rosy cheek and black hair turn their color;
> The morning smile disappears in the evening
> Like the wind which blows away.
> Changes continue in life like the water passing away,
> And my tears do not stop over the uncertainty of life.

Source: *Manyoshi: The Great Asian Religions*, p. 239.

GLOSSARY

Amatarasu Omikami   The Sun Goddess, believed to be the divine progenitor of the imperial line.

Folk Shinto   (*minzoku shinto*) A term for popular practices connected with the kami.

Ise   The most prominent shrine of Shinto, dedicated to the Sun Goddess, Amatarasu Omikami.

Kami   The indigenous gods of Japan, often associated with particular places.

Makoto no kokoro   "Heart of Truth," an attitude of reverence toward the natural world and pure moral character.

Sectarian Shinto   (*kyoha shinto*) Distinctive schools of Shinto thought and practice.

Shinto   "Way of the Gods," believed by many traditional Japanese to be the native religious tradition of Japan.

Shrine Shinto   (*jinja shinto*) A form of Shinto that centers on ritual activities connected with shrines.

Uchigami   Clan deity.

FURTHER READINGS

ANESAKI, MASAHARU. *History of Japanese Religion*. London: Kegan Paul, 1930.
GEEMERS, WILHELMUS H. M. *Shrine Shinto after World War II*. Leiden: E. J. Brill, 1968.
HOLTOM, D. C. *The National Faith of Japan*. New York: Paragon, 1965.

KISHIMOTO, HIDEO. *Japanese Religion in the Meiji Era,* tr. John F. Howes. Tokyo: Obunsha, 1956.

KITAGAWA, JOSEPH M. *Religion in Japanese History.* New York: Columbia University Press, 1966.

MURAOKA, TSUNETSUGU. *Studies in Shinto Thought,* tr. Delmer M. Brown and James T. Araki. Tokyo: Japanese National Commission for Unesco, 1964.

Australian Aboriginal Religion

INTRODUCTION

Like many other aboriginal peoples, the earliest inhabitants of Australia developed complex religious systems that emphasized myth and ritual practices designed to explain how the world came to be as it is and describing techniques for manipulating natural forces. At the time of white settlement in Australia, there were an estimated 300,000 Aborigines, divided among around 500 tribes. There were more than 200 distinct Aboriginal languages, most of which were mutually unintelligible, and each tribal group had its own myth and ritual cycles. Thus the most significant aspect of Aboriginal religion was its diversity, although there are common themes and concerns that are still shared across the country.

Australian Aborigines have traditionally viewed themselves as custodians of the land, and much of their religious lore and practice is concerned with how the world came to be as it is and the role of humans in maintaining it. In Aboriginal culture, there is a strong sense that there is a common life force that pervades the entire world, and humans, animals, and spirits are all manifestations of it. They see themselves as fundamentally linked to the land they inhabit and as having a primordial connection with other humans and animals. Their ancestors were also aware of the fragility of their environment, and so they endeavored to avoid damaging it by their actions. This concern continues today among the Aboriginal peoples who maintain their traditions, but white settlement has led many to lose this sense of connection with the land.

During the early twentieth century, the Australian government pursued the now-discredited "White Australia" policy, which led to Aboriginal children being forcibly removed from their families and raised in orphanages or in white families in order to help them become part of "mainstream" Australia. The people of the "stolen generations," as they are now called, often suffered severe psychological scarring, and in its aftermath this policy has created pervasive problems among Aborigines. Among its legacies are high suicide rates and alcoholism, along with a common feeling among many contemporary Aborigines that they do not belong either in white society or among their own people. It has also virtually destroyed traditional religious practice in areas in which European culture is most dominant, particularly the southeastern parts of the country.

The Dreaming

Before Europeans landed in Australia, Aborigines had no writing systems; nor did they build permanent structures or monuments. Most tribes were nomadic, wandering from place to place in search of food and water, and many of their myths encoded information regarding where to find the necessities of life and instructions for the making of tools, temporary buildings, hunting, etc. The most pervasive shared aspect of Aboriginal religion is the "Dreaming," which is given different names in different areas. The Aranda people of the central desert region refer to it as "Alcheringa," the peoples of the western desert generally call it "Djugurba," and the Murngin word is "Wongar." For all Aboriginal peoples, the Dreaming is a primordial time during which things came to be as they now are. It has a beginning, but it has no real end, since it continues to affect and shape the present.

In Aboriginal mythology, there is no particular interest in the origin of the world; the stories of the Dreaming begin with the notion of the world already existing in an embryonic state, but still unformed. There was no light, because the sun and moon were slumbering beneath the surface of the earth, along with the ancestral beings whose actions are the focus of Dreaming stories. Many of these were the progenitors of the species that now inhabit Australia, and stories about them often relate how they came to have their distinctive shapes and characteristics. For example, there are a number of myths that tell why emus have no wings and spend all their time on the ground, unlike other birds. In several such myths, the emu ancestors were tricked into cutting off their own wings by other birds who were jealous of them. Beings took shape during the Dreaming, and events left permanent traces on the ancestors, which continue to be inherited by their descendants. In another myth, a lizard with a black patch on its tongue is said to have inherited this characteristic because its Dreaming ancestor once carried a burning coal in its mouth in order to bring fire to its tribe.

Aboriginal myths are overwhelmingly associated with the land, and each tribe's stories are connected with specific features of its territory. In Aboriginal religion there are no churches or other monuments in which religion is practiced; rather, certain areas are considered sacred, and rituals are performed in these places in accordance with their religious significance. One of the most fundamental problems for contemporary Aborigines who want to preserve their traditions is the fact that many sacred sites are now owned by the descendants of European settlers, who have fenced them off and regard Aborigines as trespassers. Most Aboriginal religious practice is connected to specific places in a tribe's traditional area, and once this link has been severed there is no possibility of recreating the ritual in another area because each place has its own specific Dreaming associations. Moreover, the patterns of traditional Aboriginal life were concerned with re-creating the events of the Dreaming, and their lands were crisscrossed by the tracks of their primordial ancestors. In their wanderings in search of food, they emulated the examples of these beings and maintained their sense of relatedness to them. This way of life is practiced today only by small tribal groups in isolated areas, and Aborigines living in urban areas face significant difficulties in attempting to adapt traditional religious myths and rituals to their present situations.

The overall concern in most myths of the Dreaming is how the world came to be inhabitable by humans, and the power of the ancestors is thought to be available still to those with the proper ritual knowledge. In some cases the ancestors were transformed into features of the landscape, and in others they died or passed beyond tribal lands, but in most cases their spirits survive, and they continue to be as alive as they were during the primordial Dreaming, though now in altered form. They are eternal, and many are said to be self-created. Unlike the gods of other peoples, however, the ancestors are portrayed as living much like humans: they hunt their food with spears or other hand weapons, they require water in order to survive, and even the most powerful build shelters in order to protect themselves from the elements.

Despite their great power and the cosmic significance of their actions, their lives parallel those of traditional Aborigines in most respects, and Aboriginal life was seen as replicating their paradigmatic actions in their daily activities. All of life was pervaded by a sense of sacredness, and for the traditional Aborigine the surrounding landscape contained the traces of the ancestors, and their actions had a sacred quality to the extent that they followed the models that had been initiated in the Dreaming. The events of the Dreaming have a primordial quality, and the Dreaming overlaps with conventional time. It continues to affect the present, and it is just as real as ordinary reality, and in fact is intimately conjoined with it.

In Dreaming stories, the ancestors are often shape-changers, and they physically adapt to changing circumstances. Some of these changes become permanent, while others are temporary. It is important to note that in Aboriginal religion the Dreaming does not merely reflect a past time, but is significant because it is also reflected in present reality. The beings of the Dreaming had great power and shaped both the land and its inhabitants, and they continue to exist as part of the world they formed. Their actions and conflicts altered the landscape, and they also laid the basis for tribal laws, customs, and rituals. The stories that were left behind provided examples of good and evil behavior, as well as answers to the problems that faced traditional people. In some cases the moral of a Dreaming myth is straightforward: "We do this because Baiame (the all-father in many Aboriginal myths) did so and commanded us to emulate him." In other cases, the ramifications of myths are deeply encoded in layers of meaning and may be differently interpreted in accordance with changing circumstances.

Although the Dreaming establishes the basis for human society and its laws, it is in no sense a golden age. The ancestors often act immorally, and in many stories humans learn not to emulate them because of the negative consequences of their actions. For example, in some myths of the Walmadjeri people of the central desert, the first men trick the first women and steal their sacred emblems and the magical powers associated with them. But even though the ancestors in such myths behave immorally, they are generally punished for their misbehavior, and so the moral order is upheld.

Religious Practice and Ritual Lore

Because there was no writing system for Aboriginal languages, the scriptures of their religion existed only in oral form. As noted previously, they mainly took the form of stories that recounted the deeds of ancestral beings, many of which contained prescriptions for present behavior. They also encoded often complex rituals, many of which were linked with the human life cycle. Surprisingly, birth does not figure very prominently in most Aboriginal religions, but puberty, tribal initiation, procreation, and death are central concerns. In some Aboriginal societies, death is seen as final, and there are a number of stories that recount how it first appeared during the Dreaming. But other tribes believe in a form of rebirth, in which the spirit of the deceased goes to another realm, which is generally said to be idyllic, though its main features reflect this world. In most cases the journey to the afterlife is fraught with peril, and many are unable to find their way, and so remain among the living as unhappy spirits. Those who successfully overcome the obstacles find a land inhabited by friends and relatives, in which game and water are plentiful, and in which life is much like that of our world, but better and happier.

Only those who live good lives have a chance to successfully make the journey to the afterlife. Good behavior requires adherence to the laws and norms of the tribe and submission to tribal authority. Traditional Aboriginal religion is profoundly conservative, and people are enjoined to strictly adhere to past paradigms and to obey the dictates of tribal authorities, who are generally old men. Deviation from tradition is viewed as a serious offence, and this conservatism is no doubt one of the reasons for the difficulties Aborigines have faced in adapting their traditions to modern Australian society. The myths and rituals of the Dreaming tell nomadic hunter-gatherers how to live in harmony with the natural environment, where to find food and water, and how to replicate the behavior of their ancestors, but provide few clues for how to live in fixed dwellings in urban areas or how to function within the modern economy.

Male dominance was a pervasive feature of traditional Aboriginal society. Male elders generally were the dominant figures, and most important rituals were performed by men. In recent years researchers have discovered that women also were involved in rituals, commonly referred to as "secret women's business," but these were generally seen as having significance only for female members of a tribe, while men's rituals were important for everyone. In tribal rituals, women played at most a subordinate role, as supporters of the men who led them. The inferior status of women is also reflected in Aboriginal myths: while there are a number of powerful and influential female characters, women are generally portrayed as submissive to men. Marriage is often the result of a man simply carrying a woman away and ordering her to become his wife, and male ancestors commonly disciplined their women through physical force, with beatings or physical deprivation. Female characters are often flighty and undependable, and firm male influence is needed in order to keep them in line. As in all traditional societies, however, religious paradigms reflect an ideal constructed by male elites, and the actual status of women probably varied considerably in Aboriginal societies. The following stories are drawn from a variety of tribes from different parts of the continent.

AUSTRALIAN ABORIGINAL MYTHS

THE FIRST DEATH

Death is a central concern of Aboriginal religion. There is a great deal of speculation regarding how it first entered the world and whether or not it is final. In this story from the Kamilroi tribe, Baiame, the all-father, finished creating the world, and after extensive travels around the land was well satisfied with his work. Subsequently he returned to his abode in the sky along with his wife Birrahgnooloo, who some tribes regard as the Mother-of-All and his partner in creation.

As Baiame walked the world, he fashioned various animals and plants, along with important features of the landscape such as rivers and mountains. Finally he created humans out of the dust of the mountains, intending that they would be custodians of the land. The first people began to reproduce, and Baiame's world became increasingly filled with various species. The sun and rain he provided sustained both plant and animal life, and sustenance was plentiful.

Long after his departure to heaven, however, the land was afflicted by the first great drought, which is still today a recurrent problem in Australia. Although humans had been ordered by Baiame not to eat certain species, a man driven to desperation began to kill and eat some of them and shared the food with his wife. They offered a forbidden kangaroo-rat to a friend who was afflicted by hunger, but mindful of Baiame's prohibition he refused the meat and went away.

As he walked he became steadily weaker, until he collapsed at the base of a large tree. The man and woman who had offered him food saw him from a distance and called out to him, but he was too weak to respond. As they watched, a large black shape emerged from the tree and picked up his dying body and carried it up into the high branches. The monster who carried him was Yowee, the spirit of death, and the man became the first human to die. Baiame had intended that his creation would be perfect and that all of his creatures would have plenty of food and water, but in his absence they experienced severe privation, which allowed death to enter the world and claim its first victim. Since that time death has been the fate of all creatures.

HOW FIRE BECAME WIDELY AVAILABLE

There are a number of Aboriginal myths concerning the origins of fire. In some the ancestors jealously guard the secrets of how to make and maintain fire, and there is a general sense that such a wondrous lore would not be freely shared. Fire is often obtained by trickery or theft, and those who get it generally want to keep it for themselves. In the following story from the Northern Territory, two men acquire the secret of fire and refuse to share it with their tribe.

Before fire was widely available, people made their food more edible by leaving it to dry in the sun. One day Bootoolgah the crane ancestor was rubbing two sticks together and noticed that this action produced a spark. He showed this to his wife Goonur the kangaroo rat, who realized that this technique could be used to make fire whenever they wanted. They fashioned two sticks that could be carried in a pouch, which they carried with them at all times. They first used fire to cook some fish they had caught, and marveled at how much better it tasted than sun-dried flesh.

They decided to keep the secret of fire for themselves, and they always went to hidden places to make their fires and cook their food. When other members of their tribe noticed that their meat looked different from theirs, Bootoolgah and Goonur claimed that they had dried it in the sun like everyone else, but the others became suspicious. One day Boolooral the night owl followed them silently and saw them making fire to cook their food, and he reported back to the elders of the tribe. Rather than try to take the secret by force, they decided to trick the two. They announced that a huge *corroboree* (tribal gathering) would be held, the largest in living memory, and that all the surrounding tribes would participate.

Each group arrived decorated with its distinctive symbols. Some painted their whole bodies, while others had elaborate costumes made with feathers. All performed dances unique to their tribes, and no one had ever seen such a wondrous display. During the celebrations Bootoolgah and Goonur became so entranced by the spectacle that they forgot to guard their fire sticks. When their guard was down a man who had been pretending to be sick grabbed the bag in which the fire sticks were hidden and brought them to the tribal elders. They learned how to use them to make fire, and subsequently shared the lore with the rest of the tribe, so that everyone could make use of it.

THE RAINBOW SERPENT

Different ancestors figure in myths of the various regions of Australia. One of the most widely dispersed ancestral characters is the Rainbow Serpent, named Ngaljod in Northern Arnhem Land and known by other names in other parts of the continent. He is said to be an enormous snake who commonly lives in lakes and rivers. When he moves from one place to another, he makes rivers and water holes. His voracious appetite often brings him into conflict with other ancestors. He is essentially an amoral character, whose actions created important aspects of the landscape, but he has no particular love for humans. Rather, he eats them whenever he can, and many myths about the Rainbow Snake focus on how dangerous he is.

Before going off to hunt, the men of a tribe in the Northern Territory warned their boys not to venture near the sea because a giant snake lived there, waiting to eat unwary children. After they left the boys began to play, but after becoming bored decided to follow the sound of the surf to the beach. As they drew near, they saw a beautiful rainbow in the sky, but they failed to realize that it was caused by the Rainbow Serpent, who had arched his coils up from the water. The colors of the rainbow were caused by the light reflecting off his scales.

When the boys reached the water, they were so enraptured by the beauty of the landscape that they failed to notice the serpent, who swam toward them swiftly and silently. He swallowed them whole. When the hunters returned to their camp, they immediately noticed that the boys had disappeared, and when they followed their tracks to the beach they found that they ended at the water's edge. There were two black rocks in the ocean that had not been there before, and the men realized that the rainbow serpent had swallowed the boys and turned them into rocks. There was nothing they could do about this situation, and so they sadly returned to their camp. The rocks are still visible today between Double Island Point and Inship Rock. When a rainbow appears in the sky, the elders of the tribe tell this story to the younger members in order to illustrate the importance of obedience and the dangers of wandering by themselves.

DIVISION OF LABOR BETWEEN THE SEXES

This story from tribes living near the Murray River in New South Wales tells of how men and women came to cohabit and describes how each has certain duties and obligations.

During the Dreaming the Raven ancestor wanted to cross a river, but since he could not swim he decided to build a canoe. After searching for suitable bark, he fashioned one and began to carry it to the water. As he walked, he began to hear a rhythmic tapping in the air above his head, and after searching around determined that it was coming from his canoe. He set it down and discovered to his surprise that a woman was sitting in it. He had never before seen a female, and so he stared at her, fascinated by the differences in their respective physiques.

The woman said nothing to him, but stepped from the canoe and helped him to carry it to the bank of the river. After they were both in the small craft, he handed her the paddle, but she shook her head and sat in the back of the canoe. Her actions indicated that she expected him to do the hard work of paddling. Because he had never before met a woman, he was unfamiliar with the proper relationships between the sexes, but she began to teach him his role and what sort of work was appropriate for her. He found many of her lessons difficult to accept, and the learning process was fraught with conflicts, but at the same time he realized that there were unexpected compensations. Many things he had had to do by himself were now shared, and they developed a mutually satisfactory partnership. Later they had children, and raising them presented more challenges and rewards. One day when the two were searching for food their young wandered from the tree in which they sheltered. When they reached the ground they adapted by taking on human form, and thus they became the first Aborigines. All of Australia's original people are descended from these two ancestors.

FURTHER READINGS

BERNDT, RONALD M. *Australian Aboriginal Religion*. Leiden: E. J. Brill, 1974.

COWAN, JAMES. *Aborigine Dreaming*. London: Thorsons, 2002.

KEEN, IAN. *Knowledge and Secrecy in an Aboriginal Religion*. Oxford: Clarendon Press, 1994.

REED, A. W. *Aboriginal Myths: Tales of the Dreamtime*. Sydney: Reed New Holland, 2000.

STAMMER, W. E. H. *On Aboriginal Religion*. Sydney: University of Sydney, 1989.

Acknowledgments

HINDUISM

Translation of excerpts from Hindu texts, by John Powers. Reprinted by permission.

Excerpts from *The Rig Veda,* tr. Wendy Doniger O'Flaherty (New York: Penguin, 1981). Reproduced by permission of Frederick Warne & Co.

Excerpts from *Shankara's Crest-Jewel of Discrimination,* tr. Swami Prabhavananda and Christopher Isherwood (Hollywood: Vedanta Press, 1975). Used by permission.

Excerpts from *The Bhagavad-gita: Krishna's Counsel in Time of War,* translated by Barbara Stoler Miller. Copyright © 1986 by Columbia University Press. Reprinted with permission of the publisher.

Excerpts reprinted from *Encountering the Goddess,* tr. Thomas B. Coburn (Albany: State University of New York Press, 1991). Used by permission.

Excerpts from *Saundaryalahari,* attributed to Shankara, translated by W. N. Brown. Copyright © 1958 by the President and Fellows of Harvard College. Reprinted by permission of Harvard University Press.

Excerpts from *Speaking of Siva,* tr. A. K. Ramanujan (Baltimore: Penguin Books, 1973). Reproduced by permission of Frederick Warne & Co.

JAINISM

Translation of excerpts from Jaina texts, by John Powers. Reprinted by permission.

Translation of excerpts from Jaina texts, by Royce Wilies. Reprinted by permission.

BUDDHISM

Translation of excerpts from Buddhist texts, by John Powers. Reprinted by permission.

Translation of excerpts from Buddhist texts, by David Moore. Reprinted by permission.

Excerpts from *Indo-Tibetan Buddhism: Indian Buddhists and Their Tibetan Successors* by David Snellgrove. Copyright © 1987. Reprinted by arrangement with Shambhala Publications, Inc., 300 Massachusetts Avenue, Boston, MA. 02115

Excerpts from *The Garland of Mahamudra Practices* (Ithaca: Snow Lion, 1986). Used by permission.

Excerpts from *The Hevajra Tantra: A Critical Study,* David Snellgrove (London: Oxford University Press, 1959). By permission of Oxford University Press.

Excerpts from *Bar do thos grol: The Tibetan Book of the Dead: Liberation through Understanding in the Between,* tr. Robert A. F. Thurman. Copyright © 1994. Used by permission of Bantam Books, a division of Bantam Doubleday Dell Publishing Group, Inc.

Excerpts from *The Beautiful Ornament of the Three Visions* (Ithaca: Snow Lion, 1991). Used by permission.

Excerpts from *The Platform Sutra of the Sixth Patriarch* by Philip Yampolsky. Copyright © 1967 by Columbia University Press. Reprinted with permission of the publisher.

Excerpts from *Kukai's Petition to Supplement the Annual Reading of Sutra in the Imperial Palace with Special Esoteric Buddhist (Shingon) Rites,* translated by David Gardiner. Reprinted by permission of David Gardiner.

Excerpts from *Dogen's Manual of Zen Meditation,* tr. Carl Bielefeldt (Berkeley: University of California Press, 1988). Used by permission.

Excerpts from *Nichiren: Selected Writings,* tr. Laurel Rodd (Honolulu: University of Hawaii Press, 1980). Copyright Laurel Rasplica Rodd. Reprinted by permission.

SIKHISM

Translation of excerpts from Sikh texts, by John Powers. Reprinted by permission.

Excerpts from *Adi Granth: Guru Nanak and the Sikh Religion,* tr. W. H. McLeod (Oxford: Clarendon Press, 1968). By permission of Oxford University Press.

CONFUCIANISM

Translation of excerpts from Confucian texts, by Kurt Vall. Reprinted by permission.

Translation of excerpts from Confucian texts, by John Powers. Reprinted by permission.

Excerpts from *Sources of Chinese Tradition,* by William Theodore deBary. Copyright © 1964 by Columbia University Press. Reprinted with permission of the publisher.

Excerpts from *Mencius,* tr. D. C. Lau (Hong Kong: The Chinese University Press, 1979). Reproduced by permission of Frederick Warne & Co.

Excerpts from *Xunzi: A Translation and Study of the Complete Works,* vol. III, tr. John Knoblock (Stanford: Stanford University Press, 1994). Used by permission.

Excerpts from *Instructions for Practical Living and Other Neo-Confucian Writings* By Wang Yang-Ming, translated by Wing-tsit Chan. Copyright © 1963 by Columbia University Press. Reprinted with permission of the publisher.

DAOISM

Translation of excerpts from Daoist texts, by John Powers. Reprinted by permission.

Excerpts from *Early Chinese Mysticism: Philosophy and Soteriology in the Daoist Tradition,* Livia Kohn. Copyright © 1992 by Princeton University Press. Reprinted by permission of Princeton University Press.

Excerpts from *Chuang-tzu: Basic Writings,* translated by Burton Watson, Copyright © 1964 by Columbia University Press. Reprinted with permission of the publisher.

Excerpts reprinted from *Daoist Mystical Philosophy: The Scripture of the Western Ascension,* tr. Livia Kohn (Albany: State University of New York Press, 1991). Used by permission.

Reprint from *Immortal Sisters,* by Thomas Cleary. Copyright © 1990 by Thomas Cleary. Reprinted by arrangement with North Atlantic Books, P.O. Box 12327, Berkeley, CA 94712.

SHINTO

Translation of Shinto texts, by Meredith McKinney. Reprinted by permission.

Excerpts from *Kojiki,* Records of Ancient Matters in The Great Asian Religions: An Anthology (New York: Macmillan, 1969). Reprinted by permission of Evelyn Kitagawa.